POLICE CONFIDENTIAL
What Really Goes On
Behind The Thin Blue Line

Jane Doe

DISCLAIMER

The names,police forces and locations have been anonymised.
Events, places and conversations in this book have been recreated
from memory. The language in this book isn't meant to cause
offence, it is indicitive of the era in which the stories happened.

PROLOGUE

The time is the early 90's and I've been successful in my application to join the police. For reasons that will become clear I have decided to keep my name, and the name of the police force I worked in anonymous.

This book details accounts made by policewomen and a few willing policemen from various Police forces across the UK, and of their experiences during their careers. These are canteen room stories that we would talk about after the event. There are funny stories, heart-breaking stories and stories of misogyny though the years. The policewomen who have spoken to me had their careers through the 60's, 70's, 80's, 90's and 2000's yet the thread often seems to be the same. The accounts in this book often capture the humour of being a woman in the police force, but it also highlights how much harder it is for us to be seen and valued.

 As often happens when I meet up socially with retired or still serving police colleagues, we speak of our experiences and now laugh about them, but at the time some of these experiences were anything but funny.

99% of the public live in a bubble. You have no idea of what's really going on in the world and I don't think this is a bad thing. There are some days when I wish I hadn't seen some of the things I've seen. Civilian friends often say to me 'You must have seen some terrible things?'. I look at them and think in my head yes, I have, but what is it that you really want to know? They want to know something that's a bit shocking but not too much, so I moderate the stories I tell people. I tell the story of the car crash I went to where the man had suffered a compound fracture, and his femur was sticking out of his leg. My friends are shocked, but also intrigued because people have a morbid curiosity of things they wouldn't ever see. Sometimes I wonder to myself what their faces would be like if I told them stories about the incident's I have dealt with that have affected me beyond measure. The paedophile that thought I was his friend, so decided to tell me in graphic detail how he raped a small child. The 7-year-old child who is distraught because she's been raped so many times and doesn't understand why daddy does this to her. The people who die alone in their houses and have no one. The screams from the mother who has accidentally suffocated her child to death when she fell asleep on them because she was so exhausted. I can't tell my friends these stories because it's a bit much for them to hear but also, it's a bit of a conversation stopper when you're having a dinner party. So, I just smile at them and tell another funny story.

The Police service was catapulted into the limelight in 2021 with the arrest of Wayne Couzens, a serving police officer who raped and murdered Sarah Everard. A Police officer who used his position of power to gain her trust. This appalling act sparked numerous gatherings of women around the country. I, like so many of my serving co-workers and retired ex officers was appalled by this murder. The officer's retired and serving who create 'What's App' groups with horrific sexually offensive and racist or homophobic content. The officers who photographed the dead bodies of two sisters, Nicole Smallman and Bibaa Henry in a London Park, and shared them on a What's App group with the title 'dead bird's'. This behaviour is utterly unforgiveable.

More recently the new Commissioner of Police for the Metropolitan Police Sir Mark Rowley was interviewed and said that there are between 30-50 sackings of police officers every year. He believes this figure should be in the 100's, and that the police are not living up to the values the public expect of the police. Sir Mark has said that there is a weakness in the system and admits that the police should have done better to root this unacceptable behaviour out. He has said that officers have committed serious offences, that wouldn't pass vetting if an officer was trying to enter the force, yet after investigation these officers are allowed back into the force because offences are dealt with 'In house'.

Two instances Sir Mark has mentioned are one male officer who had 11 misconduct cases against him for abuse, sexual harassment and distribution of an indecent image of himself. This officer was given a formal sanction and allowed to remain in the force.

Another instance was a male officer who had 6 misconduct cases against him for harassment and neglect of duty. He was also allowed to remain in the force.

Sir Mark assures us that he has set up a new Anti-Corruption and Abuse Command to root out Racist, homophobic and misogynistic behaviour in police officers. In my opinion attitudes of male officers will not change unless bosses like Sir Mark come down on officers who persist in this behaviour, like a ton of bricks. Officers need to know that their behaviour is unacceptable and know that they will be sacked not just reprimanded. I feel this will put a stop to this behaviour as officers will be scared to voice their awful opinions in work or 'what's app' groups knowing they will be rooted out and dismissed. It won't stop officers having these opinions, but it will put a stop to them openly voicing them to their peers. There also needs to be no stigma in calling this behaviour out. If you see it report it because it is unacceptable.

What this book will demonstrate is how policewomen try to get by in a man's world, and the struggles associated with this. Every policewoman has a story and some of them have been brave enough to tell it.

The Police is absolutely a 'Boys Club'. No other occupations other than the Army, Fire service or building trade would you get groups of men together who sometimes behave in a manner that is appalling. For Policewomen it really is 'sink or swim'. If you are 'touched', 'sexually assaulted' or discriminated against and you make a formal complaint, trust me this will follow you around for the rest of your career. You learn to keep quiet, to take it, to just get on and do your best. To try and be 'one of the lads'. The Police is a man's world, and it will be for a very long time to come. Change is coming slowly. Policemen are more aware now that they must 'toe the line, knowing that if they step out of line there will be consequences. I don't think the men's opinion of policewomen has really changed. Policewomen are still seen as a necessary evil. Policewomen joining the service now are more likely to challenge inappropriate behaviour from their colleagues. Sexist behaviour is now seen as unacceptable and if reported there must be an investigation. In the 60's 70's 80's and 90's it was a very different story.

For a while now I have wanted to tell these stories. The stories I haven't told the friends who have asked me about the terrible things I've seen. Heart-breaking, funny, outrageous, and sexist stories about what really happens in the Police Force.

What follows next is a collection of stories through the years. The names of the police officers involved, and the police forces have been left anonymous as you will discover for obvious reasons!

1996

We'd just been issued with CS spray, and it was still a novelty. I was working nights and responded to a B and E (Burglary in progress). We got to the back of the house, and I saw the burglar running away. I chased him through the entries and nearly had him cornered just as a van load of Policemen appeared. Every force has units that usually deal with disorder and riot situations but on their 'down time' they would prowl the streets for prisoners listening in silently to the radio for foot or car chases and usually swoop in last minute and steal your lockup. This group were renowned for nicking your prisoners right at the last minute.

So, the van pulls up and a policeman jumps out and grabs my prisoner. The prisoner immediately starts to fight with the policeman and tries to break free. I ran over and decided this would be a good chance to try out my new CS spray. It was a perfect scenario as the prisoner was resisting arrest. I took it out of my holster, gave it a shake, shouted 'gas, gas ' and sprayed him..... And then I sprayed the officer who had nicked my prisoner, in the face with my gas. I took hold of the burglar and arrested and handcuffed him while saying to my colleague 'Don't try and nick my prisoner'. The officer was rolling round, his face buried in his hands. I found out years later this officer got back in the van with his colleagues with snot dripping from his nose, and his eyes streaming. 'Did that bird just have you off' they said. He confirmed to them that yes, a female officer had indeed sprayed him and taken her prisoner from him. We ended up working together years later and have been good friends ever since. He still laughs about the first time we met.

2001

It was a Tuesday night, and I was working a night shift 10pm-7am. Nothing much happens usually during a weekday tour of nights so if a job comes out, most of the section would turn up. On this night, there was a report of an intruder in a rear garden. So, half a dozen police cars turn up to this address, and within minutes there's several officers tromping all over this woman's garden looking for an intruder that had long gone. As we were all looking around the garden the lady householder opened the upstairs window and shouts 'What's going on'. We try to reassure the lady telling her there's nothing to worry about and to go back to bed but she decides to come downstairs and join us in the garden.

Now at this point our uniform section had a 'dog patrol' attached to it and they would also turn out to jobs with you, especially reports of intruders. So, the dog handler let the dog off on his long lead and within seconds the dog was rummaging through the bushes and started to growl. 'Bloody hell' says the dog handler, he's found someone in the bushes. We walk over and see the dog with something in its mouth. On closer inspection this turned out to be a dead bunny rabbit.

We looked round the garden and saw a rabbit hutch on the patio. My colleague quickly took the dead rabbit from the police dog's mouth and says, 'What are we going to do?'. We hastily decide to put the dead bunny back in the hutch and close the door.

Shortly after this, we're joined by the householder who is in her dressing gown wondering around the garden asking what we're doing. We explain there had been an intruder, but we've had a good check around and there doesn't seem to be anything to worry about. The lady householder walks off towards the patio. Seconds later there's a scream. We all look at each other panicking. 'What is it?' the dog handler says. 'It's the rabbit' the lady says. The dog handler walks over to the hutch, looks in and says, 'I think it's dead love'. 'I know it is' said the lady.......'we buried it this afternoon'.

2007

Executing a drugs warrant in a block of flats on the first floor. As I looked through the letter box, I can see a massive amount of cannabis drying out on washing lines that are strewn across the hallway. As I'm looking through the letter box, the male inside the house sees me and runs to the back of the flat. We thought we had all the exits covered but he manages to jump from the rear first floor window and run off. We quickly ran out of the flats and around to the rear only to see him legging it across a dual carriageway and through a park. Me and a colleague gave chase and at this point the drug dealer is about 20 yards in front of us and showing no signs of slowing down. My colleague shouts 'Stop or we'll set the dog on you'. The drug dealer stops running and puts his hands in air shouting 'alright alright'. We ran up to him and handcuffed him to the rear. As he turns round, he says 'Where's the dog'. 'We haven't got one dickhead' was the reply.

2002

2am on a freezing cold morning during a set of nights. I got sent to a report of a male who had smashed rear patio windows of a house and had run off. As he was only dressed in shorts, he wasn't hard to spot and a few minutes later we spotted him and arrested him, placing him in the back of the police car. Clearly the amount of cocaine and alcohol he'd taken gave him superhuman strength, and this coupled with massive size as he obviously like working out, he promptly kicked out the rear passenger window out of the police car and ran off up the street.

We gave chase on foot and were joined by the dog handler. The perp runs up the side of a house followed by the three of us and the police dog. We follow him to the rear of the garden where he decides to pick up a large deck chair and start swinging it around. There were two greenhouses right next to him as he's swinging away, and I was obviously concerned that we'd all end up covered in glass if he started smashing them. The dog handler let go of the police dog which then bit the perp on the knee at least 5 times.

This seemed to have no effect at all. All three of us now had hold of him as well as the police dog hanging off his leg, as he swung us all around. Suddenly the police dog let go and ran to the middle of the garden. He'd spotted a ball, and not just any old ball, it was a squeaky ball. So, in the middle of being thrown around like a rag doll all I could hear is the continuous squeak of the ball. The dog then rolled the ball from its mouth in my direction and wagged his tail excitedly as the ball rolled to my foot, obviously wanting me to kick it for him. The dog handler at this point was shouting 'No, naughty boy'. The dog oblivious to this continued to play with his new ball. We somehow managed to get the male back down the garden and eventually into the police van, not before he'd kicked out at a colleague and broken their knee and then decided to pull himself up, while handcuffed onto the top of the police carrier. The wonders of Cocaine!!!!!

Weeks later I was talking to the dog handler about what had happened, and he said he had to tell the dog training school about the ball incident. They replayed the scenario and made the dog chase a handler who was wearing a protective sleeve. As the dog grabbed the handler and brought him to the floor, they threw a squeaky ball. The dog promptly spat out the handlers arm and ran to play with the ball. #earlyretirement.

2014

Had to go to an agoraphobic lady's house to interview her as she alleged she had been assaulted by her care worker. At the house, we set up the recording equipment on a table that was in-between two couches. The lady sits on her couch, and we sit opposite her ready to press record. I settled onto the couch with my colleague next to me when suddenly I realised my bum was soaking wet through, right through to my knickers. I jumped up and said, 'Why is the couch all wet?'. The lady nonchalantly replied, 'Oh the dog pisses itself when it gets excited'!!! I realised I had sat in a huge puddle of dog piss. I then had to place the back cushion from the couch on top of the wet cushion, so I was sat about two feet above my colleague as we conducted our interview, the whole time my colleague was trying not to laugh. I then had to drive back to the station on a forensic paper sack, so I didn't get the car seat wet. Luckily, I always had spare clothes in my locker.

2013

When the police interview victims for serious assaults these are usually done in a room resembling a living room to make the experience as comfortable as possible. The whole interview is video recorded, and an officer will sit behind a two-way mirror making notes while the lead interviewer sits in the living room with the victim. One such interview was being conducted, and the lead interviewer was sat opposite the lady who was pouring her heart out. For some unknown reason the interviewer decided to sit with her leg tucked underneath her for the duration of the interview. At the conclusion of the interview, the lead interviewer will leave the room to speak to their colleague who has been making notes, to see if there is anything they have missed. As the lead interviewer stood up, she realised her leg had gone dead and promptly fell into the wall and had to leave the room dragging her dead leg behind her. This was played in Crown Court during the trial!!!

2010

Whilst driving the Police carrier, the driver can sometimes be subject to pranks. One day whilst I was driving along, I was suddenly blasted with a CO_2 fire extinguisher. This was just one prank in a line of several that had happened that day. I promptly pulled the carrier over and stepped through to the back grabbing the culprit in a headlock. In the melee that followed, the culprit ended up with a loose tooth!!! That was the last time he squirted me with a fire extinguisher.

2005

Christmas Eve driving round the city centre in a carrier playing 'All I want for Christmas Is You' by Mariah Carey though the loud hailer. The public loved it.

1992

Times have changed. When I first joined the police there were no computers. Statements were written by hand, and typewriters were used to write your summary of evidence. Photographs were either taken on a Polaroid camera (where the photo would appear from the bottom of the camera, and you would wave it frantically in the air to dry it) or a camera with a film in it. You also had to fingerprint your prisoner using an ink pad. This could be a messy experience, but one that the more you did it the more confident you got. As a young probationer you had to work as the BP (Bridewell patrol) helping the desk Sgt booking in the prisoners and generally seeing to their welfare. On one such day a female had been arrested for prostitution and had to be processed. She had been arrested many times before. I was tasked with taking her fingerprints. I squeezed the ink onto the brass pad, spreading it around with the roller, and took hold of the ladies' hand to take her prints. After me tentatively doing the first fingerprint she turned to me and said, 'Here I'll do em me fucking self', and promptly did her whole set of prints in record time.

2017

First thing in the morning as my shift started, I was sent to the hospital to deal with a sudden infant death SUDI (sudden unexplained death of an infant). These are always difficult to deal with. As a police officer you must go to these incidents in case there is anything untoward, but in the vast majority of cases this is just a tragic incident. As a police officer, attending these incidents you feel as if you are massively intruding on a family's private grief. Their initial reaction towards you is nearly always one of hostility and they often accuse you of suspecting they have hurt their child. You have to explain that there is protocol to follow after the unexplained death of a child and we have to remain with the family at the bereavement suite until the family are ready to leave the child. There will always have to be a post-mortem which can also be extremely distressing for the family.

On this day, I stayed with the family for 8 hours until I finally gained the trust of the mum who had held onto her dead child all day refusing to put her down. She was devastated and my heart went out to her. She was refusing to put baby in the cot and leave her, so my job is to wait with her until she is ready. Throughout the day we chatted, and she cried while I held her hand. She told me she was a smoker, and I could see she must have been desperate for a cigarette, so I offered to hold her baby for her while she popped outside. She agreed to this and passed me her child. I put my hand on the babys cold lifeless cheeks and my heart broke. I couldn't believe what I was doing. It's weird sometimes being a Police officer. You turn up to incidents that most people would run a mile from. The public want you to be the hero and sort things out. Sometimes, although you put a brave face on, inside you're shitting yourself. You have to get things right. You must think about everything you say to the parents before you open your mouth. It's also hard not to cry at incidents like this. Witnessing someone's utter distress is heart breaking to see. I've never cried in front of the public.

I stayed with the mum this day until she was ready to dress her baby in new clothes and leave her in the crib at the bereavement suite. I went back to the station. None of my colleagues asked how I was or what I'd been doing all day. Everyone is so self-absorbed and busy with their own work. I drove home and had to stop the car, as I couldn't see through the tears. I didn't want to cry in front of my partner when I got home and have to say what I had been dealing with that day. It feels unfair to burden them with stuff sometimes, so you just learn to bottle it up and put it away inside your head.

2003

I had to attend a report of a man that had thrown himself off the top of a block of 20 storey flats and died. It's difficult to get the body covered quickly enough before people start hanging over their balconies shouting abuse at you. The ambulance service got there quickly and put a tent over him. Checking the body for suicide notes is not pleasant but needs to be done. I remember his hip bones had come through his skin when I put my hand into his trouser pocket. His smashed femur was also protruding through his skin. Turns out he had been reported missing from home a week before and obviously felt there was no other way out.

After he was taken by the undertakers, I borrowed a mop and bucket and cleaned the congealed blood from the pavement. Then you just go onto the next job!!

1998

Shootings had become more prevalent and in response to this an advert was put in internal orders for AFO's (Area firearms officers). I'd always aspired to be in firearms and then eventually the TAU (Tactical Arms Unit). There were no females in the TAU and I'd love to be the first. The thought of abseiling off the top of a building and in through a window massively appealed to me so I applied. Firstly, I had to pass a medical and physical which I did, and then I got the start date for my course.

The morning I turned up there was me and three other females, and about 12 male candidates. It soon became apparent to me that women were not welcome. The course instructors were all male and I can honestly say in all my service I have never worked with such a bunch of wankers!!!

During the course I was shouted at for no apparent reason. Made to run up and down the firearms range holding a rifle above my head shouting 'I am shit'. The worst comment was made on my second day. I remember me and the other candidates were sat on the floor eating lunch. I was sat with the other two female officers when we were approached by one of the instructors. 'Why are you here?' he asked. 'I want to be a firearms officer' I replied. 'We've already got one split arse down here and we don't need another' he said. Now, if someone said this to me now, I'd challenge them as well as put in a formal complaint about them, but it was the 90's and this wasn't how things were done. If you complained about other colleagues, that shit followed you round for the rest of your career. So, I just sat there and didn't say anything. He walked away with his other instructor colleagues laughing. This behaviour continued for 2 weeks. The constant jibes and jokes at our expense. 'Why have women got small feet? So they can stand closer to the sink'. Throughout the course we were just treated with utter contempt and were made to look like fools. As part of the course, we had to do a silent entry into the 'hard house' which is in a purpose-built compound used for riot training. As we reached the front door of the house there was a brush leaning against the door which I took hold of to move. One of the instructors had sawed the head from the brush so that as I moved it the head of the brush fell to the floor making a hell of a noise. The instructors stopped the whole exercise calling me a 'fucking stupid prick' in front of all the other officers some of whom laughed at me, others were probably glad this hadn't happened to them. I watched on as the men all slapped each other on the back, joking around with each other. You could see exactly who the instructors were going to pass, and it was a joke. I was so annoyed. They knew nothing about me, how I policed or the good reputation I had as a hard-working officer amongst my colleagues back at the station. The commendations I'd had for my excellent arrest rate.

It all came to a head when we had to do a timed exercise at an outdoor firing range. I stood next to my female colleague as we were going against each other. Every shot I fired I made sure I missed. I don't think I hit one target. She looked over at me and said, 'What are you doing?' 'I'm going home today' I said. 'I can't take this anymore'. And so that day I told the instructor I wanted to leave. 'Yes, I don't think it's for you' he said. And so, I returned to my station. I didn't tell my colleagues what had really happened when they asked. I had to say I didn't pass the course. I had to tell then I had failed. I hadn't failed; I hadn't even been given a chance. I was gutted I hadn't had a chance of doing something I'd always wanted to do but I also realised I couldn't work in an environment where I would be so hated.

So, 5 years later I was starting on a new response group, dealing with 999 jobs. I was spoken to on my first day by my new Sgt. Also starting work on this group was a male colleague. I remember looking at him thinking I knew him from somewhere. We were given our inspirational chat and then put to work together in a patrol car. Over the next few weeks, we worked together a lot, getting in fights and watching each other's back. One day whilst chatting with him it suddenly dawned on me who he was. He was the instructor on my firearms course 5 years earlier. The conversation went 'Oh my god I remember who you are now'. He looked ashamed and said 'I wondered when you'd remember who I was. Look I'm sorry about what happened to you on the firearms course'. Then he said, 'You should apply again you know, you're really good'. I must have sat there with my mouth open when he said this, and then I just told him to Fuck Off!!!. The fact was that I was really good when I had applied to be a firearms officer 5 years before, you just didn't want women in your department. We were always civil to each other throughout our career, although he always seemed embarrassed when we spoke.

What angers me most about the treatment I and my other female colleagues received on this course is that my career at that point, and the direction it was going to take was dictated by these men who ran my firearms course. I always wonder what I could have done and how far I could have gone in Firearms. I guess I'll never know. In case you're wondering, all of the females were failed and sent home and all of their 'mates' passed and became firearms officers.

1992

I got my date to join and I was ecstatic. I got a date to attend the uniform stores to get measured up for my uniform which comprised of a skirt, ill-fitting blouses with a small breast pocket that you couldn't fit anything into, a tunic, jumper, car coat!!!!!

and a long black dress coat for state funerals! I was then issued with a handbag, a truncheon which was approximately 6 inches long so it could fit in your given handbag, a set of old-fashioned style 'chain link' handcuffs, a box of 30 denier tights and a pair of steel toe capped riot boots. I also had to buy two pairs of sturdy flat black shoes. I was also fitted for my hat. Policewomen have hard topped bowler hat. Policemen get issued with a flat cap with a peak on it and a custodian helmet known better as a 'tit' hat. This is the tall hat with the silver metal topper.

My first day I was very nervous. We were to spend two weeks living in quarters and spend our days learning about basic law and what was to be expected of us. We also did a lot of 'Fun Runs'. It was very strange putting on uniform on for the first time. Everyone was dressed the same, obviously the boys had trousers on and shirts with pockets that you could fit your pocket notebook into. The men were also issued with truncheons that were about 15 inches long. We'd been shown the basics of how to fill in our pocket notebooks and were warned of the repercussions if we failed to keep it up to date. We were told that the 3 things bound to get you in trouble in the police were policewomen, property and your pocket notebook. This was known as the 3 P's. Can you imagine having to write down everything you do every day for 30 years. A few days into my training we were all whisked off to headquarters one evening for our Attestation ceremony. This is where you individually go up to the commanding officer, in this instance it was the deputy chief constable, and you swear an oath. It is also a chance for your parents and loved ones to attend the ceremony and see you in your uniform for the first time. I arrived at headquarters all nervous. We sat through the ceremony; I was watched by my mum and friends. Then it was my turn to go the front of the auditorium. I then swore my oath, and I meant every word of it. I was so proud to be wearing this uniform

' I (Name) Do solemnly and sincerely declare and affirm that I will well and truly serve our Sovereign Lady the Queen in the office of Constable, without favour or affection, malice or ill will; and that I will, to the best of my power, cause the peace to be kept and preserved and prevent all offences against the persons and properties of Her Majesty's subjects and that while I continue to hold the said office I will, to the best of my skill and knowledge, discharge all the duties thereof faithfully according to the law'

After the ceremony there is a chance to meet family and friends in the canteen. So, there I was walking up to the canteen from the auditorium in my uniform. Just prior to walking through the doors to the canteen I put my hat on….. back to front. I proudly walked towards my mum who said, 'Why's your hat on back to front'.

So, after being together for 2 weeks doing lots of fun runs and being terrified to write the wrong thing in your pocket notebook, we were dispatched off to our respective police station where we would remain posted for at least 2 years. We had also been issued with a collar number which you keep for the duration of your service. Our collar number was a strip of metal numbers you had to put onto your epaulettes using a metal spike (not much health and safety). I got lost the first morning going to my station. You had to rely on A To Z's at this time as Sat Navs didn't exist. So, after an hour and a half I eventually found my station. I somehow managed to baggsie a locker and put my kit away.

Knowing absolutely nothing about the law I was assigned to a tutor constable for a week, who was less than impressed to be tutoring a woman!! He was a proper man's man, and I thought he was a bit of a knob to be honest. Rather than drive around all week, we spent a lot of time on 'foot patrol'. We walked around for bloody hours around the whole of the area I would be covering. I remember the first time I caught sight of myself in a shop window, I thought 'It's the Police'. Then I thought 'Bloody hell it's me'. I was 21 and knew nothing, yet everyone who spoke to you expecting you to know what to do. I had huge 'CONSTABLE IN TRAINING' covers over my epilates but this didn't seem to deter the public from asking me all sorts of questions!! My tutor Constable said to me 'Get those fucking things off your shoulders, you're going to get us battered' so I took off my constable in training epaulettes. I was also issued with a Motorola radio which weighed a ton, which fixed to my skirt by being held on with my belt. A long loopy wire then attached the microphone end to my shirt which had a little material attachment on it. Obviously over the years you get to understand what is being said by the radio operators and all of the acronyms that accompany this. At the beginning of my service, I was terrified to use the radio. Not only because I hadn't got a clue what to say but that you were effectively on talk through, and everyone could hear you!! So, your tutor constable would dictate what to say to the operator to try and help you out.

Two days into my first week in the job, whilst on foot patrol with my tutor constable he shouted up for a job than came out over the radio, a sudden death. Now, I was only 21 and I'd never seen a dead body, so I was terrified as we walked through the back of the little terraced house, through the kitchen and into the front room where the man was dead on the sofa. It was a shock seeing him and sad because he'd died on his own. As the man had a slight cut on his head and with no explanation as to why this had happened, the death was deemed suspicious. So, my tutor constable told me I'd have to search the body while we waited for CID to arrive to assess the situation. All dead bodies must be checked for any suspicious injuries or for property and valuables that would be seized.

I went over to the body that was sat on the couch sort of looking upwards. 'Check his pockets' came the instruction. I took hold of the body by the shoulders. It was stiff and cold. He was wearing trousers and a jumper. As I leant him forward to gain access to his pockets the dead man did a loud groan. I now know through experience that this is just un-expelled air that gets trapped in the body, but as a naïve 21-year-old I absolutely shit myself!!! I jumped back from the body screaming, to find my tutor constable and several old arse CID officers laughing behind me.

The CID officer decided the death was nonsuspicious, so me and my tutor constable followed the body down to the city mortuary to book it in. At the time you used to have to write the deceased's name on a tag which was attached to their big toe. This protocol has changed now due to a tag falling off someone's toe years ago and a mix up with the bodies. Nowadays you write the name of the deceased down their calf.

My tutor constable then decided it would be good experience for me to stay for the post-mortem. So, there I was stood in an old city mortuary, which was like something out of a Dickens novel. The mortuaries now are modern and bright and usually officers sit behind glass with access to a microphone to ask the pathologist questions. He or she has a microphone attached to their scrubs and will speak about their findings as the officer makes notes for them. This is called being the 'scribe'. A second officer will then shadow the pathologist and take any exhibits from them. Samples of body tissues and organ tissues are always taken for toxicology to establish a cause of death, even if the cause is obvious (a knife sticking out of them).

So, there I was in the old city mortuary. The smell was awful. Death smells sweet and sickly and when you get the smell on your clothes you can't get it off. I was pushed forward to get a good view and stood about 6 feet away from the mortuary table. They also want to see if you'll be sick, or faint. The body was laid naked on the table. The skin of the man was so pale. The pathologist first checks the exterior of the body to check for any wounds, puncture marks or anything else suspicious, turning the body as he goes. The pathologist has a mortuary technician who assists him, passing the required tools when asked.

I stood there, mouth open as the pathologist made his first cut, throat to abdomen, and then pulled the skin back over the chest. What then look like bolt cutters are used to crack open the chest and expose the internal organs. There is no blood because the heart has stopped pumping. All the blood congeals in the lower back and is scooped out like jelly. The internal organs are removed one at a time, weighed and examined and samples taken from them. The mortuary technician then removes the brain from the skull using a small circular saw. I couldn't believe what I was seeing. It was like something out of a horror film. All these procedures are done with the upmost respect for the deceased body. The brain is sliced to check for abnormalities, and then small samples are taken for toxicology.

The skin is then pulled back across the face to check for fractures and bruising under the skin. Even a healed bruise can still be visible under skin. The pathologist looked at the small cut on the man's head and deemed it nonsuspicious. The cause of death was a heart attack. The pathologist had been made aware that there was a probationer in the room, so he called me over to show me his findings. Holding the man's heart in his hands he showed me where one of the arteries had ruptured, confirming the heart attack. All the organs are then placed back into the body which is then sewn up by the technician.

I felt very privileged to have seen this. Not many people will ever get to witness a post-mortem in their life. We returned to the station and had a cup of tea. I later drove home after detailing everything in my pocket notebook (PNB) Later that evening the enormity of what I had seen hit me, and I sat and cried. I cried because nobody should have to die alone. I think it was a bit of delayed shock as well. Most people live their life in a bubble, they don't see bad things. They read about them and see them reported on TV, but they don't witness these events. Police officers, Fire fighters and Ambulance staff do. They deal with death, drug addicts and see people in the depths of despair. Then they go home to their families and often don't talk about what really happened during their day. It's all bottled up, and so when officers meet up retired or still serving it's nice to let off steam.

Anyway, I finished the week with my tutor constable. Nothing else of note really happened apart from him walking the legs off me!!

The following Monday I drove myself to Bruche. This was an ex-army establishment based in Warrington which is in the Northwest of England. Police forces from all over England and the Isle of Mann use Bruche to train their new officers. I was to stay here for 10 weeks learning about the law and how to implement it. Also, on the timetable was PT, riot training and Parade, which was basically marching like they do in the army. This was in preparation for your passing out parade in front of friends and family, swimming and self-defence were also on the menu. You were placed in a class of about 20 policemen and women from all over the country and off you went. I didn't go to university. Nowadays you have to complete a degree when you join the police, but when I joined you needed 5 O levels or CSE equivalent (or GCSE's as they are now known). You had a strict timetable that you stuck to for the first 10 weeks you were there. Every Thursday we all met up in the campus bar and got drunk. This seemed like a good idea until you had to be at swimming for 8am on Friday morning with the hangover from hell. Swimming was followed by Parade for an hour which consisted of being yelled at by an ex-army officer with a slashed peak on his cap, so it came down over his eyes, who was now employed by Bruche to whip us all into shape. You had approximately 8 minutes from the end of swimming which consisted of being 'beasted' in the pool doing length after length before you had to be on the parade square with your number 1 uniform on. Sit ups in the deep end with someone sat on your legs which would be out of the pool while you kept up with the instructors demands. The only rest you got was to lean back, thus putting your head under the water until you came up for air.

We also had routine fitness tests throughout the weeks of your probation. I'd had to do my first fitness test prior to joining the Police. This consisted of as many push ups and sit ups as you could do in a minute. A standing long jump (explosive power). A grip strength test for the men and women and the bleep test, which consisted of you running between two fixed points and having to get to the end before the bleep went off. It also consisted of a 'body fat' test. This involved certain points on your body being measured for fat mass. Women have a naturally higher fat mass than men. Measurements were taken using callipers on the back of your arm, your stomach and your back, just underneath your bra strap. As women's fat density was higher than men's this usually meant we would have to do more push ups or sits ups or go further in the bleep test to out way the fact we naturally have more body fat. A totally unfair process and one I would come to realise years later precluded a lot of women from entering male dominated postings in the Police as they just couldn't get to the required level to pass the fitness test. The average woman has 25% body fat. Even when I was very fit on joining the Police my body fat was

19%. The men I was up against, many of whom were ex-military had less than 10% body fat. The odds were stacked against us from the start. The fat test has since been abolished along with the sit ups, push ups and standing long jump. Can you imagine the uproar nowadays if women in the Police were subject to a 'fat test'.

Parade was very 'Army' based. You had to line up using your arm held straight out to your right, so it touched your colleague's shoulder, thus giving you a perfect straight line. You were then marched up and down, arms swinging, feet stomping while unintelligible commands were shouted at you. And you marched in all weathers!! Every week we had a mass parade on Wednesday morning. Your class had to have someone who would march slightly in front of you, usually a police colleague who was ex-army, and as you passed the Commanders they would shout 'Eyes right', and everyone would look to the right, directly at the row of commanders all stood there with their night sticks. Night sticks were given to police officers in the rank of Sgt or above. They are a piece of carved wood about 3 foot long with a metal tip. The history of these stems back years, when prior to Constables patrolling in cars they would each have a 'beat'. When your Sgt pegged you (checked up on you) on your beat they would tap their night stick on the ground so you could hear them coming, as the metal tip would be tapped on the cobbles. All the classes would congregate on the parade square in front of the Commanders and march around in the formations we'd been taught. It was like 'Trooping the colour', but on a much less grand scale. In front of the parade square was a building with a tower on it. In the top of the tower was an officer, usually one on light duties because they'd broken their arm or something similar. This officer was responsible for playing the music for everyone to march to. At the time this music was played on a 'record player' with a vinyl record in the 1980's or a CD as we moved into the 90's.

On one such occasion I remember a colleague telling me that when he was in Bruche in the 80's he had been banished to the tower on parade day due to an injury he had sustained to his ankle when he was nearly caught in a female's room and had to jump from the window to make his escape. He was sat in the tower on his own, and with the needle at the ready, he steadied himself ready to put it down on the record as the classes waited to march onto the parade square. He popped the needle down and the record crackled into life as the classes, arms swinging, marched onto the parade square towards the commander. Then he had an idea. He hadn't seen eye to eye with one of the instructors who had banished him to the tower so just as all the classes had entered the square, he put this finger on the record slowing it down. This resulted in marching carnage. Everyone lost their timings and were banging into each other. The instructor looked up at the Tower yelling my colleague's name. As penance for this he had to parade on at 5am every morning for a week to be inspected.

Every Wednesday on parade, the classes would be pitted against each other to win the lanyard for best class uniform. Every Tuesday night we would gather in our respective classrooms and polish our kit. We would bull our shoes together, getting tips from the ex-army lads who taught me to use spit and polish. We would then press our uniforms using a towel. If you put the iron directly on your tunic, trousers or skirt it would leave a shiny mark. You'd steam your hat to get the edges to sit up and then use rolls and rolls of Sellotape to get any flecks off your finished article.

Riot training was basically being fully kitted up in your boiler suit and boots and running with a 6-foot shield that weighed a ton up and down the parade square. Running together in a line and then sprinting as fast as you could. Riot training was clearly still in its infancy, as nowadays things are a lot more sophisticated. We didn't have body armour or utility belts to hold your kit on. Everything was attached to the leather belt that held your skirt or trousers up, and by everything, I mean your handcuffs. One of my female colleagues was only small and the riot shield towered above her.

After spending 10 weeks at Bruche, you returned to your respective station for 5 weeks with your tutor constable. My previous tutor constable had left our section, so I was allocated with a different one. He was and still is one of the best officers I've ever worked with. A truly well-rounded copper who taught me a lot. This 5 week period was a 'baptism of fire' as we say in the police. I completed a 5-week shift pattern which at the time included a tour of 'nights. At the time your night shifts lasted for 7 nights. The powers that be have now decided that working 7 nights in a row isn't good for your health and so nights now consist of 4 nights followed a few weeks later by a tour of 3 nights. I can see their point as during this shift you really did live it. You worked your shift, went home to bed, got up and came back to work for a whole week. During my 5-week shift pattern you worked days 7am -5pm. Lates 2 pm- 12 pm and nights, 10.30pm – 7am.

During my 5 weeks with my new group, it really was 'sink or swim'. I was the only woman on a group of very capable male officers. I got loads of 'stick' but as I was eventually told, 'They wouldn't give you stick if they didn't like you'. I was called a 'Doris' which is a derogatory name for a policewoman. I was known as a WPC whereas now a days women police officers are just known as PC's. I was also known as a 'Plonk' which is also a slang name for a policewoman. I also became aware from listening to stories in the canteen that policewomen were either a 'Dyke or a bike', meaning you were either a lesbian or a female officer who would sleep with the men on her shift.

So, there I was as a 21-year-old who knew absolutely nothing, going to all sorts of jobs with my tutor constable. Yes, in Bruche I'd learnt the caution 'You do not have to say anything but anything you do say may be given in evidence' and arrested my colleagues for pretend offences but this was a whole different ball game. I was posted to an inner-city area which was very rough. It had a very high crime rate and a lot of drugs problems. I'd never taken drugs or even seen them so the first time I came across cannabis resin I didn't know what it was. To me it looked like an oxo cube. I really had to learn fast.

I was attending 'domestic disputes. Now I'd been brought up in a 4-bedroom semi-detached house in quite an affluent area and now I was policing in an area predominantly filled with terraced housing and is classed as one of the most run down and drug fuelled areas of the country. I remember the first domestic dispute I went to. As I walked into the small hallway I thought 'Where's the carpet'. It was just floorboards. It didn't' occur to me that some people didn't

23

have or couldn't afford carpets. People had some real issues, and it made me realise what a privileged upbringing I'd had. Drunk parents looking after several children. Children running around with full nappies crying because they were hungry. We'd deal with the job and walk away. You just put a sticking plaster on the incident. The same care wasn't taken like it is today to inform social services of the issues within the household. You arrested the man usually for being drunk just to get him out of the house. There was no point arresting him for assault because his wife/girlfriend would refuse to provide a statement of complaint, and without a statement you'd never get a charge. When I first joined the police, it was your desk Sgt who agreed to charge your prisoner. This is still the case for a majority of cases, but more complex cases now have to be sent to the Crown Prosecution Service or CPS as they're known. A lawyer will review the evidence and decide if there is enough to charge your prisoner. This can and does take hours on the phone!

After 5 weeks of being a police officer for real, I returned to Bruche to finish the remainder of my training. This lasted another 5 weeks. We were again put into mixed classes and were given a timetable. I remember during one of the self-defence classes in the gym. We had been issued with Judo suits, as the class was quite Judo based. I'd done a bit of Judo from aged 5 to 13 so I knew a bit but didn't say anything. You learnt to keep your mouth shut or you'd be pulled to the front of the class to help with demonstrations. Anyway, this day I'd been grappling with one of the male officers and I was getting the better of him much to the amusement of the male instructors. I could hear them saying, 'She's going to have him'. I put my colleague in an armlock and he tapped his submission. I got up off the floor and the whole class were looking at us. I'll be honest, when I heard them say this there was no way I was getting up unless I'd won. My male colleague was mortified and the rest of the men in the class took the piss out of him relentlessly over this for the remainder of the course.

So, we continued with our training. A lot of emphasis was placed on our final parade which would be in front of friends and family. This was called your 'Passing out parade' so we marched and marched as it had to be perfect.

The night before your passing out parade there was a formal dinner, and all the female officers had to have a male escort who comprised of one of your colleagues. As a gay female officer who wasn't out to any of her colleagues, I wasn't overly happy about this. I was also expected to wear a dress. I didn't even own a dress, so borrowed one from a straight friend of mine. I asked one of the male officers in my class if he'd accompany me and he agreed, picking me up on the night in his tuxedo. I felt so uncomfortable throughout the whole night tottering around in my heals. It was the very early 90's and people just didn't 'come out'. I knew some of the female instructors were gay, but you didn't talk about it. Being gay was only declassified as being a mental illness by the World Health Organisation the year I joined the police, and hate crimes weren't even a thing, so you just stayed in the closet and kept your mouth shut.

The day before our passing out parade the weather was terrible with wind and rain but the morning of our parade it was frosty and cold with bright sun and not a breath of wind. I was so excited. My mum came to watch me. She died 18 months later so I'll always cherish the fact that she saw me that day and was so proud of me.

We all stood in our classes at the foot of the parade square ready to march on in front of friends and family. At the front of the parade were the police horses and riders in full regalia and the police band whose music we would march to. I couldn't see my mum as we marched past our families as there were so many people there. The parade went like a dream with everybody marching in time. Sometimes during the hotter months when we were training officers would faint. If they did faint you just left them. God help you if you broke ranks!!! After the parade is finished, we threw our hats in the air and cheered. Then there were photographs on actual cameras. The photo of me and my mum still sits on my mantlepiece. Me all fresh faced and my mum with tears in her eyes. You then said your goodbyes to friends from other forces and made your way home. Roll on the next 30 years! I was now in 'The Job'.

1992

Every police force has a main police station usually called a Bridewell. I was very young in service and attended the Bridewell probably to deal with a prisoner we'd lodged there. To me, the men that worked there were old, experienced, and very intimidating. You learnt to keep your mouth shut and do as you were told. Whilst at the Bridewell it was customary for new WPCs to have their 'arse stamped' with the Bridewell stamp. This is called 'station stamping', where you could choose to either have your arse or your tit stamped. This is an ink stamp with the name of the police station written on it. I had to sit on the desk, lift my skirt up and get my arse stamped. This was a tradition for policewomen in my force and if you didn't take part .... Well, you just weren't fun were you!!!!

(Bridewell – A small prison or police station that has cells. Named after St Bride, an area of London that once had a house of correction).

1994

I was working a night shift and at about 3 am a report came in of a riot in a prison about 20 miles away from our station. Our Inspector and Sgt were responsible for organising a 'serial' of officers who would get kitted up in riot gear to attend the prison and deal with the disturbance. I was so excited. I ran to my locker and got my riot bag which contained my overalls and boots etc and went to the parade room with all my male colleagues. My Sgt approached me 'You're staying here to 'man' the phones' he said. I was gutted. I really thought I'd be going with my colleagues to the prison riot. I had more service than two of the other policemen who went.

So off they all went laughing and joking and I 'manned' the phones!!! On the plus side when my shift finished, I got off at 7am and they still weren't back until after 10am. I think at that point I realised that some people think very little of policewomen. They let you be part of the gang until they didn't want you. It was disappointing, but you just got on with it.

1997

I was sent to a report of a drunk female who needed removing from a pub. Usually at these kinds of jobs, you turn up, they're drunk, they swear at you, and you lock them up. Not so at this job. I arrive at the pub and there is the culprit. An 80-year-old lady with dementia who is very drunk. I speak to her and she's quite calm with the occasional outburst of obscenities. I go through her handbag and find a home address for her. She tells me she lives with her son. She agrees to come with me, and I decide to take her home. Usually with prisoners you place them in the rear of the car behind the front seat passenger for safety reasons. A colleague would usually sit next to the prisoner in the rear of the police car, but on this occasion, I was just giving the drunk old lady a lift home wasn't I? I was also single crewed for the day. A practise that to this day I find dangerous.

I helped her out of the pub and into the front passenger seat of the police car and we began our journey to her house. She got a bit agitated on the journey and as I attempted to calm her down, she suddenly punched me in the face splitting my lip. I manged not to crash the police car and got her home in one piece. I returned to the station with a fat lip and subsequently got the piss taken out of me by my colleagues.

2005

It was Saturday and I was working a night shift and had been sent to a report of burglary just after midnight. The Sunday would be Mother's Day. When I arrived at the address there was a man standing in the window of the house next door. I thought nothing of it as I walked up the path, us both looking at each other. I dealt with the job and left.

At 5am on the same night shift I'm again dispatched to the same street but this time to the address where the man had been stood looking at me, to a report of a hanging.

I got there with my colleague to find his girlfriend and small child stood in the front room shouting at me through the window. I asked her to open the door, but she tells me they've lost the front door key and the only way to get in and out of the house is through the top window. This was an old Victorian terrace house, and the top windows were high. A fleeting thought of 'How do lose your fucking front door key and keep climbing in through the window?' I quickly took off my belt kit and hauled myself up onto the window ledge, telling my colleague to throw me my utility belt when I was in. I teetered on the top ledge while his girlfriend was screaming at me help her. I just let go and fell into the living room. I put my right arm out to save myself as I landed on a small side table. Unbeknown to me I had broken my wrist but due to the adrenaline surging through my body wouldn't realise this until later. The girlfriends still screaming 'Help him'.

I run into the hallway and see him, the man who had looked at me through the window 5 hours earlier, hanging by his neck in the footwell of the stairs. I moved his body and got behind him. Hangings aren't really like you see on the TV where the body is swinging, most hangings happen when people place a noose around their neck and just let their body go floppy, so their neck takes the weight of the body which cuts off their oxygen supply. This is what this man had done. His legs were slightly bent, and his body was still. His girlfriend and small child had followed me into the hallway, her now screaming. I took the weight of him on my right knee to try and take some of the pressure off him. He had used an old fleecy bed blanket to make the noose. The type you had in the 1970's that was fleecy with pastel stripes. He had tied it to the top of the banister and then knotted it around his neck and I couldn't get the knot undone. He emptied his bowels, and it dripped down my leg. I remember thinking 'I had one of these blankets as a child'. I screamed at his girlfriend 'get me a knife'. She ran off retuning a short time later. All the while I was holding him up trying to keep the pressure off his neck. She returns and hands me the knife and I managed to cut though the blanket. I took his weight and eased him down onto the stairs and then slid him down onto the floor.

At this point I heard a large smash and realised my colleague had smashed the front room window to get into the house. I remember thinking' Why didn't I do that'? Anyway, she joins me in the hallway, and I loosened the noose around his neck. We'd called for backup, paramedics and someone to bring a door opener (big orange key) I took my mouth cover out of my utility belt and placed it over his mouth and began breathing into him as my colleague did chest compressions. All this, while the girlfriend was screaming hysterically. I realised there was nothing we could do, he was dead, had been for a while by the looks of him.

The front door suddenly smashed open, and my colleagues were there. They realised there was nothing they could do and took his girlfriend into the front room to comfort her. The paramedics had arrived a short time earlier and had climbed in through the broken window and realised there was nothing they could do for him either. I left the house to sit in the police car. I was in shock. I couldn't believe what I'd just done. It didn't even occur to me to be scared during all of this, you just get on and do your job. No matter who the person is you just want to do your best for them, and you're gutted when you don't.

I went home, undressed in front of the washing machine and took off my shitty trousers to wash them. This incident affected me beyond measure. What this man didn't know was that my mum had died suddenly years before, and Mother's Day was always hard for me to start with, and now this!!! Mother's Day for me is now ruined. Not only do I not have my mum, but every Mother's Day I remember dealing with this hanging. He wasn't to know this and was hurting when he took his own life, I get that.

This incident still plagues me today 17 years on. I have PTSD and struggle to deal with anything that's knotted, wires, string, Christmas lights. As soon as I see something knotted, I see his face, I hear his name. I had counselling to work through my issues which has helped immensely.

2014

I'd just started working in my new post in child protection and was sent to speak to a lady who'd found indecent images of children on her partners laptop. Statement taken from her, I went and got a warrant for his address. A couple of days later, armed with a van load of uniform cops, we went to his address to execute the search warrant. He opened the door and to coin a phrase 'The world fell out of his bottom'. I handed him the search warrant for his address and explained why we were there and that we'd be taking his computer equipment, of which he had lots!!! He told me while shaking violently 'There's stuff on my computers'. We seized a lot of hard drives and laptops. He was arrested and interviewed and advised by his solicitor to say 'no comment' as I hadn't viewed the content on the hard drives at this point. Then he was given a long bail date because to view what he had on the laptops was going to take a while.

What used to happen was that the police staff who worked in the indecent image's unit would view your exhibits (laptops and hard drives) and then they produce a report on their findings. Unluckily for me this was no longer the case due to cutbacks of staff. I had to go to the indecent images unit to view all the indecent images and videos myself that had been found on this man's hard drives.

The night before I first went to view these images I sat in the bath with a glass of wine and cried. I had a knot in my stomach that just wouldn't go. I've always said that 'once you've seen something you can't unsee it'. I was dreading it. The next morning it was worse than I could ever had imagined. There were 57,000 indecent images and videos of children on this man's devices. I won't go into detail about what I saw as it's very distressing, but it was truly the most awful thing I've ever seen in my life. The look on the children's faces, just blank and accepting of the horrors that were about to befall them. Children being raped by men and women. Children tied up and indecently assaulted. Horrific things done to children with animals as well as videos of animals being sexually assaulted and killed. The children were very distressed, and I found this incredibly upsetting. During one 'snuff' video I watched I had to stop halfway through because it was so horrific to go and be sick in the toilets. A man was murdered on a video in front of me. Nobody knew who he was. There was no way of telling who he was. His body was mutilated and dismembered and then sexually assaulted. To this day it is probably the most shocking thing I have ever had to view in my career. In total I had to re bail this man a further 3 times to give me more time to view the videos and images he had on his devices. I only went down to view the images once a week. I tried to do it twice a week but found it too distressing.

He eventually answered his bail, and with overwhelming evidence confronting him admitted possession of the images. I discussed with him the snuff video I'd had to view, his reply 'Oh I couldn't watch that it was too bad'. I just sat there open mouthed looking at him. At court he received 12 months in prison for possession of the images. He would serve only half of his sentence, so 6 months. It had taken me longer to view the images than he got in prison. I would love to speak to the home secretary about this and ask for an increase in the sentencing for possession of indecent images of children. Make it a mandatory 5-year sentence when you get caught.

These images stay with me to this day. I have flashbacks about certain very distressing images I saw. Many of these videos are made in European countries. You can tell this if you look beyond the image and at the plug sockets in the room. It really plays on my mind about the children. There's literally 1000's of images of different children and I'm just sat there grading them. No one knows who they are and I'm dealing with one man who has been caught with these indecent images. There are literally 1000's of people viewing these images daily. I subsequentially had a breakdown and started having flash backs of indecent images of children I had viewed. After numerous sessions of counselling, I've been able to come to terms with what I saw but it'll never leave me.

2017

Whilst working in CID in the Child Protection Department you deal with some harrowing incidents. What I've come to realise in my career is that when I was in other departments, like the drug squad in the late 90's, I'd go to court with my colleagues, and we'd have a laugh. We would all give our evidence and invariably the suspect would be found guilty. We would then go to the pub and toast ourselves laughing and joking over the prison sentence the drug dealers got. Child Protection I was about to learn, was a whole different ball game.

You get the complaint; you attend the medical examination with the child and the specialist paediatric doctors. You interview the child, and they eventually open to you telling you they've been assaulted, sexually assaulted or raped. To see the effect this has on the children is very upsetting. These paedophiles have no idea the lasting effect their actions have on these children. It makes you think about your own childhood and the carefree days you had playing with your friends and how incredibly lucky you were. I then interview the offender. I've had offenders say 'no comment' during interviews as well as offenders who have admitted everything. Historic offences are notoriously hard to prove as there is no forensic evidence. It's basically just one word against another. Thankfully the jury see through this most of the time and find the offender guilty. I've had historic rapes go to court and the offender is found not guilty. The offenders turn up with walking sticks when they've never used one before. Requesting to use the 'hearing loop' in court. It's all for show, for the jury to make them feel sorry for the frail old man stood in the dock. Old men who have been accused of horrific sexual offences appear at court wearing a smart blazer adorned with war medals.

I was at court years before with a case of possession with intent to supply controlled drugs. At the scene when I had initially arrested the man, I chased him up the stairs and across the landing and he flushed the drugs down the toilet. Luckily, we had someone stood with a bucket by the open drain and retrieved it all. This offender turned up at Crown court in a wheelchair!!! Being pushed by his wife. The wheelchair even had a tag on the back of it as I suspect he'd either just bought it or more accurately probably hired it for the day. He got off with a suspended sentence.... Well, he was in a wheelchair!!

The truth is the kids and adults involved in these cases are broken. The children suffer terribly. Over sexualised at such a young age. Some have carried their baggage around for years and then bravely come forward to tell the police what has happened to them. They go to Court, get pulled apart by the defending barrister (who I understand are only doing their job) and the jury comes back and says, 'Not Guilty'. These jobs tear though families forcing parents and grandparents to 'take sides', forever ripping families apart. When this happens, I feel devastated for them and have come home and cried on many an occasion. Sat on my own downstairs when my partners gone to bed. Sometimes it's just not fair. Why would a victim of sexual abuse come forward and bear all to risk being ripped apart by a defence barrister in a court full of family members. Why would you choose to put yourself through this unless it had happened. What's important is that I believed them, and I always made sure I told them that.

2002

Crown Court is great. I've always loved going to court. The whole drama of it!! On one such occasion I'd attended Crown Court due to me arresting an offender for indecent exposure. If you get arrested for a 'summary' offence ie shoplifting or minor traffic offences these usually get dealt with at Magistrates Court and a solicitor will represent you. If the sentence you might receive is likely to be greater than 6 months, your case is transferred to Crown Court. At Crown Court you are represented by a barrister in a wig and gown. Over the years I've met some very good barristers, and a few not so good ones. There's nothing like the drama of seeing them in full flow during a cross examination. Anyway, my indecent exposure job ended up at Crown Court.

The incident went something like this. I was sat in my patrol car at 2am looking through my A to Z trying to find the location of the incident I'd just been dispatched to by the radio room. I was suddenly aware of a man banging on the bonnet of the patrol car shouting at me. As I looked up, he turned away from me and pulled his trousers down showing me his arse. I was going to put this down to him just being pissed when he then turned round grabbing his dick and starts waving and gesturing it at me. As I got out of the police car to arrest him for indecent exposure, because in my mind he was totally taking the piss, he runs off down the street followed by me and my colleague. He ran into his house and slammed the front door in my face. Not to be deterred I go around the back of the house and find the back door unlocked, so I go in. I find the culprit in the hallway behind the front door undressing. 'What do you want, I've just got out of bed' he says. I arrest him. There's an almighty struggle. My colleague fearing for my safety, kicks the front door in to help me. We drag him outside followed now by his screaming girlfriend. I'd managed to shout for back up, which arrived quite quickly. In the scuffle the girlfriend managed to grab and unclip my radio from my body armour and throw it under a parked car. Several of the local neighbours joined us on the pavement shouting the usual 'leave him alone, he's done fuck all'. Little did they know he'd been waving his dick at me minutes earlier. Anyway, he came in for indecent exposure and his girlfriend got arrested for a public order offence.

Fast forward some months later to his appearance at Crown Court. He was having none of the evidence and had pleaded not guilty?? You seriously couldn't make this shit up. It's all really funny when you're waving your dick around at a police officer, but when there's a possibility you're going to be placed on the sex offenders register it isn't so funny. My barrister approaches me on the landing outside Crown Court. Now, what can happen at Crown Court is that the indictment (the offence you're charged with) can be changed. My barrister was asking if I agreed to the accused male being charged with a lesser offence of public order, causing harassment, alarm or distress, as he was willing to plead guilty to this. As I said I quite like going to court, so I said 'No' it's indecent exposure or nothing. Then I said to her 'what's he going to ask for next, for it to be dropped to a charge of 'possession of an offensive weapon?' 'That would be no good as an offensive weapon has to be bigger than three and a half inches'. The barrister who was female burst out laughing when I said this, at which point the accused male turned around and scowled at us. My barrister made her way back into court and returned a few minutes later. The accused had now spoken to his barrister and had agreed to plead guilty to indecent exposure. If you plead not guilty and opt for trial and are found guilty, you run the risk of getting a higher sentence, usually imprisonment, so sometimes it makes sense to plead guilty.

I then go into the court room. The accused is in the dock and the judge is sat ready to pass sentence and he said, 'This is just high jinks, a bit like when I was in University', and gave the accused a bit of a fine and sent him on his way. I thanked my barrister and left the court room shaking my head and thinking, 'I give up'! So, the Crown Court Judge thought that flashing your dick around in public is 'just a bit of fun'. I'm sure if I was flashing my tits at a member of the public, I would lose my job.

2007

I was a probationer, 21 and out on patrol with a male colleague. He drove to a popular area where kids would park up and smoke weed. If we found anyone it would be a nice easy arrest for me. This area was quite secluded and out of the way. As were driving down the track he stops the car, undoes his utility belt, reaches across me and runs his hand up the inside of my leg, and touches my vagina over my trousers. I just wasn't expecting this to happen and in no way had I encouraged any sort of behaviour like this. I jumped back and grabbed his hand, twisting it round hard. He yelled 'You nearly broke my wrist'. I quickly got out of the police car and walked off shouting up on my radio for someone to come and collect me. My Sgt, knowing I was out with a colleague must have thought this was strange and so came to collect me. Prior to my Sgt arriving my male colleague had turned the police vehicle around and was now driving alongside me slowly with his window down saying, 'I'm sorry, I misread the signs'. 'I didn't give you any fucking signs' I shouted back at him. He was pleading with me to get back into the police car.

A short time later I'm collected by my Sgt and driven back to the police station where I tell him what has happened. He gives me two choices. 'You can either report this as a sexual assault and forever be the girl who reported one of her colleagues, or I can have five minutes with him in the rear yard and I guarantee he'll never do this again because I'll give him a beating. Being new to the job I opted for the second option as I didn't want this stigma following me around for the rest of my career. I never did find out what happened during the 'five-minute chat' but the officer who basically sexually assaulted me was happy to go into the yard with the Sgt and take whatever was about to be meted out to him which I suspect was a good hiding.

2008

I was on patrol with a male colleague late at night when I saw a male stood by a wall, pants around his ankles looking like he was having a wee. I walk up to him saying 'Stop that, you can't do that there'. The man carries on facing the wall as I shout a bit louder 'Stop that'. He just carries on facing the wall, so I took hold of him by the arm and turned him around to find he's masturbating, penis in hand, just as he ejaculates up the arm of my florescent yellow coat. I screamed as this was quite horrific as his semen is now dribbling down my arm. 'I'm sorry miss I'm drunk' says the man. My male colleague joins me on the pavement to see what all the fuss is about, and I tell him what has happened. He bursts into fits of laughter and shouts up on the radio 'Can we have a cage. Some fellas just spunked all over ....' The radio operator replied 'say again over' as she can't quite believe her ears. In the meantime, I'm still shouting and screaming in the background. My other colleagues hearing this, and hearing me scream think it's a 'Con requires' (officer needing urgent assistance) and so make their way to my location. When they realise, I'm not getting beaten up but in fact have just been jizzed on they all laugh as well. The prisoner is escorted to the police station along with me. I end up stood in the yard shouting 'Get this fucking jacket off me its covered in jizz'. My colleague was telling me to calm down as I could see them all bent double laughing. I had to get someone to peel the jacket off me as I screamed 'Get it off me'. The jacket was then put in the bin.

2016

I was dealing with a SUDI (sudden unexplained death of an infant). The baby had been taken to the bereavement suite where I was to meet them. When I got there, there was all the family, three generations. Mum, grandmother and great grandmother who was terminally ill and didn't have long to live. The baby was being passed around the family members for a last cuddle and was handed to the great grandmother who sat cradling him in her arms saying to him 'I waited to meet you. You're all that's kept me going. It won't be long until I'm with you now'. It was so sad to see. I felt extremely privileged to be present with the family at this very sad time. The family then asked if I would like to hold the baby and of course I accepted. I held his cold little body and commented as to how gorgeous he was before I handed him back to his mum. I heard from the family that the great grandmother passed away before the baby's funeral. True to her word she was now looking after him. I always think with SUDI's that when you attend them you can't make things better for the family, but you could make things a hell of lot worse depending on how you deal with the incident. I've lost count of the amount of SUDI's I have dealt with. All you can do is offer some sort of comfort for these families on the worst day of their lives. You really feel like you are unavoidably intruding on their grief. Jobs like this make you hug your own kids a bit tighter when you get home.

2010

Sent to deal with a male wanted for a DV incident one afternoon. I arrived with my male colleague to see a man stood on the pavement with his arms outstretched saying 'come on then'. We walked towards him and pulled out a large, serrated bread knife and is waving it around. My colleague, quick thinking, ran towards him and grabbed hold of him pulling him close as we then wrestled him to the floor. It was obvious the man had taken a lot of cocaine as he had the strength of ten men. He was on the floor still holding the knife refusing to let go of it. I literally was stamping on his arm to try and get him to drop the knife which he eventually did. My colleague ended up with a black eye. I had to go to hospital to get an x ray as I'd taken a nasty dig to the stomach.

We had to stay with the prisoner while he was getting seen to at the hospital. He apologised to us about threatening us with the knife as he laid there with his wrist and arm smashed to pieces where I had stamped on him. 'It's alright girl it's not your fault'. You don't mind when they apologise!!!

2010

Arresting a teenage girl who was a lunatic. I had her handcuffed to the rear and was dragging her to the police car and as we reached the car door she turned around and gobbed in my face. She was charged with assault, and I was awarded £80 which she paid at the amount of 20p a week!! I'd occasionally get a cheque through the internal mail for £2.45.

2010

Dealing with a prisoner at the custody suite. We placed him in the cell when he suddenly pulled his trousers down and did a massive shit on the cell floor. We hurriedly slammed the cell door shut as he picked up the shit and threw it at the cell door. I heard it 'splat' on the other side.

2022

The graduate police entry scheme. We are sleep walking into a disaster in policing because of the degree entry now. I understand you want a professional style of policing but you're losing 'life experience'. You need people who can speak to people on their terms because they know what it's like. I grew up poor, I know what it is like to be poor. I know what it's like to go without. I'm from a council estate. I can reach people that graduates from an affluent area cannot. We're losing all this experience. When you've had nothing, you can communicate with people, you can understand what they're dealing with. You know about vulnerability.

2014

I attended Family Court with my Sgt in December in relation to an application for children to be returned to the family home for Christmas. This was my first experience of Family Court, and it has stuck with me ever since. The circumstances were laid out by the prosecution solicitor working on behalf of the police. The children had been removed from the family home some months earlier and placed into foster care due to neglect. Neglect can be physical harm, sexual harm, emotional harm, medical neglect or educational neglect. This was general neglect. Lack of schooling, medical neglect (not being seen by a doctor or dentist) by the parents which in my opinion had caused emotional harm. You go to some houses, and I know you can't apply your own personal level of cleanliness on other people but some of the houses we are asked to visit are dirty. There's no food in the house, the children have very little or no toys. The children are sleeping on the floor on dirty bedding and just a mattress. Social services get involved and tell you that they've given the parents money to spend on a new bed. Well, here's some fucking news for you, they spent it on drugs and alcohol. Sometimes you feel like banging your head against the wall.

The facts were laid out to the judge about the neglect the children had suffered. The solicitor on behalf of the parents then puts their case forward and says how they've improved and turned their life around. The judge believes all this and says, 'It's clear that these children should be with their parents on this 25th day of December', like we're in some Dickens novel. I left the court shaking my head. The children would be returned to their parents over Christmas. What I wanted to do was stand up and shout at the judge 'Do you think they sit around a log fire on Christmas Eve having a cheese board and a glass of Port? What they do have is 12 tinnies (beers) and a punch up. Not forgetting that the parents over Christmas would then be entitled to all the child support again. I'm sure that had nothing to do with the parent's decision of wanting their children home.

1995

I attended a sudden death. The deceased was an old man who had died in his living room sat on the couch. There was nothing suspicious, so we waited for the ambulance to arrive and for the ambulance staff to pronounce life extinct. We then asked for the undertakers to attend. This usually takes a while, so you settle down and wait. My colleague could see the man had died whilst doing the crossword, so he sat next to him on the couch, picked up the paper and finished the crossword for him saying 'There you go fella' and popped the newspaper back on his lap.

1997

I was at Crown Court on two separate jobs in the same week, so it was going to be a busy one. The first day was a drugs trial. Myself and my colleague gave our evidence against the two men and then made our way home. We go back to Crown court the following day for the second trial. Now at Crown Court you can get out of the building two or three ways. Down the stairs that are usually situated at either end of the building, in the public lift, or in the barristers lift which is only really for barristers but we sometimes sneaked in it.

After giving our evidence on the second trial me and my colleague left the floor of the crown court and decided to take the stairs down. We were both dressed in full police uniform at this point. As soon as we got through the doors there was an overpowering smell of(weed) cannabis. I looked, and one flight of stairs below us were the two men from the trial we had been on the previous day smoking a massive joint (cannabis cigarette). I mean how cheeky can you be. You're on trial for PWITS (possession with intent to supply) and you've brought drugs to court with you. I shouted 'Oi' at which point they look up at me and then begins the mother of all foot chases down the numerous flights of stairs.

Every landing has three flights of stairs, and we were on the 6th landing, he was near the 5th when I saw him. I chased him and his friend all the way down to the bottom floor, down 18 flights of stairs, where I jumped on him and we landed in a heap on the floor, him still holding the massive spliff in his hand. Just at this point the doors to the barristers lift open and four barristers are stood there looking at me horrified as I'm rolling round with this man trying to arrest him, and his friend trying to drag me off him. Now, thinking that barristers uphold the law I shout to them 'Help me will you'. No, they all scurried away through the doors and back into chambers. Well thanks a fucking lot! At this point I'm joined by my colleague who helps me restrain the man while again the second male is hitting my colleague trying to rescue his pot head mate. My colleague drew his arm back and elbowed the second man in the face breaking his nose. They both got arrested, one for possession and the other for obstruction. My opinion of barristers went down a lot that day.

2003

Legislation had just been passed making it illegal to use your mobile phone while driving. What happens in the police is that when a new law is passed you want to either arrest someone for that offence or give a ticket out for it straight away because its new and you've not done it before. One evening I'm in my patrol car when I spot a lady on her mobile phone whilst she was driving. Bingo! I quickly turn the police car around and go after her, using my blue lights and klaxons to stop her. I get out of the police car an approach her driver's side window ready to give her a dressing down and a ticket. As I start to speak to her, I realise she's in floods of tears. I ask what's wrong and she points to the back seat of the car. I look and see a large dog sat on a towel on the back seat, and lots of blood. 'She had puppies a couple of days ago, she's started bleeding and it won't stop. I'm trying to find the emergency vets. You only had to look at dog to see it was very unwell and with the amount of blood it was losing this didn't look good. This explained why the lady was on her mobile phone.

I told her to follow me, and I would take her to the emergency vets. 'I'll put the blue lights on just stay right behind my police car'. So off we set me leading the way and the lady following. I got my colleague to contact the radio room and notify the vets that we were on the way with a dog that was haemorrhaging badly. We reached the vets in a matter of minutes to find the staff and vet waiting for us in the carpark with a trolly for the dog. The dog was whisked into theatre straight away and the lady said a teary thank you to us. I hope the dog made it through.

2015

I was at a post-mortem acting as 'scribe' (making notes for the pathologist). My colleague had drawn the short straw and was in the room with the pathologist collecting exhibits as they were handed to him, standing next to the pathologist as he conducted the post-mortem. The death had been deemed suspicious so a 'home office' post-mortem' was taking place. This is a much more detailed examination of a body than a run of the mill post-mortem where the deceased has died of natural causes. I was sat comfortably behind glass watching the proceedings and thankfully getting none of the smell. As part of the proceedings, fingernail clippings need to be taken, so the pathologist took hold of the dead man's hand as my colleague held open the forensic bag ready to collect the clippings. The first snip was made and suddenly my colleague jumped backwards 'Oh god it went in my mouth' he shouted. I nearly fell off my chair laughing.

1992

All the police stations still had bars on the top floor where officers would congregate after work for a pint. As the probationer on the group, it was my job to run upstairs on a late shift when we'd handed over the cars to the night shift and order the drinks. The order was like some massive shopping list. I'd run upstairs and into the bar, handing the list over to the lovely lady who'd worked behind the bar for years. Ten minutes later we'd all head upstairs for a well-earned drink. This was the place to discuss what had happened during your shift. For the elders on the group to give you their wisdom and advise. All the police bars have closed now, and I feel sorry for the probationers who won't get to experience this camaraderie. I'm not joking when I say that the number of drinks on our order was huge. It covered the end of the bar. We'd all laugh and joke about the jobs we'd dealt with that day and drink our pints, vodka and cokes or glasses of wine. Then we'd all drive home!! There was probably a good reason why the bars were eventually closed.

1993

I'd completed my initial riot training at Police training school, but actual riot training once you were posted to your station was a whole different ball game. Every Tuesday when we had finished our tour of earlies, we would all pile into the police carrier and head off to an old aeroplane hangar for riot training. Unlike nowadays where there are purpose-built arenas for riot training with hard houses and football stadium seating, the aeroplane hangar was not like this. It had an old wooden structure built inside it which was a two story 'house'. There was also a huge hole in the roof of this building which caused a puddle to form on the floor as the rain just poured in. This was an extra obstacle, as you had to try not to slip over as you ran around. The flame proof overalls were kept on a massive hangar. There must have been 50 of them. You'd go into the room housing the overalls and pick one that you thought you would fit into. This overall had probably been worn by countless sweaty men over the previous months and not been washed. Being the only female there I was allocated a separate changing room. This was just a small room full of spiders and two old rusty chairs. Your overalls were to be worn over you police uniform as you must have a 'second skin' under your flame proof blue overalls which usually consisted of your black work trousers and white shirt.

You were then run ragged for two hours, sweating profusely through your woollen trousers and police shirt. Occasionally you would do a six-man entry into the wooden house which comprised of three men in front with shields facing forwards and three men (obviously he didn't think any women were there!) behind them with their shields placed on top of the front three shields forming a roof. You would then attempt to enter the building while car tyres are thrown on top of your shield roof. This was a far cry from running up and down the parade square in a line. In your serial, you would chase the instructors around the hanger as they pretended to be rioters throwing wooden blocks at you as you tried to advance on them. Suddenly there was a huge flash in front of me. The heat was immense like I'd opened an oven door in my face. One of the instructors had thrown a petrol bomb at our shields. It hit the shield of the officer running next to me. The fire engulfed us both for seconds, the heat intense and the fumes unbearable. We'd been given no warning there would be petrol bombs thrown at us, and no training on how to deal with petrol bombs when you're hit by them, we just had to get on with it. It's true to say health and safety were in their infancy!

2009

My male colleague was searching his prisoner at the custody suite in front of the Sgt who was elevated behind his desk. As my colleague patted down the front of the man's trousers he said, 'what's this?' as he patted the suspicious bulge down the man's leg. 'It's my dick' came the reply.

2002

I was at the custody suite dealing with my prisoner and as there were no male custody assistants free, the prisoner agreed I could search him. I began my search of his clothing eventually patting down his legs when I felt a small lump. I patted the lump down to the hem of his trousers where a lump of shit then fell onto the floor.

2007

Working in uniform, I was called to bring a caged vehicle to the city centre to transport a prisoner who had been arrested for a public order offence. I arrived and walked towards the location of my colleagues. The area was a pedestrianised area surrounded by shops. I reached my colleagues who were stood together with no sight of the arrested male. 'Where's your prisoner?' I asked. They pointed to a tramp who was sat quite calmly about 25 feet away from them on some steps. I was confused. Usually, people who have been arrested for a public order offence are shouting and swearing. 'What's he done?' I asked. Without saying a word, they pointed to a wedding dress shop. I noticed two staff members stood behind the glass doors, one of them holding a mop and bucket. They were pointing outside the shop to the biggest pile of human shit I've ever seen! The tramp had dropped his trousers and pooed in front of the shop door. We lead the prisoner to the van to put him in the cage. I have never smelt anything like I did that day. The man was literally caked in human shit. Normally if a prisoner is not 'kicking off' you don't need to blue light to the custody suite, but on this occasion, I had to put my foot down. Blue lights whirring and klaxons blaring, hanging my head out of the driver's window trying to breathe. We eventually made it to the station. Rather than pull up slowly to the metal shutters to be let in I slammed to a halt outside the police station, got out of the van and was sick all over the road. Not my finest moment in front of the public.

1998

My colleague was searching his prisoner in the custody suite. I see him patting down the prisoner's leg until he eventually brings out a small brown lump. Thinking this was Cannabis he says, 'Oh yeah and what's this'. That's shit, replied the prisoner.

2009

Whilst working on a drugs team I dealt with a 'crack house closure'. The police had been given new powers to get rid of problem tenants and neighbours who were causing anti-social behaviour and basically making other people's lives a misery. This incident was in an enclosed gated community which housed people aged 55 and over. One of the people housed in this community was a 55-year-old drug addict who was causing havoc. He would have fellow drug addicts calling around all hours of the day and night. Drug dealers would we selling their gear though the windows to the occupants inside waking the other residents with their constant shouting. During the daytime, drug addicts were congregating in the communal garden and would sit with their dogs' drinking cans of beer which they left littered around. Alcohol really is a recurring theme in so much of policing. They would also dig up the flowers planted by other residents and throw them around the gardens. I decided I was going to sort this out. I spent months collating statements from the other residents. Most residents were too scared to put pen to paper but agreed to complete a questionnaire about the impact this drug addict resident was having on their lives.

I conducted several drug warrants at the address due to information I would receive from the other residents living in the flats. During the warrants we recovered heroin and cocaine from the tenant of the flat and other drug addicts that would 'sit off' in his flat. I eventually put all my evidence, photographs of damage and findings of drugs possession together and present my evidence to the court. My hard work paid off. I had run this crack house closure alongside my regular drugs jobs, and it had been majorly time consuming. The magistrates issued a closure notice, and he had 7 days to move out. I called around to the flats that evening to find out from one of the other residents that the drug addict had moved out that afternoon. The old man was crying as he shook my hand and said 'thankyou'. I felt so proud of myself that I'd made a difference in the resident's lives. He told me that he planned to re plant the gardens again so that he and his neighbours could sit outside. I sincerely hoped the council would vet the new potential resident of the empty flat a bit more thoroughly next time.

1997

I was working a night shift and it was a weekday so it can be quiet. We received a call from the radio room that a male was continually ringing 999, asking for the Ambulance service. Once he was connected to the female operator, he would begin a barrage of 'dirty' talk to her. He would start heavy breathing and was obviously masturbating whilst talking to her. This went on for a few nights, with the culprit never caught. On the Thursday night at about 4 am again the calls started. By this time several Ambulances were circling the area that the male was calling from. The ambulance crews were so angry, as the female operator was quite distraught about what was happening. Even our Sgt had offered a crate of beer to whoever caught him. Suddenly another call came in. It was him talking to her again. I said to my colleague 'I reckon I might know where he is'. There was a tiny telephone box on a dark side road. One of those phone boxes that's just a small free standing one. I switched off the headlights on the police car as I drove down the road. The phone box had no sides to it, it was just a small triangular structure on the pavement and there he was. I switched on the headlights of the police car. The culprit was stood, erect penis in one hand, phone in the other. I jumped out of the police car and ran towards him. He didn't even see me he was so engrossed in his 'business'. Just as I reached him, he ejaculated onto the phone box. I took hold of him and placed my handcuffs onto his hands that were dripping with semen The phone box was also covered in semen. God help the next person that uses that I thought. I told the radio room to let the ambulance operator know we had him. As I placed him in the police car, several ambulance crews drove past us shouting obscenities out of the window at him. I told him he was lucky we caught him and not them! Some people do the strangest things. I also never got my crate of beer.

1997

I was working overtime at a premier league football ground. My duties that day were as a pitch officer. Nowadays stewards do this duty but, on this day, it was me. Just before half time I took my place at the side of the pitch and began walking between the halfway line and the back line. To this day I don't know how I didn't see this woman. Suddenly a woman ran onto the pitch with just her g string on, waving her shirt in the air, tits flying. The whole ground erupted in a cheer. I tried to stop her, but she dodged me and headed across the pitch waving her shirt above her head. We are told not to chase streakers onto the pitch and to leave it to the stewards. To my surprise they didn't do anything and just stood there. She continued across the pitch to the centre circle where she did a celebratory cartwheel, cheered on by the baying crowd.

I looked across the field and saw one of my female colleagues. The streaker was heading towards her and in my head, I thought 'Thank god for that'. This was not to be, as she completed her cartwheel and then headed back in my direction. 'Oh shit' I thought. She ran up to the side line and was greeted by her boyfriend who tried to hand the streaker her clothes. I took hold of her and told her she was under arrest and told her to put her shirt on and cover herself up. She refused, and to be honest if she wanted to flash her tits so be it. I handcuffed her, popped her clothes on top of the handcuffs and started to take her up the steps to the underneath concourse of the stadium. A few people barred my way shouting their protests, but I managed to get through the crowds with the assistance of a colleague. The funniest thing about the whole episode was that the whole stadium booed me! I later found out that several streakers had simultaneously streaked at Premier league football grounds on the same day. My streaker was the only one to be arrested and charged for her trouble.

2003

I was called to hospital following a serious car crash where a young male had been thrown through the car windscreen and was 'likely to prove' (likely he was going to die). I arrived at the hospital and had to go into Resus to remain with the young man while the hospital staff tried to save his life. It is always amazing to watch Doctors and nursing professionals in full flow, and I am always in awe of them. I was asked by the attending Doctor to get his parents to the hospital as soon as possible as the young man was not going to make it. I contacted my colleague who was with the young man's mother and asked him to 'blue light' the mum to me straight away. She was obviously aware of what had happened to her son and must have been terrified. The Doctor informed me the young man had died but he was being kept alive on a life support machine. He intended to ask the mother for permission to use her sons' organs for donation.

A couple of minutes later my colleague ran through the hospital doors with mum and she ran down the corridor towards me and the doctor. She must have just known her son had died by the look and my face and the doctors. Her knees buckled and she collapsed to the floor, a guttural wail leaving her body. It was so sad, but you can't cry, it's just not professional. You are there to try and help people, to make things better and there was no good news this lady was going to get this evening. She was taken into a side room, I remained outside listening to her wail and cry as the doctor asked for her son's organs, obviously needed for vital emergency transplants. The mum agreed and by doing this her son unknowingly saved the lives of several other people who were desperately ill. Sometimes my job is just sad.

2008

Whilst searching a male prisoner at the custody suite, my colleague got a 'needle stick' injury. The drug addict she had arrested failed to mention the used hyperaemic needle in his trouser pocket and it went straight into her hand. Then ensues the panic. You need to get to hospital as soon as possible for injections and tests. The custody Sgt asked the arrested male 'Have you got HIV', his reply while laughing 'You'll have to wait and see won't you'. My colleague had to endure 6 months of HIV blood tests before we finally found out she didn't have HIV. That's six months of it being on your mind every single waking minute. Being scared to have sex with your partner in case you infect them. The male in question was sentenced at court to 3 months in prison and served only half of that. As I said, my colleague had to wait 6 months to find out she was HIV negative.

1996

While working a quiet night patrol we were all called to attend a certain location as one of my colleagues had found some graffiti scrawled on a wall relating to another of our colleagues. On arrival we found 4-foot-high letters written on a huge wall. It said '........ .... IS A DICK BRIAN'. We all stood there open mouthed trying to make sense of what we were reading. I think it should say 'BRAIN' we eventually deduced. So much for the total DICK BRIAN that wrote it.

1996

In the 90's a lot of mental health establishments were closed, and the residents placed into housing to live on their own. As a result of this, the calls we received regarding mental health issues went through the roof. On one such occasion I was sent to a report of a female who had been banging on the internal wall of her terraced house for 48 hours singing hymns. We got there and had to force our way in with shields as we didn't know if she was armed. We found her inside wearing a dress and covered from head to toe in human shit. She had shit in her shoes then put them back on. Her internal wall had thousands of dents in it where she had hit it with the ball end of the hammer she had. Since living on her own she had also bought a kitten which I found drowned in the kitchen sink. I remember she had large tins of chopped pork open in the living room that she had been scooping out with her hands and eating. There was also a box of chicken crisps that she had been eating. The crisps were opened and strewn all over the living room floor. To this day if I smell chicken crisps it makes me feel sick. It was obvious that she hadn't been taking her medication. She was removed from her house into an ambulance for a hospital assessment no doubt to be returned weeks later to live on her own again.

1999

I was called to possibly one of the most distressing incidents I've ever dealt with. The rape of an old lady in her 90's. The lady through kindness had housed one of her grandchildren who had decided that he was going out to town on Saturday night. He returned in the early hours of Sunday morning with a male friend who had taken a lot of cocaine and told the grandson that he was going to 'shag' his granny. The grandson panicked and ran to a nearby police station telling the officer on the desk that a man had broken into his grans house. The officer dispatched a patrol to check it out. In the meantime, the male had gone upstairs and subjected the 90-year-old to horrific sexual assaults and rape. The neighbours in the terraced house next door were alerted something was wrong when they heard a man voice shouting 'open your legs'. They too called the police who arrived minutes later, kicking the front door in and finding the male walking downstairs pulling his trousers up. He was arrested, and I dealt with the lady.

To say it was harrowing was an understatement, but she seemed to take it all in her stride. She was taken for a forensic medical examination, and I remember she was too small to get on the examination table, so I had to up end a bin which I placed on the floor. She then stood on this to help her get on the table. Prior to being examined, the lady was questioned by the examining Doctor who asked her 'When did you last have sex?' The lady couldn't remember because it had been so many hears before. She had been a widow for over 30 years. During the examination copious amounts of the man's semen was found. She also had horrendous cuts and bruises about her body. She was taken home and cared for by her family. They were a lovely family, children in their 50's and 60's. I was in Crown Court when weeks later the man appeared for sentencing. He'd pleaded guilty due to the over whelming DNA evidence. He sat with his head in his hands. The family had to sit through the evidence before sentence was passed. To their credit they remained seated and dignified throughout the proceedings. It's more than I would have done if someone did that to my mum. It again never ceases to amaze me the horrors humans inflict on other humans.

2015

I had dealt with a horrific child sexual abuse case. All the children had been removed from the parents who were both subsequently convicted. The children were all placed into care with foster carers. I remember speaking to one of the foster carers who said that on the first morning of having the children they had given them cereal for breakfast and had put milk on the cereal. The children had questioned what was on their cornflakes as they had only ever eaten cereal with water on it. They didn't know what milk was.

2014

Whilst dealing with a SUDI (sudden unexplained infant death) it transpired that the mother had been keeping the baby in a draw within the chest of drawers in her bedroom which was a makeshift cot. It's 2014 and you couldn't make this shit up.

2014

I'd come on duty on an early shift and was reading through the 'night report'. One of my colleagues had been killed in the early hours of the morning while on a night out with colleagues. He'd been recognised as 'police' and had been attacked along with his other colleagues. His head was stamped on, and he died. I just sat there in shock. He had only been married for a few months. It was spoken about briefly by our supervision who then told us to get on with our work. I spent the day trying to work but just not comprehending what had happened. I had worked with this policeman a few years before and he was one of the funniest, nicest, kindest men I've ever worked with. He didn't deserve what happened to him on his night out. He wasn't an aggressive man and would always diffuse situations at work if they arose. It is because of this man that I met my wife. I remember coming into work with my new computer and he set the whole thing up for me. Got my e mails sorted amongst other things. I went on a dating website and a few months later met the love of my life. I don't know if his wife knows this, but I will always be eternally grateful to him. The men who attacked him eventually got convicted but have now been released from prison. I still think about him as I do my other colleagues who have died either suddenly at home, have taken their own life, or had cancer. You think about the laughs and the daft things you got involved in with them, and what absolute gentlemen they were.

2017

I was dealing with a neighbour dispute and rang the perpetrator up to speak to her. There had been a lot of comments put on 'Facebook'. A lot of 'he said, she said'. I tried to reason with the lady as to be honest I had a lot more pressing things to be getting on with. I said to her 'Do you not think that what you wrote was quite provocative?' She replied, 'I've not wrote nothing sexy'. I gave up trying at this point as you can't reason with stupid.

2003

Whilst attending riot training, I was getting changed when I realised there were a few female probationers with us in the changing room. You could tell they were new as they were full of enthusiasm! We all got changed into cotton underclothes and then flame proof overalls on top of that. I saw one of the probationers holding up a 'box' which protects your lady undercarriage. These must have been newly issued because I had not been issued with one. She held it up looking confused and asked, 'How do I wear this?' I couldn't help myself and said 'It goes on the outside of your overalls'. The probationer then put the protective box on over her blue overalls, looking like some sort of weird 'Superman'. The other probationers followed suit and we all left the changing room minutes later and walked into the main arena to be confronted by the instructors who laughed at them, and then sent them back to the changing rooms to put the boxes on 'under' their overalls.

1996

I've lost count of the number of times I've had to leave my 'scoff' at my designated mealtime and attend 999 jobs. You were lucky if you ever got a full meal break. One meal break that does stick in my mind is Christmas day. If your shift falls on Christmas day you must have volunteers to work. Over the Christmas period it's always best to work a day shift on Christmas day. You were almost guaranteed to get off on time at 3pm as at this time people are still opening presents and being nice to each other. The alcohol also hasn't started to properly flow. By 6pm the jobs start coming in and the fights begin. Christmas cheer has well and truly gone out of the window. Boxing day isn't called that for nothing when you're policing. This Christmas, we all sat down at a long table together, having brought into work a selection of party food. It is quite a special memory. You just make the most of the situation you're in.

1992

Having joined the police, you see lots of different styles of policing by your colleagues. The thing you must decide, is what sort of officer you are going to be. As a probationer in the police there is much to learn. You see various styles of policing throughout your career and it's fair to say some officers I've met are absolute idiots. The problem I found is that if you're too trusting with certain members of the public, they just take the piss and see you as weak. I took the stance that I'll tell you once and if you don't do what I'm asking you'll get arrested. This realisation came to me when my colleague had arrested a drug addict. She was adamant that she was innocent and me being young in service believed her. I mean you wouldn't lie to a police officer would you? I remember when I realised that she was lying to me, and I was so shocked. I had been raised to tell the truth and couldn't even imagine telling lies to a police officer. It was a steep learning curve for me but after that day I never trusted anyone again.

I would describe my style of policing as being firm but fair. There was one drug addict I have arrested countless times. She is harmless enough, and having been arrested over 100 times for shoplifting she should probably rethink her career. I was working one Boxing Day morning. It was cold and frosty, and the streets were deserted when I saw her. I recognised her quick walk a mile off and I knew she was wanted on warrant for failing to appear at court. Some drug addicts have children, and many keep them in squalid conditions, collecting their child allowance weekly and spending it on drugs and alcohol. This lady had given her children to her mum to look after, realising she couldn't look after them herself. This chilly Boxing Day morning she was off to her mums address to see her children. I drove up alongside her and saw the look of panic on her face. Winding the window down I said, 'You're wanted aren't you'. She pleaded with me to let her go. I took pity on her and said 'I'll come to your house tomorrow to get you; off you go to see your kids'. She turned to me and said, 'You're a twat you, but you're dead sound'. I think this was a compliment.

2011

It was on patrol in a Police carrier with a colleague when I was flagged down by a bus driver. I pulled up alongside him asking what the problem was? He explained he had an aggressive female on his bus and could we please get her off. We boarded the bus and there she was sat near the back. This lady is very well known in the city centre for being a gobby drunk. She's one of those people who, when sober is actually alright, but as soon as she has a drink, she is an absolute arse with a foul mouth. As I walked up to her, she started shouting at me 'You fucking rat', along with various other obscenities. I peeled her fingers from the top of the front seat she had hold of and decided she was getting ejected from the bus. She wasn't very happy with this and starts struggling with me, staggering from side to side. I was called all the mother fuckers, rats, knob heads!!! She was so drunk, stinking of alcohol. I manage to get her off the bus and stand her on the pavement as she continued her rant at me. This woman must have been 70. She was dressed in a brightly coloured top and jeans and had on a lot of makeup. Her lip stick looked like she'd put it on in the dark! It was smeared all over her lips making her look like a demented clown. I decided she was getting arrested for being drunk and disorderly. I unclipped my handcuffs, took hold of her wrist and then managed to handcuff her to her handbag. She's now struggling and were gathering a bit of a crown around us, intrigued no doubt as to why we are arresting an old woman. You must think about public perception when dealing with incidents like this. To a member of the public, we are seen as bullies, arresting an old lady. They have no idea what she was like a couple of minutes ago in front of the shocked passengers on the bus. Thankfully this was pre mobile phones with cameras so there was no chance of this ending up on you tube. I managed to untangle her from the handbag and again placed her in handcuffs to the front. We then walked/dragged her across the road as she had decided she wasn't coming quietly. We decided against putting her in the rear cage of the police carrier as there is a large step up and again it would have looked awful trying to bundle an old lady into the van. We instead decided to put her in the back of the carrier in the seated area. As I went to help her in, her jeans fell down by her ankles and it became clear she had decided to 'go commando' for the evening. We are now stood on the pavement with a pissed 70-year-old who's naked from the waist down. She's now shouting at my male colleague 'Do you like my pussy?'. I tried my best to pull her jeans up, careful not to get hit in the face with the 70's style 'full bush' she was sporting. We then took an arm each and got her into a seated position on the floor of the van with my colleague sat behind her holding her up. She was very taken with him and was now chatting him up with such lines as 'Do you want to lick my pussy?'. He declined.

We arrive at the custody suite and she's still shouting abuse at us. I stand in front of the custody Sgt and relay the circumstances of arrest. As I'm searching her clothing and putting her belongings on the custody desk, she's grabbing them back. I noted that she seemed very well known to the custody staff and wondered how I'd never met her before? She replies to the custody Sgt's questions about her mental health saying she's going to kill herself. As a result of this the Sgt asked if we could take her to her cell and place her in a safety blanket. These are basically like thick dressing gowns with no cord on them so there's no way you could rip it or injure yourself with it. You are also naked underneath the safety blanket. Thankfully there's three female custody assistants on duty so they take hold of her and are walking her to the cell when I hear a 'ripping' noise. I genuinely thought the drunken woman's coat had ripped. The drunk started complaining her arm was sore. I had a quick look at it and could see her arm bone (humerus) sticking through her skin. Yes, she now had a compound fracture to her upper arm. An ambulance was quickly called, and the drunk sat down on a bench. Even trying to get her to the ambulance was a struggle. I remember the ambulance staff saying, 'Oh I can't look if it's a compound fracture'. I did say to her 'well it's your job to help her as I don't know what I'm doing'. We eventually got her to hospital and into A and E on a trolly. She was placed into a cubicle with me waiting with her. For whatever reason she now decided this would be a good time to start shouting racial abuse, who at god knows, but she was shouting loudly. The nurse then came into the cubicle to assess the drunk who decided to tell the nurse that 'I' had broken her arm. I looked at the drunken woman incredulously as she said this, because I hadn't! The nurse tuned to me and scowled, then carried on tending to her patient who she now thinks had been beaten to a pulp by the police. This small defenceless 70-year-old. I left the patient in the very capable hands of the nursing staff and returned to the station. With this type of incident, the custody suite must be shut down and a full-scale enquiry carried out. I'm just thankful to this day that we have cameras everywhere in the custody suites as apparently some weeks later after her operation and having been released from hospital the lady decided to make a complaint and say that 'I' had broken her arm when I arrested her! Which I hadn't. It turned out she had osteoporosis. The complaints department managed to track down the bus driver who confirmed my story. I never did see this woman again but did hear from a colleague recently that since this date she has been arrested a further 200 times for being drunk or racially abusive to the public.

2017

Whilst working in 'child protection' I have dealt with numerous jobs involving children who have been sexually abused either historically or jobs that are happening now. I've also dealt with adults who bravely come forward and tell their stories of historic sexual abuse and rape. Everyone is believed. Their stories are heart-breaking. Interviews about sexual or physical assaults with children and teenagers are conducted at interview suites. These are called ABE interviews (achieving best evidence). These are designed to look just like a living room with sofas and comfy chairs but there are cameras recording you. So rather than give a written statement, your primary evidence can be played to the jury as it is a recording of your interview. Children are also often assisted by an intermediary who is usually a speech and language therapist. They assist children by using props and drawings. It's all designed to get the best evidence from your victim. Before interviewing victims of abuse, specialist courses must be attended and a portfolio completed, accrediting you as a specialist in your field. Interviewing children can be incredibly tricky, as you can't ask leading questions, 'Did he do this?' as children will invariably want to please you and will agree with what you are saying. There's nothing like the feeling of talking to a child and they just open up and tell you what's been going on. Sometimes it's quite matter of fact with them. They sit in front of you on an oversized couch, their feet not touching the floor, telling you of the most horrific sexual abuse that has happened to them. These interviews can be incredibly powerful when shown to a jury. On numerous occasions I have seen jury members crying when watching videos of victims telling their story.

One colleague interviewed a child about sexual abuse and the child's parent was also present. This is not the norm as we prefer to interview children either on their own or in the presence of an intermediary, but the child would not talk without the parent in the room. You must make a judgement call. The child disclosed what had happened to her and at the end of the interview when the recording was still running my colleague asked, 'What are you doing when you get home?' 'Making cakes' came the reply from the child. We get to Crown Court with this job and the evidence had obviously been reviewed by the prosecuting and defending barrister before the trial started. Prior to a trial starting there's discussion amongst the barristers about 'plea bargains', defendants agreeing to lesser charges to save time with a trial. This barrister, who was defending the sex offender decided to raise with the judge the fact that the child had mentioned they were going to make cakes after their video interview and suggested that the child had only made disclosures because they knew they would get the reward of 'making cakes'. The barrister suggested this was coercion. The judge agreed and the child's evidence got 'thrown out', disregarded and was never shown to the jury. My colleague was devastated and felt she had let the family down. It was just a comment the child made. The abuse had happened to her. The sex offender in that case walked free from court. The jury couldn't make an informed decision when they hadn't heard the victims evidence. I understand the barristers are simply sometimes only doing their jobs but it's hard when you feel you've let the family down. You feel a pain and anger inside yourself. You try not to get emotionally involved, but are resolved to prosecute the person responsible for these crimes against children and adults. It still to this day never ceases to amaze me, the horrors human being will do to each other.

What I came to realise when dealing with sexual offence jobs at crown court is how different you feel when you get a conviction. I have lost count of the number of times I have been to court, and I quite enjoy it. The rush of adrenaline you get. There's not another job like it. The difference is that when I worked in the drug squad and you had a massive seizure of class A drugs, you would go to court, give your evidence, the defendant would invariably be found guilty, and you would feel elation when they were sentenced to 10 years in prison. You would go to the pub with your colleagues, patting yourselves on the back about a 'job well done'. I quickly came to realise that working in child protection is completely different. I've had defendants plead guilty in court when presented with overwhelming evidence and I've had defendants that have been found guilty by a jury. The judge will 'sum up' the case and pass sentence. Big sentences, sometimes over 20 years. But there's no elation at the end of it, there's just a broken child who's still been raped hundreds of times. There's the adult, who when they were a child in the 70's was sexually abused. There's the broken family who can't come to terms with what's happened to their child. There's even the defendant's family who must come to terms with what their son has admitted to and live with the stigma of this. No one is a winner. It's just very sad. I came home one day after a big day in Crown Court. I had one man plead guilty to sexual assault, one man plead guilty to raping a child and a woman found guilty of child neglect. I sat in shock on the train coming home. This would be one of the biggest days in my whole career, but I didn't feel elated I just felt numb. I got in through the front door and cried. I cried for what these children had been put through, for the heartache they felt. The worry that some of the children wouldn't be able to have families of their own one day because the sexual abuse had caused irreparable damage to them physically and emotionally. They will never have 'normal' physical relationships as adults. There are no winners.

1999

I was circuit training one afternoon at a gym where a serving police officer was running classes. I arrived with a colleague only to see a couple of police carriers outside the gym. My heart sank as I knew the gym would now be filled with about 16 male officers who worked on the 'riot squads'. Me and my colleague were both gay females and I was only newly 'out' in the police. It wasn't anything like it is now being gay in the police. There were no LGBTQIA+ groups to support you as a gay officer you just had to get on with it. In the gym, they were all 'titting' about pushing and shoving each other. We got started and were working our way around the different circuit stations with them behind us. Then started all the homophobic comments, 'Dyke this' 'Lesbo that'! My colleague had had enough and went to speak to the police instructor and asked him to ask the men to leave. His response was to tell us to move away from them! We left and went home. Thankfully things have changed now.

1996

I was working nights when a car chase came out. I was the front seat passenger with my colleague driving so it was down to me to give the commentary if we got behind the stolen car. Just then we saw it. My colleague gave chase with me giving commentary as to the vehicle's location, speed and direction of travel. We were chasing the vehicle down a wide carriageway when suddenly the front passenger tyre on the stolen vehicle blew off. The tyre bounced down the road towards us and we both ducked as the tyre bounced over the police car. The stolen car then continued on its way with sparks now flying off the wheel. The car crashed a short time later and the driver was detained. Its only after you think 'That tyre could have gone through the windscreen'. It just doesn't occur to you to be scared sometimes. The adrenaline takes over. Sometimes you do think when you're driving fast to jobs or getting into fights 'Are they really paying me to do this?'. Being in the police really is the best job in the world.

2014

I was working in a domestic violence unit having just moved to the CID. Now I'll be honest and say I haven't got a lot of time for domestic violence perpetrators as I think they are bullies. I had been the victim of domestic abuse some years earlier and had managed to get out of that relationship. I dealt with a job where a lady had been in a violent relationship with this male on and off for years. During this time, she had been subject to broken bones and numerous cuts and bruises at his hands. What I've come to realise is that with domestic violence victims they won't necessarily report that they have been assaulted by their partner, even if they have been beaten terribly and hospitalised. Sometimes all it takes is a push to tip them over the edge and say, 'That's enough'. This is what had happened with this lady, and she now wanted my help to get him out of her life. As well as the push she wished to report there was also an historic broken arm he had given her some months before. He was arrested and pleaded guilty at Crown Court and received a 7-year sentence. I went back to speak with the lady some weeks later to see how she was doing. It was now January, and she said to me 'This is the first Christmas for 10 years that I've not had a black eye'.

2010

We were executing a drugs warrant at a block of flats that were less than salubrious. Normally front doors are inward opening so that when you hit the front door with the door opened it goes straight through allowing you access. However, the front door to this flat was outward opening so we had to use a large crowbar to get it open which took several minutes due to the ample locks fitted behind it. We eventually gained entry to find the male householder naked in the front room on the phone to the police. As we were in full uniform, I informed him we were the police and asked him to get some clothes on. Also, in the flat was his girlfriend. I noticed as we entered the flat, a bathroom on the right. As I looked in briefly it was spotless as if it had never been used.

We all congregated in the living room, handed them the warrant and commenced our search. His girlfriend was a bit gobby, not happy we were in their flat. They were obviously both drug addicts as the living room was very unkempt, and they were sleeping on mattresses on the living room floor and not in the bedroom? The girlfriend also had feet like a Griffin with long toenails. Imagine having size 4 feet but needing a size 7 shoe. During a drugs warrant one officer will be responsible for keeping a record of the search and any items seized as well as details of persons on the premises. My colleague stood making his notes when he suddenly dropped his pen…. into a washing up bowl full of piss. It floated to the bottom where it was to stay. 'Oh no that was good writer' he said. I asked the couple why there was a washing up bowl nearly full to the top with urine and toilet paper. She replied that that was from last night and she had a urine infection. We're talking litres of urine! The sad fact of the matter was that they couldn't be bothered to walk the 10 feet to the spotless bathroom that had obviously never been used.

2010

During your lunch breaks you are often encouraged to use the gyms provided in police stations. These usually consist of items that have been donated from other gyms. On one such occasion I was using the running machine in the gym while one of my colleagues was using the weights bench and was in the process of bench-pressing heavy weights. As he was doing this, another colleague entered the gym dressed to work out in his shorts. Seeing my colleague holding the bar containing heavy weights he walked up behind him lifted his shorts to one side and sat on his face, covering it with penis and balls. This apparently is called 'teabagging'. The joys of working with men!

2009

I had executed a drugs warrant at a Cannabis factory. These usually consist of hundreds of cannabis plants in various stages of growth. The fully grown plants can reach 6 foot tall, weighed down with cannabis buds which are then taken from the plant and dried before being placed into small snap sealed bags and sold. An established 6-foot cannabis plant can 'yield' £100 per foot so each plant is worth £600. At this warrant, we had seized hundreds of plants. Nobody was present at the property when the warrant was executed, so you rely on intelligence and fingerprints retrieved from the scene by the scenes of crime officers (SOCO). Once the plants had been seized and booked in it is the responsibility of the investigating officer to take several cannabis plants to the drugs laboratory. They are then looked at by a scientist who will then establish the 'yield' the plant would give over a 12-month period. This would then give you the value of the plant and therefore an estimation as to how much money the drug dealers are making.

I looked through the cannabis plants and selected several to take to the laboratory. I then loaded these into the back of a plain police vehicle and set off with my colleague, both of us in plain clothes for our day trip out. A short time later we stopped at a set of red traffic lights and a car pulled up alongside us. He looked over at us then beeped his horn repeatedly. I wound the window down to see what the problem was to which he said, 'Watch it with all that weed in your car, there's loads of bizzies round here'. I thanked him and we drove off laughing.

2007

I was on plain clothes patrol with three colleagues in the city centre. It was a hot day, so we decided to stop off at a local public house for a round of diet cokes. My colleague went to the bar, and we all sat at a table in a corner awaiting his return. He came back a short time later and we all sat chatting quietly enjoying the break. A man walked up to us carrying a large black holdall. He looked around him and then said, 'Do you want to buy some t shirts?'. One of my colleagues says, 'yeah what have you got?' The man with the holdall then proceeds to empty the contents of his holdall next to our table and spreads them out lovingly on the floor taking time to display his ill-gotten gains. He spent several minutes doing this while we all sat there in silence looking at each other. The man suddenly looked up at us and said 'You's are all bizzies aren't you?' We all nodded, and he looked devastated. He began to pack his stolen t shirts back into his holdall as my colleague got hold of his by the collar saying, 'You can wait here till we finish these drinks, they cost me £10'. We got him a chair and then sat the thief with us at the table while we finished our drinks.

2000

I was working undercover in a different police force posing as a drug addict. It's usual for UC officers to be placed in different forces so they are not known or recognised by anyone. I had been there for a few weeks and had started to mix with the local drug addicts and had gained their trust. I was then introduced to the 'dealer' the other addicts used. At this point I looked awful. You had to fit in, so I hadn't washed for about a week, my clothes consisted of a dirty old tracksuit and worn-out trainers. My hair was matted, and I smelt terrible. I was wearing a tiny camera hidden inside my clothing to capture the exact moment the dealer passed me the drugs. I waited my turn and was introduced to the dealer by one of the other addicts who I'd befriended. It was my turn. The male dealer was stood with a female who appeared to be working alongside him. I asked him for two bags of brown (heroin). He then motioned towards the female who was stood with him, and I watched as she turned away slightly, placing her hand down her trousers. Her hand then appeared seconds later, and she handed to me two small bags of heroin.... Covered in period blood. I looked at them horrified. There are times when you ask yourself why you're doing this job!

1992

I had parked the patrol car up in the rear yard of the police station and was bent over the rear seats collecting my paperwork and hat when a male colleague came up behind me, pulled his trousers down and began to dry hump me from behind. Obviously, I couldn't move because he had me pinned in the car. This was watched by numerous male colleagues who were all laughing and jeering him on. At the time I was the only woman on a section of 15 Policemen. As I stood up from the car and straightened myself out, I looked to an upstairs window of the police station and saw the female Superintendent watching the whole incident. She laughed, shook her head and walked away. Seriously, how could you complain about things like this when the officer in charge of the station even thought it was funny?

2012

I had just joined the CID department after many years in uniform. I thought 'I'll just keep my head down and get on with my work'. CID was a whole different ball game to working in uniform. I was in Crown Court for the morning dealing with a case and my colleague was in a different court but in the same building. I needed a lift back to the station, so she agreed to take me but said she just had to quickly call in to a local station to re-bail a prisoner. If you were released on bail, it was common for prisoners to attend police stations to have their bail extended while enquiries were ongoing.

We arrived at the police station and went to the bail desk that was situated away from the main custody suite at the rear of the station. One Sgt was working here just dealing with re-bails. The prisoner who was an adult, was brought in accompanied by his father who was acting as his appropriate adult. The pair of them were quite agitated when they arrived and began shouting at me (even though I hadn't got a bloody clue why they were even there?) so I moved with my colleague out of sight. No sooner had I done this than the station panic alarm sounded. I ran back into the bail suite to see the Sgt who had obviously vaulted over the custody desk as the prisoner was trying to slash his own wrists open. The Sgt had hold of the prisoner trying to stop him as the dad (appropriate adult) was hitting the custody Sgt, obviously not realising the Sgt was trying to help his son. I ran in grabbing the father from the Sgt and tried to restrain him. This was less than easy as he was a big man. He continued to struggle and grab at the Sgt so I decided to 'knee strike' him. I drew my right leg back and hit him hard. He went down on the floor clutching at his leg, but at least now I could get him under control.

At this point a man in a suit appeared at the bail room door. 'Get some cuffs will you' I yelled at him. This was the thing with CID you just had no kit on you when you went out! The man disappeared and reappeared quickly with some handcuffs which we put on the prisoner and began to take him through to the custody suite. I looked at the officer in the suit that was helping me and suddenly realised it was the Chief Superintendent of the station. He seemed to be pleased to be getting his hands dirty for a change. The prisoner was eventually dealt with and accepted a caution for 'violent conduct in a police station'. This would be the only time I arrested anyone for this offence. I returned to my respective police station hours later thinking no one will know what's happened. As I walked in through the door, I got a round of applause.

Weeks later I received yet another complaint against police from this man who stated I had permanently damaged his leg and was asking for compensation. Full enquiry later, he got nothing. I had acted completely appropriately.

1993

When it was quiet during a weekday tour of nights, we would have a competition. How far could you get during the shift. You had to travel to another station and get your PNB (pocket note book) stamped with the station stamp. We won.....Liverpool to Birmingham and back!

1998

Whilst working at a very famous horse racing ground I was with a group of officers who were responsible for vehicle searches. You usually had a 'clean' pair who would search the inside of the vehicle, and a 'dirty' pair who search the outside and underneath of the vehicles. On this day we were searching the cars as they came through when we noticed our Chief Inspector parked in her car in the queue. Now this lady had been our boss and had overseen us for over a year and knew the officers by name. As her car got to us, we waved her through, not stopping her car for the routine 20 minutes search. She waved back to us as she went through. At the end of the day, we were spoken to by our Sgt who said a complaint had been made. We were all confused as we had acted with the upmost professionalism throughout the day. He explained that the Chief Inspector who had driven through our check point during the morning had complained to the Chief Superintendent that her vehicle had not been searched at the check point.

The following morning, we were again searching vehicles at the same checkpoint, when the Chief Inspector drove towards us. She went to drive through but was stopped by us. Wanting to do our jobs thoroughly, she was stood in the rain for 20 minutes whilst her car was gone over meticulously. For good measure the drugs dog who had been rolling in mud some minutes earlier was put through her car, standing on her coat and slobbering dog drool all over her hat. After the search we thanked her for waiting and allowed her on her way. We could see she was absolutely fuming. We heard that afternoon that she had again complained to the Chief Superintendent that she had been subject to a 20-minute vehicle search and the dog had ruined her police hat. 'What did you think they were going to do to you after you complained yesterday' was the Chief Superintendents reply.

2011

I was working at a party-political conference, and we oversaw vehicle searches prior to cars parking up at the conference or in the multi-story car park. A huge canopy was erected which could fit 8 cars underneath so that if it rained, we would at least be dry. Throughout the day huge queues of cars were dealt with. Some of these occupants were going to the party conference, others were groups of stag do's and hen do's using the multi-story car park and going to various nearby hotels, before heading out on the town. During our 'down time' the drugs dog handlers who were assisting us would take their pooches for a walk and a wee around the area that had been cordoned off for vehicles to queue up. That week the number of drugs found by the dogs was incredible. Huge bags of cocaine thrown into the bushes by panicked 'hen and stag do's', knowing they would be searched and arrested. By the end of the week, we literally had a carrier bag full of cocaine. A lot of parties were ruined that week.

2012

I was dealing with a domestic violence victim who was male. During the investigation he would ring me constantly complaining if things weren't going his way. He was one very rude and obnoxious man. One day while I was particularly 'snowed' under' with work the phone rang. My colleague picked it up as I frantically waved at her mouthing 'If it's him I'm not here'. She spoke to the caller then said, 'I'll just pass you to her'. My colleague told me it was him! I looked at her dumfounded and took the phone from her. As I said 'hello', the whole office burst out laughing. One of my colleagues had rung my landline on her mobile pretending to be him. Bastards.

2009

I was dealing with a SUDI (sudden infant death) and we had gone to the hospital to meet the family. Whilst there one of the aunties appeared and started to cry when she saw the deceased child lying in the cot. She went to pick her up and was told she wasn't allowed to do this at that moment, as the child need to be examined by a doctor. To my surprise the woman stops crying and says, 'Oh ok I'll go for a ciggy then' and left the room. More and more family arrived. The two aunties were now in attendance, and one was heavily pregnant. It transpired on the journey home when we said we would drop her off, that she was pregnant to her sister's fella. They had been on a break though! This family went on to have numerous appearances on Jeremy Kyle as well as Benefits and Proud. There was one instance with this family when a male family member had been arrested for a sexual assault. He was interviewed and denied this allegation and then went on to appear on Jeremy Kyle where he admitted the sexual assault?? We had to contact ITV who provided the unedited version of his 15 minutes of fame which was used to prosecute him when it was played in Crown Court.

2008

I was working on a shoplifting squad and my colleague said she was having trouble arresting a male who was wanted for theft. I went with her to the flats, pressed the buzzer and when he asked me who it was, I just said my first name. The door opened and we were in. I turned to her asking what she had said, 'I always say it's the police and he never opens the door'. We got upstairs and knocked on his door. He opened the door and saw me and my colleague standing there. He looked at me incredulously and said 'You said it was ….. and you're the police'. I explained that that is my name, I just failed to mention I was a police officer.

We took him to the police station and interviewed him, showing him the CCTV of him stealing items. He then laughs and says, 'Well that's not me, that fellas got a bald patch'. I stood up from my chair and looked on top of his head. 'I hate to break this to you but you're bald'. He got charged!

1995

One of the stations I worked in had a very odd policeman working there. He would regularly change out of his police uniform during his break time and walk around in just his underpants. He then went into the station gym where he would strip naked and work out.

1996

I had taken my prisoner to a custody suite to be booked in. The Sgt on the night shift used to 'moonlight' working on the side playing the piano at weddings. As I had arrived at the custody suite the Sgt had obviously just finished one such gig and was dressed in a full tuxedo. He proceeded to set up his electric organ on top of the custody desk and do a request for the drunk I had just brought in. The look on the drunks face was priceless.

1995

Very often you would arrest shoplifters who had been arrested 100's of times before and knew the procedure better than you did. They would fingerprint themselves because it was quicker and during the interview, in which you would ascertain what that had stolen and why they had stolen, you would try and find out a little about them. They had different ideas. My seasoned shoplifters would get into the interview room with you and as soon as you switched on the tape they would say 'Yeah, I did it. I went to the back of the shop took the item from the shelf, put it down my top and then made my way to the front of the shop past the last point of sale and left the shop making no attempt to pay for it. I was then going to take the item to a local pub and sell it because I've got a drugs habit. All this was reeled off in about 30 seconds. There was nothing more to say. They were charged and out the door in 30 minutes. Back to the shops to steal some more. Time is money!

1994

I was called into the main police station in town to answer questions as part of an enquiry. An enquiry into numerous polaroid photographs that had been found containing pictures of policewomen's breasts. Some photos were taken down their shirts, some were taken with just their bra on. I hadn't been involved in this but being one of the few WPC's working town I was questioned. The actual WPC who was involved in this denied it when first asked, until they showed her a polaroid with her face showing, then she said it was her. Nothing happened over this.

1989

Whilst working in the 'radio room' in which jobs are dispatched to officers, I had cause to go to a store cupboard. I was bent down trying to retrieve something from a box. At the time I was wearing standard police issue uniform of skirt, stockings and shirt. As I went to stand up, I felt someone was behind me, it was a male colleague trying to put his hand up my skirt. I jumped back shocked as he said, 'I suppose a wanks out of the question?'. I did speak to my supervisor about this and decided not to take it further, but it transpired some 18 months later that this police officer was under investigation for following home policewomen and sexually assaulting a civilian he picked up in a police car. He was sacked following a tribunal.

1992

I was at a police station when the male officers decided I should follow tradition. I was hoisted up onto a filing cabinet my skirt pulled up and my arse stamped with the station stamp. We just became conditioned to accept what the male officers would say and do to us. I have daughters now and if somebody did that to them, I would be raging.

1997

I was tasked to watch some CCTV footage following an assault in the town centre. I trawled through hours of footage when one man caught my eye. I watched as he placed his hand down the back of his trousers, pulled out a lump of shit and threw it in the street.

2000

The females in the force were periodically receiving e mails asking them to go to open days at the firearms department. This was because females just weren't applying to go to Firearms. This is called positive discrimination. I refused to go on principal because when I'd applied years before I was refused, but you want me now because you're short of females.

1994

I had attended a terrible RTA (road traffic accident) where a lady had been run over. I stayed with her at the scene while medical crews attended and made the decision to amputate her legs which were stuck under a bus. It was horrific and she subsequently died. Back at the station our Sgt ordered that we all take some time to have a cup of tea and cakes together which he had bought. We sat trying to process what had just happened and it wasn't long before the jokes started. 'She wouldn't have felt anything because she was legless'. The Police like all emergency services have a coping mechanism, and that is humour.

1993

During a quiet night shift or quiet early morning shift, going to a motorway services miles away for a breakfast.

2013

Whilst interviewing a very old man for historic allegations of sexual abuse he kept leaning forward in the interview room and shouting into the microphones placed on the wall 'I geographically deny that allegation'. That'll be categorically then! Do you know how hard it is not to laugh sometimes during an interview?

1994

We were called to a report of persons at a graveyard with torches. It was 2am in the morning so we made our way down there. I got out of the car with my colleague, and we started to make our way through the graveyard looking for the culprits. It was eerily quiet as we tried not to step on the graves and made our way deeper and deeper into the graveyard. Suddenly two male colleagues with masks on jumped out from behind a gravestone to frighten us. I screamed and nearly shit myself. The whole job was a set up. There's nothing worse than a 'bored bobby'.

1995

Whilst working in a particular station, one of the desk Sgts would bring her dog in on a night shift to potter around the station, much to the annoyance of some other officers. During your 'scoff break' you would go to the rest room and pray you would get an uninterrupted 45-minute break to eat your meal. The dog would come into the rest room at break times and go through everyone's sandwiches which was starting to piss people off. The first night this happened the Sgt was told to leave her dog at home because it was annoying staff who were trying to eat. She ignored this and brought the dog in for a second night, and it again snuffled through officer's sandwiches in the rest room. On the third night as it was walking around the rest room one of the officers fed the dog a bar of laxative chocolate. At about 5am the Sgt did as usual and put her dog in her car for a sleep before she would be heading home at 7am at the end of her shift. We all watched at 7am as she went to her car to discover the 'shit fest' inside her car. She didn't bring the dog in again after that.

2005

I attended a seminar on 'Women in Industry' which was being run by a very successful businesswoman. She pointed out that when applying for jobs a woman will look at the criteria and think, 'I can't do that' whereas a man will look and think 'I can't do that so I'll wing it and say I can do it'. This is the difference between men and women in business and why women don't apply for postings within the Police because they don't want to let anybody down. To be a good or successful policewoman in the police service you must be very good at your job otherwise you're seen by your male colleagues to be 'shit'. You must work so much harder just to be accepted as good. Policemen can be just average and 'he's alright'. It's as if you must prove yourself all the time.

The number of times I have dealt with incidents where male supervisors don't know what they are doing. I was dealing with a SUDI (sudden infant death). The male Sgt told me he didn't know what to do. I had to literally talk him through every aspect of the incident. Getting a blood sample from the baby, asking the parents to provide blood samples to be sent for toxicology, getting an Inspector to attend the scene of the death, asking the Sgt to ring social services for a 'strategy meeting'. As we were leaving the hospital, I overheard him say to another male colleague 'I'm applying for my Inspector's board'. It obviously didn't occur to him that he was useless at his job. He is now an Inspector!

2014

I was sent to deal with a hanging of a child. This was extremely upsetting for the officers attending and the family. It appeared the child had accidently hanged himself whilst playing. Emergency services managed to cut him down and he was taken to hospital and placed on 'life support'. It was discovered that he was brain dead, and the family were asked if they would agree to donate his organs which they agreed. I had to remain in the room with the family and the child whilst the child was taken to theatre to have his organs removed. He died a short time later.

Due to this incident, along with the amount of work I was dealing with, going through menopause, being on HRT, and a colleague dying I had a breakdown. I ended up being off work for months and having counselling to help me process what had happened. I was asked if I was ok to return to child protection and I said I was. This was because it was what I was very good at and where my friends were. You don't want change.

2013

I was dealing with an historic allegation of child sexual assault that had occurred between a child and teacher from their school in the 1990's. I attended the offenders home address to warn him in for an interview rather than arrest him. His house was a disgrace, with walls that were dripping with grease. He was now a wizened old man, not the towering monster the victim had described him as. He attended the police station and settled in the interview room to speak to him. To our surprise he admitted sexually assaulting his victim over a period of years. Sometimes you feel that elderly sex offenders just want to get things off their chest before they die. I drove him back home and to my surprise he invited me into his house for a cup of tea. I wanted to say to him 'not in this lifetime' but instead I politely declined. This job progressed to Crown court where he pleaded guilty and received a custodial sentence. That was all the victim wanted. She wanted him to go to prison. He only lasted another 2 months in prison before he died. Not much justice!

2021

The graduate entry schemes. In my opinion this is not a good thing. I think people will take advantage of getting a degree paid for and then leave prior to joining the police or leave soon after. It also stops older potential candidates from applying. Who wants to start a degree in their 40's? New graduate entries are also leaving when they realise, they must do PSP (self-defence using batons) because they 'don't agree with hitting someone'. Let's see if that view changes when you're faced with someone waving a knife in your face. Graduates are also leaving when they realise, they must work weekends and nights. I give up!

2014

I dealt with a very upsetting assault. The victim had been married to her abusive husband for 50 years and they had children together. He wore the front door key around his neck and would control when she left the house. He would also switch the TV off and say 'bed' at 7pm and she was not permitted to watch anything else. The couple slept in separate bedrooms and during the night the husband came into her room and tried to strangle her. She managed to dislodge the bedside drawer and hit him over the head with it. Police were called and he was arrested for attempt murder.

During the victim's interview which was conducted on video she described how in the 1950's she had taken herself and her week-old baby to a local police station to complain that her husband had hit her and given her a black eye. The advice from the desk Sgt was 'Go home, put some lipstick on and make him some supper'. The domestic abuse continued throughout their marriage until he tried to kill her. Her husband was charged with attempt murder and remanded in custody. I called to see this lady the day after and she told me how that now she had the house to herself she had watched Coronation Street the previous night while having a glass of wine, and then she watched Scott and Bailey (police drama) and loved it. She planned to sell their house and split the profits and buy her own flat. She was now in her 80's and told me that she could now start 'Living her life'. This is the only time I have ever cried whilst interviewing a victim. The tears literally ran down my face as she told of this terrible life she had suffered. I hope she finally got some peace.

2014

I was at Crown Court watching evidence be given at a murder trial. The witness, a drug addict was getting tied in knots by the prosecution barrister and I watched as the drug addict got more and more agitated. She suddenly shouted,' I don't fucking know', and then turned to the Judge and said, 'sorry for swearing lad'.

2007

While executing a drugs warrant we burst in through the front door with the door opener. We all ran in shouting 'Police'. The men in the kitchen had been bagging up drugs and tried to run but were stopped by my colleague who jumped on them. They proceeded to struggle in the kitchen, knocking into the units which then dislodged from the wall and fell on top of them. I ran into the living room with my colleague and noticed two large Rottweiler dogs in front of us snarling and frothing at the mouth. Our fourth colleague who fears dogs, slammed the door shut behind us locking himself in the hallway and refused to open the door for us. I shouted to him 'Just open the door', to which he replied, 'I can't'. I managed to grab a mountain bike that was propped up in the living room and wave it in front of me hoping to keep the dogs from killing us. My colleague who had been fighting in the kitchen had managed to restrain the drug dealers and eventually brought them into the living room to subdue the dogs. A few stern words were had with my colleague when he eventually opened the door to the hallway.

1994

There had been a spate of industrial size homemade fireworks being seized over the Bonfire night period. These fireworks were being set off in the old-style red telephone boxes, therefore blowing them up. We had managed to recover one of these fireworks before it had been lit and brought it back to the police station. There is a saying, 'There's nothing worse than a bored bobby'. We decided it would be a good idea at 3am to place a traffic cone over the top of this firework and set it off. This resulted in the firework sending the traffic cone about 100 feet in the air. We hadn't thought of this and all panicked as it came crashing down in a yard full of expensive police vehicles. Luckily it missed the cars.

2008

We had executed a drugs warrant at an empty house. My colleague who was scared of dogs always entered the houses we raided with a CO_2 fire extinguisher. This is common practise to spray any aggressive dogs in the house with the fire extinguisher which would usually make them run away. As there had been no dogs in this house there had been no need to use it. We searched the house and found nothing and had requested 'boarding up' to secure the front door. As we stepped outside, he noticed a wasp's nest which had been built inside the porch and without giving it a second thought he sprayed the nest with a large blast of CO_2 from the fire extinguisher. Suddenly a whole swarm of angry wasps descended on us from the nest. I screamed and ran for the police carrier which was painted yellow. The wasps followed us! We managed to get inside the van with only several wasps who had snuck in. These were swiftly dispatched with an old newspaper that was lying around. My colleague looked at me and said, 'I think I've been stung on the neck'. I looked and he had indeed been stung. I spent the next ten minutes getting the sting out of his neck while calling him a tit.

2004

I was working a night shift in the height of summer with a dog patrol officer. It was great working nights at this time of the year as it was only dark for about 5 hours between 11pm and 4am. It was particularly quiet, so we headed to the local park to exercise the dog which was a large black German shepherd. The dog seemed friendly enough. It had spent the whole shift trying to stick its head out of the driver's window as I drove the van. We arrived at the park, and by now it was getting light. 'I've got an idea' he said. 'You go and hide in the bushes and then I'll send him to find you'. My response was quite simply 'Absolutely no chance'.

1992

I was coming into the police station with a colleague who was driving the panda car when I saw a new in service probationer standing by the store cupboard door. He had all of the orange and white traffic cones out of the store and was weighing them on a scale. 'What is he doing?' I asked. The reply 'The Sgts just taking the piss and making him weigh all the traffic cones to see if they contain the same amount of sand'. To my knowledge, the young man was out there some 3 hours before he finished his task.

2010

The winter of 2010 was particularly harsh with temperatures reaching -15 on some of the shifts I worked. On one such shift it was Christmas Eve and very cold. We were working an EP until 5am in the morning, so when we got back to the station to go off duty it was bitterly cold. One of my colleagues had mentioned earlier in the shift that he was driving some 150 miles to go to his parents for Christmas day. Also in the police stations at this time were large water barrels attached to a tap to keep the officers hydrated. We decided at 11pm to go outside to his car and pour a whole barrel of water over his car. At 5am the result of this was 2-inch-thick ice that had set all over his car. We found out after the holidays that he couldn't defrost or get into his car until 8am and was late getting to his parents' house.

1997

I was posted to a plain clothes drugs squad, and it was brilliant. We had managed to acquire a blue Golf GTi car to drive around in and it was fast! We were in the office one afternoon when a job came out over the radio of drug dealers in our area that were selling gear now. Me and a colleague ran downstairs and jumped into the VW Golf with him driving and me in the passenger seat. We set off out of the station at breakneck speed hoping to catch the culprits in the act. As we drove along the road, he shouts to me 'Put the blue light on the roof'. Now with it being the 90's we didn't have the new-fangled equipment that plain police vehicles have nowadays. We had a blue light on a wire that you plugged into the cigarette lighter and then you would reach up through the open passenger window and place the light on the roof of the car. I plugged the blue light in and went to reach up through the open passenger window but the force of the magnetism on the base of the light was too strong. My hand was forced downwards with the magnetic pull and the whirring blue light ended up stuck on the outside of the passenger door. There I was hurtling down the road at about 60 mph hanging out of the passenger window trying desperately to pull the light from the side of the door with my colleague shouting at me 'What the f**k are you doing?'. The blue light remained attached until we reached our destination and I managed to prise it off by putting my foot on the door and yanking at it.

2013

It was first shift as the night detective, and it didn't get off to a good start. I was called to a house fire where a mother had left her two children at home alone while she went to her mates to get 'vino collapso'. The result in this was one of the children tried to make some food and a fire started. The neighbours called the fire brigade who attended, rescued the children and put the blaze out. I arrived just as mum staggered down the road wondering what the hell was going on. Having worked in uniform for so long and feeling very uncomfortable ordering my uniform colleagues around I went to speak to the woman who was a bit worse for wear and told me to 'Fuck off'. After making several attempts to calm her down and explain what was happening, she continued being abusive towards me so I arrested her for child neglect and for being drunk and disorderly. I took her to the custody suite and waited with her in the holding area, which is where you wait prior to entering the custody suite and booking in your prisoner. I then get a radio message asking for my location. I replied I was in the holding area with my prisoner. The radio operator sounded confused and said, 'Say again'. I again gave my location which was met with silence. I subsequently got the mother of all bollockings from the night Detective Inspecter who told me the night Detective Constables do not arrest people. I was slightly confused. Apparently, I should have told one of the uniforms to arrest her. But being old school and having a power of arrest myself I decided to do it. And I would go onto do it again months later.

1994

I was involved in a foot chase. I chased the suspect along the alleyways and up onto a roof where he was eventually detained. Only problem was I was stuck. The suspect jumped from the roof onto a narrow wall and down to my waiting colleagues. I however had to be rescued by neighbours who had to get me down with a ladder.

1998

Whilst posted to a Support group (so a van full of policemen) in our down time you would have a bit of a laugh. We would park up in a plain car, we were in uniform and peep over a wall which gave a very good vantage point for the local prostitutes selling their wears on a busy road. It didn't take long for a punter to stop beside her, she then climbed in his car and off they went. We knew the area they would be going so we got in the police car drove to the car park frequented by the prostitutes and punters and got out of the police car. A quick peep behind the wall confirmed to us that the punter was parked up getting what he paid for. We would wait a couple of minutes then run in and surprise them by opening the car door. We caught many a punter in some compromising positions. Sometimes the punter was laid back in his seat while the lady wanked him off. Other times the lady would be legs akimbo with the punter bashing away on top of her. No one ever got arrested but it did make us laugh. We just used to make sure the ladies got their money and then told the drivers of the car to 'do one'.

2004

I was in uniform in a plain police vehicle, and we were responding to a job. I was the front seat passenger, so it was my job to plug the blue light into the cigarette lighter and put the light on the roof of the car. The wire attached to the light was a long curly flexible wire probably about 10 foot long. Having plugged the connecter into the cigarette lighter I reached through the open window and placed the blue light on the roof of the car. My colleague who was driving then took a sharp right causing the blue light to fly off the roof still attached to the car by being rammed into the cigarette lighter. It swung off the car narrowly missing a lady who was waking on the pavement pushing a pram.

1991

We set up a pretend hanging. This was for a WPC who didn't like walking on a night shift and would continually cadge a lift with colleagues to avoid walking her beat. We decided to wind her up. Everyone was involved, supervision and the radio room who would despatch you to jobs. She was asked to attend a derelict property as there were 'possible intruders on'. With this being her foot beat, she was dropped close to the location and made her way there on foot the short distance to the house. Prior to her getting sent there we had borrowed a shop window dummy and dressed it in some police issue overalls and put a balaclava on it for good measure. The dummy was hoisted up on a noose high above where the policewoman would be walking with a colleague waiting in position to drop it in front of her. She walked into the derelict building with a colleague who was also in on the prank. As they reached the area the dummy had been set up, he pointed out to her a discarded torch on the floor. Picking it up, she switched it on just as the hanging dummy was released and fell in front of her. She screamed, her torch now lighting up the balaclava covered face of the hanging man. She continued screaming and ran from the building. This wasn't bullying it was character building.

1991

As a probationer I was sent on nights to walk along the riverside' and check the life rings. The length of the riverside was some 5 miles. I was also asked to make a note of any serial numbers on the said rings. Only on my return to the station prior to going off duty did I realise the whole thing was a big piss take.

1992

There was an annual 'Horse drawn carriage' parade in the local park and I was sent down along with several colleagues and my Sgt to police this gathering. There were upwards of 20 horse drawn carriages to be paraded around the perimeter of the park for the publics delight. My Sgt approached me 'You need to ride in the front carriage'. I did as I was told and approached the front carriage, climbing aboard much to the bemusement of the carriage driver. 'What are you doing' he asked me. 'I have to ride with you' I told him and settled in. He pulled the reins back and we were off trotting around the park. My colleagues who were spaced at different locations around the park pissed themselves laughing on seeing me trotting past them. I soon realised this was another piss take/wind up. I couldn't get off and had to go round the whole park.

1994

On nights in the summer our block would meet a block from a neighbouring station, and we would play rounders in the local park at 5am much to the bemusement of local dog walkers who could hear the cry of 'rounder' as I was cheered on running around the field.

1993

We would play 'Off ground tick' in the vans. One van would give clues as to their location and we would have to find them using these clues. When you found the van full of colleagues you would chase them, put your arm out of the window and 'tick' the van. Then you'd drive off and give clues to your colleagues as to where your next location would be. This was all done on a 'back to back' channel on the radio.

1992

Whilst dealing with a horrible drunk female I had arrested, she kept shouting at me 'I'm going to hit you'. I said, 'Go on then', so she did right in the mouth and split my lip open.

2011

I was working in a prison recall dealing with offenders who had broken their terms of release and needed to be arrested and brought back to prison. I was tasked with going to Manchester Airport Terminal 2 to arrest a male wanted on a recall. I got to the airport and the lounge in Terminal 2 was packed with thousands of people. My colleague and I were dressed in plain clothes. We had a couple of options. We could walk amongst the people with the photograph of the male until we spotted him, or I had another idea. I went over to then reception desk and introduced myself explaining why I was there and asked if I could use their tannoid system. I took hold of the microphone and pressed the 'Bing bong' before I spoke, 'Could Mr John Smith (false name) please make his way to the reception desk'. My colleague looked at each other wondering if he would fall for this. A minute or so passed and then we saw him walking towards us in shorts and flip flops. He reached the desk, and I took hold of him, identifying myself as a police officer. He looked at us in horror as I explained he was being arrested on a recall to prison. 'I'm going to Mexico on an all-inclusive' is what he replied. 'Well, you're not now are you' I said back to him.

2008

I was working in a drugs team, and it was well known amongst my colleagues that I was gay and lived with my partner. One of the men on my group spoke to me one day about another gay colleague. 'When you see her can you tell her this'. I looked at him and said, 'I've not seen her for years, do you think we all live together in the same house?'. I shook my head and walked away from him.

2008

We had been tasked to carry out a drugs warrant as it was believed the owners of this house were dealing from that address. When we arrived, the door was opened by an old lady well into her 70's. A sound of 'oh shit' went through the group as we realised, we may have been given false information. We were invited inside the address and explained why we were there. The householder looked at us stunned and said 'drugs?'. The lady explained she lived with her friend who was also her age and was due back any minute. Most of the team went back to wait in the van while a few of us stayed in the house to have a quick look around. Two of my colleagues had gone upstairs while we chatted to the old dear downstairs. It was nearly Christmas, and we were commenting how nice her decorations were when one of my colleagues shouted down 'mate you need to come and see this'. I went upstairs, and in the study, lined up along the desk were numerous small bags of cocaine and cannabis bush. We all looked at each other stunned. My colleagues began to bag up the exhibits as the second old lady who lived in the house arrived home.

A further search of the house had also revealed that one of the ladies had been growing a crop of cannabis in a downstairs room next to the bathroom. We all eventually sat down in the living room to go through with the ladies what was going to happen. One of them had admitted to the lot and was getting arrested. The other lady was pleading complete ignorance. As we were sat in the living room, the lady who was getting arrested pointed to a card on the mantlepiece which she said was addressed to her nephew. She said that as we were searching the house we better open it. On opening the Christmas card, we discovered a bag of cannabis and a bag of cocaine sellotaped to the outside of the card wishing her nephew a very happy Christmas. As a result of this she also got arrested for attempting to supply class A drugs. I remember that as we waited in the house for the search to be completed, we had quite a laugh with the pair of them. One of the ladies even opened a Christmas tub of Quality Street chocolates that we passed around. I checked months later, and she didn't get a custodial sentence which I was glad about.

1994

I was working on a uniform response group and one day the lads on the group decided to play a trick on one of the female probationary officers. The Sgt was in on the prank as well and told her that she had to make her way to a pelican crossing where she would be escorting school children across the crossing at the end of the day. She was told she had to wear her fluorescent yellow tabard and her white gloves (white gloves are only ever worn for funeral occasions, not for school crossing patrols). It was decided I would drive her to the crossing and drop her off. Ten minutes later she appeared in the yard dressed in high visibility jacket and white gloves carrying her lollipop which had she looked closer read, 'Stop Children'. Underneath this in permanent marker someone had written 'wear a condom'. She placed her lollipop sign in the back of the panda car with it sticking out of the window and off we went. I couldn't help feeling sorry for her as I drove her around the station, so I decided to tell her it was a joke rather than make a total arse out of her. Girl code and all that!!

1992

It was Christmas day 1992 and we were all working a day shift 7am-3pm. It was a bit like 'Life on Mars' back then. Our group decided to celebrate properly so we all decided what food we were going to bring in for our Christmas lunch. As well as food there was alcohol. At lunch time we pulled a load of table together to make one long table which was adorned with sausage rolls, quiche, sandwiches crisps and numerous bottles of beer and wine. We all had a fine old time toasting and wishing each other a very merry Christmas until a job came out. This was quite unusual on Christmas day as people normally don't start battering each other until at least 6pm. As we'd all had a few drinks we decided that we would all go to the domestic disturbance because it would be a laugh.

So off we went in a convoy of about 5 police cars to the address that was less than desirable. The whole family were kicking off and very drunk so we all collectively decided to arrest the whole family for a breach of the peace of for the ones who ventured outside with their arguing, drunk and disorderly. We all arrived back at the station thinking we were hilarious. Our Sgt called us all a bunch of dick heads as he had to then book them all into custody which took him hours.

1994

I was in a plain clothes police vehicle with two other colleagues, and we were responding to a call. With this being a plain police vehicle in the 90's it wasn't all fancy like unmarked police cars are today. We set off and I grabbed the blue light from the glove box and plugged with wire into the cigarette lighter. The blue light started to whir round, and I reached up through the open passenger window to place the light on top of the police car. I didn't realise that the car had a sunroof which was open so the blue light fell back into the police car through the sunroof hitting one of my colleagues on the head.

1987

After the Liverpool riots of 1981 police officers were continually given overtime to work in the troubled areas of Toxteth every evening between 11pm and 2am patrolling the streets in a police car. I had put my name down to work overtime and had been drawn 'out of the hat' to work it. The only problem was that women were not permitted to be involved in the riots in 1981 and this tradition had continued. I was told to go to the police station in the area where the overtime would be being policed. I had to speak to the male officer working as the BP (bridewell patrol officer assisting the desk Sgt) and tell him that he had to take my place in the van with all the male officers while I 'manned' the bridewell until 2am.

On one such occasion as my male colleagues were getting ready to go out on patrol in the vans, one of the men got his riot boots out of his kit bag only to realise that someone had sprayed them yellow with red dots on them.

1991

It was a regular occurrence in the prison vans for stink bombs to be sellotaped to the clutch pedals.

1990

I was working in a station and my Sgt was not liked by anyone on our shift hence his nickname was 'knobhead'. He had private number plates on his personal car and would drive his car to the station every shift, carefully reversing into his parking space. Someone had the bright idea of making a new number plate up for his car that said 'knobhead'. One tour of nights while he was hard at work inside the station two of us unscrewed his rear number plate and replaced it with 'knobhead'. It came to 7am and he left the station and headed home, reversing his car onto his driveway and then headed to bed. A few hours later his wife left the house and went shopping in his car. A short distance into her trip she was pulled over by the police who wanted an explanation as to why she was driving around with a number plate that read 'knobhead'. That night in work the Sgt came bouncing in, clearly not happy about the prank and demanded to know who had done this. Obviously, no one owned up, so the number plate was submitted for fingerprints. No prints came back because whoever put the plate on the car wore gloves. He's still a knobhead.

1991

I was working as the BP (bridewell patrol officer) assisting the desk Sgt. This particular Sgt was a drunk and would regularly turn up for work drunk, although in those days if it wasn't obvious nothing was done about it. I was approached by another female colleague about this Sgt and she told me he had touched her sexually. She was devastated about this, but it wasn't the time or the place to accuse of colleague of this. What I did do was get him in a quiet corner and grab him by the throat and told him that if he ever touched her again, he'd get a hiding. He didn't touch her again.

I remember working with him one evening and a colleague had arrested a prostitute. Prior to being placed in a cell I searched this lady and recorded her property on the custody sheet. She had a few belongings and absolutely no cash on her. This Sgt oversaw her welfare whilst she was in custody. When it came time to release her, I collected her from the cell and noticed she was holding something in her hand. On closer inspection I saw this was a £10 note. I asked where she had got this from as she didn't have any cash on her when she arrived at the station. She basically told me that the Sgt had given it to her when she'd given him a blow job in the cell. Again, I couldn't do anything because the culture was you didn't grass on your colleagues or that would follow you round for the rest of your career.

1991

You have a refs or scoff time every shift and on nights this is usually between 1am and 3am. In one particular station I worked in I had to knock on the canteen door before I went in so that the policemen in the canteen could switch off the porn they were watching on the old Betamax video.

1995

I applied to go on a bodyguard course but was told that as a woman my hands were too small to hold the gun and reach the safety catch at the same time, so I wasn't allowed to progress any further.

1997

I had worked on a surveillance unit for 9 years and had briefly returned to my uniform role in a police station when I noticed a job that was being advertised internally for a surveillance trained motorcycle officer. This was perfect for me as I was surveillance trained and I had been riding motorbikes for years. All I needed to have was a Police motor cycle course. I applied and was told 'Don't bother, we're going to take the traffic boys and train them up' 'We've never had any women bikers. 6 years later I applied again and was accepted. On my advanced motorcycle course the male instructor said to me 'you've got balls'. I later went on a course at Wyboston and bumped into the man who had years before told me not to bother applying because I was a woman. He said to me 'Actually you're really good'.

1995

I had arrested a man for disqualified driving. During the arrest he slammed my hand in the car door and assaulted me. Weeks later flowers and chocolates arrived at the station for me with a card which read 'Sorry, if I'd known it was a woman I'd not have done it'.

1990

Drug dealers and generally nasty people were regularly taken off the streets in the police van, driven to a local park and thrown in the lake.

1991

I was sent to a report of a sudden death. When I got there, it was an old lady who had passed away. The radio room said it was going to take a couple of hours for the undertakers to get to me, so I put the kettle on and made a cuppa and sat with her chatting away.

1994

I had gone to a report of a student having an asthma attack. When I arrived unfortunately, she had died. As we were dealing with this the phone rang in her flat and I picked it up. It was the girls mum wanting to speak to her but then also wanting to know why the police were in her daughters flat. I felt terrible but I had to tell her over the phone that her daughter had died. I bottled this up for years as were not really encouraged to talk about things in the police, or at least we weren't in the 90's you just got on with things. I was really devastated about this job for years after.

1993

I attended a car crash involving two children who had been run over. I ran to the little girl and held her in my arms. I remember her face was all cut open. The ambulance staff came over but realised there was nothing they could do for her so continued to help the small boy who had also been run over. I laid in the road with her, and she died in my arms. The way we dealt with things like this was to go to the bar over the police station after work and just have a chat with your colleagues. I often think about her.

2022

My opinion of the new graduate entry scheme is that it won't be recruiting people who have basic common sense. Some of these kids are still going to 'wet behind the ears' after 4 or 5 years. Their technical ability may be better but that's all.

2021

I retired but stayed on in my role as a civilian as most detectives are being asked to do due to a national shortage of detectives. When I was younger, I was always first in through a door when we did warrants but nowadays, I tend to leave this to the youngsters. This happened at a recent job I had attended. The occupant of the house was wanted on a big drug importation and had been sentenced by the courts in his absence. The front door went in, he ran from the back of the house and began fence hopping. At this point I was stood on the corner of the road holding a handbag so no way would he have thought I was a cop. I saw him run towards me and just as he got near me I rugby tackled him. I went straight up in the air upside down and full circle landing on him. My colleagues had followed him and detained him. I ended up with a massive bruise down my leg which I proudly showed my colleagues in the office by dropping my pants. Even at 54 I've still got it.

1994

I was sent to a domestic dispute. When we arrived, a man opened the door very agitated and seeing it was the police he reached up above the door frame and grabbed a knife he kept stashed there. Me and my colleague grabbed him taking hold of his arm holding the knife as he slashed it in our direction trying to cut us. I took out my baton and hit him on the wrist as we finally managed to subdue him and get him in handcuffs. You just got him booked in at the nearest police station, did your paperwork and carried on with going to the next job.

1989

I had gone through my probation and was now independent, so I could now be sent to jobs on my own. I was on foot and was sent to a report of squatters who had taken over a house. In the good old days, every radio room was staffed with actual police officers and a Sgt on every shift, and you always knew your radio room staff by first names. Nowadays radio room staff are made up of police officers and civilian staff. The radios used to be on 'talk through' so that if you spoke everyone on your section could hear what you were saying and know where you were going which made things much safer. Nowadays no one apart from the radio room staff know where you're going and what you're doing. Jobs are even allocated now via your mobile phone.

It was handy having a Sgt in the radio room as they would often give you advise about jobs you were going to. This happened on the day I was sent to my first independent job to remove several squatters from a house. I arrived at the house and the door was answered by a 'tree hugger hippie type'. I asked him if he would like to leave, and he answered 'No'. Luckily my Sgt was listening in keeping an eye on me. He soon turned up to the job and they all got turfed out.

2022

I had retired from the police, but due to the national shortage of detectives I had been asked to stay on in my role. One morning I attended a briefing as a civilian detective. The brief was we were executing a drugs warrant at an address. When we arrived the front room window was open. We had officers at the front and back of the address. I shouted through the window for the female inside to open the door. She ran to the back of the house and threw the drugs she was holding out of the window. These were collected by the officers waiting at the back of the house. The front door was smashed open, and we all ran into the house where all of the were detained. In my excitement I took hold of the female who had thrown the drugs out of the window and arrested her. A short time later I realised that I no longer had a 'power of arrest' so I had to take one of the officers to one side and ask him to arrest her. I've also noticed a difference with the way I'm treated in custody suites now that I'm a civilian.

1993

We used to play practical jokes on the prisoners and the desk Sgt. Once a prisoner had been booked in at the custody suite they are lodged in a cell. Many prisoners, after they have been interviewed and charged, are remanded to court the following day. Remand prisoners were often given a printed menu and asked what they would like for their dinner? What would actually happen is that one of the officers would be sent upstairs to the station canteen and would collect a dinner of sausage chips and beans for the prisoners, whilst they poured over the menu in their cell wondering whether to order the steak and chips. Prisoners were also asked what newspaper they would like to be delivered to their cell in the morning. One particular Sgt lost his temper one morning when the prisoners began banging on their cell doors to attract his attention. When he went to see what the problem was the prisoner asked to change his newspaper from the Mirror to The Sun.

1993

I was attached to a plain clothes unit. As well as getting a 'plain clothes allowance' you were also expected to use your own personal car to work in. I have lost count of the number of prisoners I have arrested and put in the back of my own car. I also would regularly be involved in chasing stolen cars in my own car. This would not happen nowadays.

1990

We used to work a shift system and do 7 nights on the bounce. On Sunday morning after our shift finished at 7am we would regularly go to the bar above the station and drink beer together as a team before driving home. It really was like 'Life on Mars' back then. We would work a shift together on Christmas day and bring in food and alcohol and all sit together not doing any work, just enjoying the day. Obviously, we'd respond to jobs if one came out, but generally it was quiet on Christmas day.

Our shift pattern also contained a short-change where we would finish our late shift at 11pm and must be back on duty at 7am the following morning. Most of the time we didn't even bother going home. We would all head off to the pub after our shift finished at 11pm, drink and then sometimes sleep in the pub as we all knew the landlord well. We would also sleep in a spare bedroom in an old people's homes home which was round the corner from our station, or in the Police rest room. We would all then turn up for work at 7am the following morning, slightly hungover and wearing the same clothes, ready for the next shift.

1995

There was a high-ranking officer working in our force who had an unusual name. He had a female's name and for the purposes of this story I will refer to him as 'Lyndsey'. Lyndsey was sent to oversee our unit to try and instil some order as we had gone a bit 'off the rails'. Lyndsey walked into our briefing room which was full of probably 100 policemen and a couple of policewomen. Everyone was dressed identically, complete with hats on pulled down over our eyes. He proceeded to talk down to us and continually used his first name to try and intimidate us. 'My name is Lyndsey and I'm going to sort this unit out'. 'My name's Lyndsey and what's going on in this unit is going to stop'. This carried on for several minutes with him repeating his name and threats to set things straight with his no mess approach to supervising us. He stood up to leave the room and with his hand on the door he turned and said, 'Has anybody got any questions?'. There had been silence in the room up until this moment. One voice from the back of the room then broke the silence, 'I've got a question for you. Why have you got a fucking birds name?' Lyndsey then stormed out of the room as it erupted in laughter.

2014

I was working in CID and our office had several plain police vehicles allocated to them. When I was working a late shift, uniform officers would regularly come into our office and ask if they could borrow a vehicle. My thought was, these are not my cars, they belong to the police, so, if you fill it up with fuel when you've finished with it go ahead and take it. This continued for some months with our uniform colleagues asking to borrow our vehicles. One day I realised that one of our cars was missing. This was nothing new, as often police vehicles would disappear only to be replaced with a new 'pool car'.

Some months later we found out that one of our uniform colleagues (a sgt) had been arrested for sexual offences against members of the public. This was a shock to hear but even more shocking was finding out that the plain police vehicle he had been borrowing from our office had been taken away for a 'full forensic lift' as he had been using this vehicle to pick up prostitutes who would then perform sexual acts on him in the police vehicle. His semen was discovered on the dashboard, the front and back seats and the steering wheel. I was horrified, as I used this vehicle daily. He was subsequently prosecuted and sent to prison, the dirty bastard.

1995

I had driven into work in my own car and as I was driving through the back streets, I saw a well-known thief stealing York paving flags from an entry and loading them into the boot of his car. York paving flags are very expensive, they are also very heavy. I quickly drove into the station and jumped into the back of a colleague's police car and told them to drive to a local stone mason's yard. We arrived and hid out of sight waiting for the thief to arrive. Sure enough 30 minutes later he drove into the stone mason's yard with the arse end of his car dragging on the floor. I let him park up and unload all the York paving flags from the boot of his car. He looked absolutely knackered as he lifted the last flag from his car. I swooped in taking hold of him. He was too knackered to fight and just sat down on the floor trying to get his breath back. I let him have 5 minutes then took him to the police station.

2017

I was working in a highly respected CID department which was twinned with another department. The Sgts office was situated in-between both offices and one day I had cause to go and speak to the Sgts. On this day, it was Halloween. I walked into their office and saw one of my colleagues from the neighbouring office stood there in a full witch's outfit. Long black dress, witchy makeup, witches' hat, false nose, and broom. I stood there open mouthed as she waffled on about it being Halloween and how she liked to embrace this time of year by dressing up. Unfortunately, this also meant that as she was dressed like a total idiot she couldn't be expected to deal with any in custody prisoners. Can you imagine what it would have looked like getting interviewed by someone who looks like they have stepped out of the cast of 'Wicked'. Now I was just a Constable, but I stood there looking at the Sgts wondering what they were going to do? What they did was nothing, which currently does not surprise me. What they should have done was send her home to get changed and then come back into work and do the fucking job you're paid to do. She left the office to continue prancing round like a dickhead for the rest of the day. I looked at the Sgts who basically said, 'What can we do?'. She was the sort of person that if you called her out over her behaviour, she would either go off with stress or accuse you of bullying. I walked out of the office shaking my head. The Police has gone to shit in my opinion.

1997

I was posted to a drugs team, and it was brilliant. We spent our days prowling the streets looking for prisoners or coming in early at 6am and putting a drug dealers door in. The adrenalin rush you get driving to a drugs warrant is unbelievable. Most of the time its quiet in the van driving to the address, your mind whirling with a million different scenarios about what may happen once the door goes in. Once you approach the house its fast. You've worked together so long, you know what your role is. Get the door in fast, assess who's in the house and grab them. Sometimes were had to cut a hold in sewage pipes attached to the side of the house and get a bucket ready for the drugs that would get flushed, along with the tick list of drug supplies they had made. Lifelong friendships are made with police officers who work in teams like this. There's a close bond. You trust each other with your life. You could enter a house where you get shot or stabbed so you've got each other's backs.

On one such day the RCS (regional crime squad) had approached us and asked us to execute a drugs warrant on their behalf. There was a bigger picture, and they couldn't blow their cover by doing the warrant. We hit the house within 30 minutes. I remember as we went in there was a girl sat blow drying her hair in the living room. She's obviously just loaned her house out for a short time for the dealers to come in and do their business. Then we saw them in the kitchen, 4 men making Crack Cocaine. They had the lid off the kettle, so it was on continuous boil with the Crack getting cooked. Prior to it setting rock hard, Crack cocaine is the consistency of blancmange.

There were about 8 large balls of Crack and about 8 ounces on the draining board so about £80,000 Enough to put the dealers away for 10 years plus. Everyone was handcuffed and sat in the living room. They said nothing but you could see their minds were whirring as to who had grassed.

I began collating the evidence documenting when the drugs and other items of paperwork were seized. One of the dealers had been wearing a leather jacket and when I looked inside the pocket there was a strip of negatives. I seized them up and thought I'd get them printed out by the photographic department. They were all eventually taken to the police station and interviewed, all saying 'no comment'. Prior to the trial at Crown Court, I was getting all of my exhibits together which included the now developed photographs. These were 4 holiday snaps taken somewhere obviously quite exotic. Fast forward to the trial and I'd thought nothing more of the photos until our barrister produced them while cross examining the main drug dealer who I'd noticed was sporting a rather fabulous tan. He swore blind that the pictures were taken by his girlfriend when they had gone to Mauritius. Now he wasn't working, and when she appeared the following day to give evidence on behalf of her 'boyfriend' it transpired she worked in retail in a not very well-paid job, but she confirmed she had paid for their expensive holiday. For reasons that I still can't fathom, the jury could not decide if the 4 were guilty so the CPS (Crown prosecution service) ordered a retrial.

Prior to the retrial I decided to spend the afternoon visiting local travel agents asking them to put the main drug dealers name into their system to see if he'd been on holiday anywhere before the first trial because as I said he had a tan. The last travel agents I went in confirmed he had come in a few months prior asking to go to the Maldives. She remembered this as it was her that dealt with him. He asked her to ring a specific hotel as he wanted to lift heavy weight s in the gym. She remembered him dripping in tacky gold jewellery. She then got out the travel details and there it was, he travelled with his girlfriend, but it wasn't the girl who'd given evidence in court for him a few weeks earlier, this was his actual girlfriend. And the cherry on the cake was he had paid in cash for the holiday on the day he booked it.

So now he had a dilemma. The woman pretending to be his girlfriend was a liar and would be questioned over this in the re trial. He would have to explain how he paid £10,000 cash for a holiday when he wasn't working and why he had agreed the woman giving evidence was his girlfriend. It was all crumbling around him.

We went to Crown court for the retrial. Surprisingly this didn't happen. Drug dealer's barrister must have realised he would have to pull something out of the bag to get his clients off, otherwise none of his other drug dealing clients would employ him to represent them would they? The trial collapsed because the defence barrister wanted to know who the informant was who had initially tipped off the RCS that Crack Cocaine was being cooked up in the house. Due to the policies of this police force it was decided to let the trial collapse rather than reveal the name of the informant. I mean this would have ended up in somebody getting shot.

This was disappointing but it's just a game. I've always said that no matter how big or small you are, if you're dealing drugs on a massive scale you'll eventually get caught and if you're some little rat riding round the streets on your electric bike you'll also eventually get caught.

I then received a phone call from a Detective Sgt who said one of his 'Snouts' now known as a CHIS (covert human intelligence source) had rung him panicking. Apparently, the main drug dealer who had been in the holiday snaps was very angry with me because I'd made him look like a dick head, proving him to be a liar. As punishment for this he was going to petrol bomb my house. To make this easier for him he'd seen me arrive at Crown court in my personal car and had got a corrupt police officer to run a check on my car which provided him with my home address. There was just one floor in his plan, I had sold my house some weeks earlier to a lovely couple who I now realised would be less than impressed when the police descended on their new home fitting a 'panic alarm' which would go straight through to the police station, and fireproof bags fitted behind their front door. It all blew over and nothing happened to my former house or me. I know the drug dealers thought they had got one over on us and I admit we were momentarily disappointed, but you move onto the next job. I did however find out that the informant who told the RCS the Crack Cocaine was getting cooked in the house and the phone call made to the Detective Sgt about my house getting torched were from the same person. Sometimes there's no honour amongst thieves, but he did have some conscience and I thank him for that.

1997

Another day on the drugs squad and a call came in that there was a flasher in the park. We were just round the corner so hurried down there for a laugh. There was no flasher but what I did find was a local drug addict obviously waiting to be dealt to. I hung around out of sight until another man showed up. We pounced and detained them both. Now bearing in mind that when I searched my prisoner, he had nothing on him but his physical reaction to getting stopped was very unusual. I can't explain this other than to say you just get a feeling when something isn't right. Both males got arrested for a full drugs search as this can't be done in public. Once I was back in the station, I decided I was going to get a drugs warrant for my prisoner who lived with his mum. I had to go to the out of hours magistrate as the courts shut at 4pm. I spoke to the magistrate and was very honest saying it was a massive hunch. The men were both known drug users, but I needed to get into his house as I just knew there was something there. I got the warrant signed and rushed back to the station. The address wasn't far away so a few of us shot over there. The door was put in as there was no one at home. The prisoner's mother who was in her 70's was out at bingo. We started to search and discovered under the stairs in one of those old lady shopping trollies, a stash of heroin, cocaine and cannabis probably totalled £10,000. I was ecstatic as my hunch was right. We continued to search and there was a knock at the door. We were all in plain clothes and in a plain police car so whoever it was at the door had no idea the police were inside. My colleague opened the door and there was a man stood there. For a second, he didn't quite compute, then he realised something was very wrong and he ran, chased by two of my colleagues. They chased him for a few hundred yards and saw him throw a big bag of white powder into a garden as he ran. He was stopped, arrested and brought back to the house. The powder was recovered which turned out to be 8 ounces of cocaine. Then the old lady who owned the house came back from bingo and was obviously shocked to find her house swarming with police. We explained her son had been arrested and told her what we had discovered in her shopping trolly under the stairs. She listened to what we said and then said, 'Well that explains a lot'. She went on to tell us that she had attended a police event the previous weekend with her shopping trolly in tow. During the display with the drugs dog, the dog had sat by the old lady and her trolly basically telling the police handler the old lady had drugs on her. The policeman had apologised to the lady and told the dog off on several occasions.

1994

It was a common practise in the police if you left your PNB (pocket notebook) lying around that it would get defaced usually with a 'cock and balls' or a 'cat' right through your evidence. If you had to attend court with your note book you then couldn't get it out to refresh your memory as it would inevitably be passed to the defending solicitor who would see the offending cock and balls, so you had to memorize your evidence. If you really couldn't get out of it and knew you'd have to show your notebook in court, it was always handy prior to your trial to pop it in the washing machine on a 90 degree wash, always guaranteed to stick all the pages together, therefore rendering it unreadable.

1998

We were executing a drugs warrant when I worked in the plain clothes drugs squad. The front door was a wooden one with wooden squares at the top of the door. My colleague ran up to the door with the door opener and hit it on one of the wooden squares.

He then for reasons unknown he let go of the door opener and it fell into the house landing inside on the hallway floor, breaking one of the tiles it fell on. We then had to knock on the door. The householder came to the door, looking through the hole in her door at us as my colleague said, 'Can we have our door opener back please'.

2014

I was working in CID in a child protection unit which dealt with on going rapes of minors, physical assaults of minors and historic sexual offences of children who were now adults. One such job I had been allocated was a teenage girl who had been raped by a family member. My job was to collate all the evidence I could, be that forensic, or obtaining interviews from the witnesses. I interviewed the young girl and had no reason to doubt what she was telling me. I believed every single victim that I dealt with. My way of thinking was why would you put yourself through this rigorous process and a possible trial at court if it hadn't happened. I interviewed the offender and he flatly denied raping her. After I had collated my evidence, I then had to submit my findings to the complex case unit at the CPS (crown prosecution service) for a lawyer to then review the file. This can be a nightmare. You have victims waiting for an answer as to whether the offender will be charged, and it can take months. Some CPS lawyers would deliberately ask for a piece of evidence you had already submitted or merely a question that could be answered straight away. This gave the lawyers a further 28 days to then reply to you once you had submitted their questions. It was a very frustrating process for us and the victims. I have no doubt that this was a delaying tactic with some lawyers as they were probably as snowed under with investigations as I was.

I have seen countless times on TV, people questioning the percentage of offenders convicted for rape or serious sexual offences. I often found myself shouting at the TV wishing I could tell them the truth. Well, the truth is that an investigation will only progress to Crown Court if there is a realistic chance of a prosecution. I was once told by a lawyer that it cost upwards of £15,000 a day to open the doors of a crown court, so with austerity like it is, unless your job is cut and dried the chances are a lawyer will write it off as NFA (No further action). I used to dread making calls to the victims, hearing them breakdown as I explained that the CPS were not going to take their investigation any further.

Anyway, back to my allocated investigation. I was allocated a lawyer and spoke to her on the phone. During this conversation we spoke about the victim who had said she had been raped. The lawyer asked me 'Is she flaky?'. I think by this she meant how will she stand up being cross examined in Crown Court. The lawyers watch the video recorded evidence, and this lawyer clearly wasn't very impressed with the timid victim she saw on screen. I was utterly incensed by this question and argued that the girl had been raped. We had statements questioning the account given by the offender. We had a good shot at a guilty verdict. The CPS lawyer's decision was NFA. I was gutted when I had to tell the girl and her mother. I always think they thought it was my fault, but it wasn't. I couldn't be honest with them and tell them what the lawyer had said. It's to do with money, and the certainty of a guilty verdict. Never mind the victims left by the wayside thinking they haven't been believed.

2007

I was posted to a disruption team. Our brief was to deal with anti-social behaviour and self-generate prisoners. We would also get called upon to execute warrants in the local area. Some of the warrants we did were at properties that were disgusting. You had to wipe your feet on the way out. We did warrants in flea infested houses where you could see the fleas jumping round in front of you. And the smell in some of the houses, it was indescribable. A mixture of dirt and often lots of pets who would shit in the houses. We would often play a game when searching the houses, especially the bedrooms. The bedrooms would often consist of a 'floordrobe' where numerous clothes were just strewn all over the floor. The windows had never been opened and the room would be covered in dust and pet hair and would smell of sweat and other unmentionable bodily fluids. There would be no sheets on the bed or pillowcases on the sweat stained pillows. A dirty brown stained duvet would be strewn across the bed. The question would be 'How much to sleep in the bed overnight, with your head on the pillow'. Everyone used to go 'uggggggh no chance' but they would usually crack and admit they would do it for £5,000.

2010

I was working on a drugs unit with two policemen. We would execute several drugs warrants a week often recovering thousands of pounds in cash and large seizures of class A drugs such as cocaine, crack cocaine, heroin, amphetamine, ecstasy and cannabis. The thing was our team had started to get complaints of cash being taken during these warrants. If we did a warrant and there were no drugs in the house, a complaint would be made that £300 had been stolen from the mantlepiece. I was very confused over this. I knew I hadn't taken it, but I also worked closely with my two colleagues and had no reason to suspect them of stealing. I initially put it down to people making malicious complaints. As the months went on the complaints continued to roll in and I wondered if anything was going on? During one warrant we did I searched the kitchen and found thousands of pounds stashed in pots hidden in the units. I was with my colleague who had come to help me search. I asked him to go and get me a cash seizure bag from our kit and he told me to get it. The truth was I didn't want to leave him with the cash. I didn't voice my concerns to anybody else on the team as I had no proof of what was going on. I can't say for sure if he took money from the cash, I found in the kitchen, but it wouldn't surprise me if he did.

Another warrant we executed found a drug addict in a terrace house. The house was known as a 'safe house'. A premises the police would have no reason to go to and an occupant who is usually not known to the police. In this house the drug addict had been holding drugs for a gang of dealers as well as a large carrier bag full of cash. The dealers on bikes would come to the house and collect several small bags of drugs at a time then go and deal them. If stopped by the police, they would just swallow them as they usually carried them in their mouth. I seized from the house about 300 bags of crack cocaine and heroin, each small bag was a £10 deal. There must have been thousands of pounds in the carrier bag she kept down the side of her chair. The house we were in was a small terrace, so we were all sat in the front room. The policy with seizing cash is that you don't count it, it is seized in a cash seizure bag which is then signed by me and the arrested person across the seal of the bag so that you can see it has not been tampered with. I could see my colleague was fuming at the situation and it was at that point I knew. I knew he had been stealing cash from warrants we had done, and I was so disappointed with him. We got back to the station with the prisoner and my two colleagues left me on my own to deal with the prisoner. The following day our Sgt bollocked the pair of them for leaving me. They were obviously angry that they hadn't had chance to take any cash from the bag I had seized. The thing is with cash seizures from drugs warrants. Say if the arrested person had £10,000 in a bag and this corrupt policeman stole £5,000 of it, the arrested person isn't going to say 'hang on there was much more money than that' because that infers that they are dealing on a massive scale. So, my colleagues were stealing from people who were never going to complain, because by complaining, you were making out you were dealing drugs on a large scale due to the amount of cash you had stashed in your house.

Shortly after this I left this group and the team got disbanded. We all moved to different groups. Unknown to all of us an investigation had been launched into the numerous thefts. I then found out that one of my former colleagues from the drugs team had been arrested for theft. He had conducted a drugs warrant and had recruited some probationary constables to go with him on the warrant. It was a set up. The occupant of the house to be raided was occupied by an undercover officer who had befriended my colleague at his local gym over a period of months. So, when the front door was opened, and my colleague saw a man he knew from the gym things got interesting. My colleague established by asking the occupant, that there were drugs and cash in the house. The drugs were fake and were left by my colleague with the occupant. The occupant told him there was £3,000 in the living room. My colleague out of sight of the other officers took this money and put it in his pocket. They then left the house. On the way back to the station the police van was stopped by undercover officers who searched my colleague and found the £3,000 in his trouser pocket. He came up with a story saying he was unsure what to do with the cash as he knew the occupant from the gym. He was suspended from work and eventually charged with corruption and sent for trial at Crown Court. What surprised me during this investigation was at no point did anyone from the anti-corruption team speak to me. I'm aware that all three of us were followed an no doubt out personal finances looked at. This initially annoyed me, but I understand they had a job to do, but I still don't understand why they didn't ask me anything. I was incredibly upset by all of this. On one hand I felt completely betrayed by my colleague. It went against everything I stood for. The job is hard enough without your colleagues being corrupt and stealing. I was also incredibly worried for him in case he went to prison. I can only imagine how awful it would be for a serving police officer to go to prison for stealing cash belonging to drug dealers.

The trial went ahead, and he was found 'not guilty'. He was dismissed from the police due to this investigation. I want him to know I think he's an absolute disgrace. The second policeman resigned a short time later. Although he wasn't involved in the 'set up' warrant they knew he was involved in the thefts and wanted shut of him as well.

After this I would walk into a room in the police station, and everyone would go quiet. I really hoped people didn't think I had anything to do with what had happened. It was a terrible time and one thankfully that has not been repeated during the rest of my career.

I saw the ex-policeman who went to crown court years later when I had cause to visit a hospital for work purposes. He looked over at me and I turned my back on him. My silence said more than anything I could ever have said to him.

2007

I was working in the city centre late one Saturday evening when a call came out of a man who had been assaulted. This man had been fighting with another drunk who had grabbed a fire extinguisher and had pulled the pin out of it which was now wrapped around his finger. During the fight the man with the fire extinguisher pin had punched the other man in the neck causing the pin to puncture his carotid artery. He was bleeding badly and losing consciousness. My colleague radioed for an ambulance, but we were told there weren't any. Yes this also happens to the police! My colleague made a split decision. He decided to take the man in the police carrier to the hospital. This was a brave decision, because if the man died en route of which there was a distinct possibility he could, we would get in a lot of trouble. On the other hand, if we left him lying on the floor waiting for the non-existent ambulance he was going to die. We put him in the police carrier and drove like maniacs to the hospital. The man lost 3 pints of blood en route, but the NHS staff saved his life when we got him there. The carrier had to be put off the road to be cleaned as it was swamped with blood.

1993

I was working a night shift in the summer and at 5am we were called to a report of a domestic disturbance. It was very light with it being the summer, and we raced down the road in the patrol car. With it being the early 90's we didn't have the all singing, all dancing klaxons that are on response vehicles now. We had two pull out buttons in the car, one to activate the single blue light on top of the police car and the other to activate the two-tone horns on top of the police car. There were literally two horns on top of the police car. As we zoomed down the road with the horns blaring away they made a 'nee naw' sound. The road ahead was clear apart from a flock of pigeons that were sat in the road. My colleague couldn't slowdown in time as we drove through them. Suddenly we were engulfed in a cloud of feathers. A few seconds later the klaxons began to sound funny, going from 'nee naw' to 'naw'. We arrived at the job and when I jumped out of the car, I looked at the top of the police care and noticed a dead pigeon stuck head first in one of the klaxons.

1996

One of the men I had worked with on the first section I was posted to, moved a different group. We were gutted when he left as he was one of the best policemen I had ever worked with. What we would call in the police a natural thief taker.

He told he a short time later that he had been asked to be part of the arrest team. This arrest team was part of an operation to crack down on a local 'dogging' area for gay men. The area was right by the beach in the sand dunes. It was the height of summer, and the plain clothes cops were dressed in shorts and t shirt. He told me that he had never been involved in anything like this before and had asked his colleagues for advice. He wasn't sure how far to let the gay men go before he arrested them. He was told not to worry and that if he just walked through the sand dunes, the men would pop up like meerkats and then approach him asking for sex. That's where it should have ended, but his colleagues, realising this was an opportunity to really take the piss told him that he also had to wait for the men to touch him sexually before he arrested them. This of course was utter bollocks.

At the end of the operation my colleague had arrested a man for 'importuning' (attempting sex in a public place). When his colleagues asked him how far he let the man go with him he replied, 'Oh I let him put his hand in my shorts and grab my dick, then I arrested him'. He never lived this down.

2003

I was attending a domestic dispute. The female in the house had covertly rung and had asked for assistance from the police due to her abusive partner. I arrived with my colleague. The house was a detached new build and looked very smart. I knocked on the door which was answered by a lady who had a black eye. She took one look at us and told me to take my boots off before coming in. I told her 'No' and pushed my way into the house to find her husband stood behind the front door. He immediately started shouting telling me to 'fuck off' and that it was 'nothing to do with us. We managed to calm the situation down slightly and took him into the kitchen to talk while leaving her in the living room with me. The policy with domestic incidents is to arrest the offender even if you haven't got a victim statement. Quite often victims will ring the police for help but all they really want is for the offender to be removed from the house while the situation calms down. This solves nothing as the domestic will more likely than not continue when the offender returns home.

I had spoken with the female who point blank refused to make a complaint of assault against her husband although it was clear he had given her the black eye she was sporting. We handcuffed him and brought him through the living room past his wife. He was seething, struggling against us as we walked him to the front door. His wife was not happy with this as she had point blank told us she didn't want to make a complaint. As I walked past her, she jumped on my back screaming for me to leave him alone, or as she put it 'he's my world'. I managed to shake her off me as she continued to try and reach her husband. I dodged the scratching hands and managed to get her in handcuffs. She was also arrested for a breach of the peace. You just can't help some people.

1992

I was working lates and we responded to a report of a fight in the street. The street was a main road and as we drove towards the fight, I couldn't quite believe what I was seeing. Stood in the middle of the road was a bride and groom dressed in full wedding outfits, and they were both battering each other. Her veil was flying in the wind as he swung her round and she hit him on the head. They had obviously headed to the local pub after getting hitched and it seemed that wedded bliss had run its course. They both got arrested for being drunk and disorderly as they were steaming drunk. Him with his suit ripped and tie askew, her with her veil pulled from her head, makeup streaming down her face. We managed to bundle her and her enormous meringue wedding dress into the back of the panda car and her groom went into a separate car. We arrived at the police station and due to the conversations on the radio a crowd of police had gathered to see the arrested newly weds. Bride and groom were taken into the custody suite where they continued to argue with each other, him being a 'bastard' and her being a 'fucking bitch'. They were both booked into custody and then as they were being taken to their cells the bride said, 'Can we share a cell with it being our wedding night'. Her request was denied by the desk sergeant.

2002

We were executing a drugs warrant at a well-known dealers house, but having raided this address on numerous occasions we could never find his stash. On this day I found myself stood in his lounge once again wondering where the hell he kept it all. As I looked at the wall, I noticed a strange seam in the wallpaper which had a cabinet in front of it. I moved the cabinet out of the way and ran my hand down the seam managing to prise my fingers behind it. A panel in the wall suddenly opened revealing a staircase behind it that lead downstairs underneath the property to a cannabis factory housing hundreds of plants. Just proving that sometimes you look but you don't see.

1998

It was New Years Eve and our group had been tasked with policing the local drug dealers who had decided to throw a large party in a house they had bought in a very rough area where I was stationed. We parked up and were greeted with a hail of 'fuck offs' from the occupants of this house, who stood in the window flicking the V's at us. They continued to arrive in a hail of taxi's as more and more of them crammed into the house, music blaring out through open windows. We decided to speak to some of the local dealers who were arriving in taxis about the fact they weren't wearing seat belts pointing out if the cab crashed, they could be seriously injured. They were also issued with fines for 'not wearing a seat belt. Obviously, we wanted to get the night started on the right foot. This had the desired effect and wound them all up to fever pitch. The music got louder with empty cans being thrown from open windows, littering the street below. The 'Fuck offs' continued through the windows. Then we decided we had a better plan. They were causing a disturbance with it being a residential area, so we rang the electric board who attended a short time later and we all stood guard around the men as they dug up the pavement and cut off the electric supply to the house plunging it into darkness and cutting the music dead.

Shortly after the local dealers began to leave and couldn't help themselves shouting their 'fuck offs' and that we were a load of 'twats', only now they were drunk so several of them got arrested for being drunk and disorderly and spent the night in the cells. Happy New Year!!!!

1989

For whatever reason I had been given a crappy foot beat where nothing happened. It was the dead of winter on nights and the snow was deep. I trudged through freshly laid snow trying to keep warm when my radio suddenly crackled into life. Could I go to a possible sudden death. A lady had rung saying she hadn't seen her neighbour for days and feared the worst. I arrived at the house and had to remove several pieces of slatted glass from a window at the rear of the property to gain entry. The house was freezing, but it wouldn't be for long once I got the fire on and waited for the funeral directors to arrive. I felt quite pleased with myself getting out of the cold. I walked through to the living room where I found the old dear slumped in an armchair with what appeared to be several coats stacked on her. The room was bitterly cold as I leant in towards her face to check for a pulse. As I put my finger on her neck she shouted, 'What do you want'. To say I shit myself is an understatement!!

1993

A prisoner had made a malicious complaint of assault. As usual a few days later, police officers from the unit that investigates such allegations arrived at our station to 'serve' the bald officer who it was alleged had assaulted him with 'disciplinary papers'. He was greeted with several officers who were all bald because the male officers on the group had all taken part in a 'sponsored head shave' for a cancer charity that week. The investigating officer just shook his head. I later found out that one of the officers wives had gone ballistic when he had returned home from the head shaving event as he had completely forgotten they were attending a very posh dinner a few days later, and now he looked like a thug!!.

1990

Canteens in police stations are now a thing of the past with most stations now having a small kitchen area for officers to prepare their food, and a 'rest room' usually with a TV in it for officers to sit while they eat. Years ago it was very different. Canteens were subsidised with meals being very cheap. You could get food from 7am to 7pm usually and canteen culture was rife. You'd talk about your jobs and take the piss out of each other. The Constables would sit in the canteen with each other but attached to the other side of the kitchen was the 'officers dining room' which had a long dining table in it, because obviously the officers couldn't be seen to be eating food with the workers. It really was a very different era, very much like the army. What the officers didn't know was that police officers who would frequent the police bar in the evenings and weekends and get drunk would often use the officers dining room to have sex on the table.

1994

Occasionally on nights you would be asked to come in in plain clothes. This was exciting as you'd get to drive around in a plain car just looking for prisoners rather than being sent to jobs. On one such evening I was working with a male colleague when we saw a drug deal taking place. The addicts would wait on the corner and the dealer would arrive in the car and deal to them, but we had to get closer. My colleague decided to get out of the police car. He put his beanie hat on and walked over to where the drug addict was waiting. My colleague used to run a lot and so looked quite gaunt. He pulled his collar up and sat on the wall next to the drug addict who engaged him in conversation. They waited for several minutes, and the car pulled up again. The dealers looked at the two 'addicts' and asked the first one what he wanted. He asked for 'brown (heroin)' and as the dealer went to hand it to him my colleague swooped grabbing the dealer and the stash he had in his hand. I quickly drove over detaining the driver and both were arrested. The poor drug addict ran away empty-handed wondering what the fuck had just happened.

1997

During a suspect interview we were sat in the small interview room when the suspect began to look a bit green. He suddenly grabbed the bin and vomited into it. The smell was horrific in such an enclosed space. After a few minutes he composed himself and we continued the interview.

1998

A brothel had opened up on our area but before we executed a warrant there, we had to sure of what was going on inside as at the time we just suspected this is what was going on with the amount of men frequenting the establishment and the amount of girls that would arrive at the beginning of the evening and stay until the early hours. It was decided that one of the policemen would be given £20 and would go in and see what was going on. Off he went, disappearing behind the door only to return 30 minutes later to confirm it was a brothel. He'd spent the £20 on services!!

We hit the premises a short time later and found numerous girls working inside servicing the many men who had paid for sex, in the small rooms. I walked into one of the rooms and there was a man spread eagled on the bed. I threw a pillow over his genitals to spare his embarrassment. The men's details were taken along with the girls and the brothel owner was arrested. He was a piece of work. The girls told us that prior to being given a job he would get the girls to perform oral sex on him to make sure they knew what they were doing. A lot of the girls were University educated but said the money was just too good to turn down. The owner was eventually charged with running a brothel.

2004

I was working as a UC (under cover) cop. UC's are usually deployed to different forces away from their own so they are not recognised. On one job I was posing convincingly as a drug addict. I hadn't washed in weeks and looked terrible. I was sat in a house with other 'actual addicts' and as I went to leave, I was stopped in the hallway by one of the dealers who held a knife to my throat and accused me of being a 'bizzie'. I managed to persuade him I wasn't, but I got pulled from the job a short time later for safety reasons. One of the drug addicts was interviewed and was told that the woman he thought was 'Sharon' was a police officer working under cover. He was dumb struck and devastated as he told the interviewing officers 'I can't believe it. I was going to shag her!!!'

1991

I was working lates with a colleague. It is usual as the passenger in the police vehicle to check junctions as you approach and give a 'clear left' so that the driver can get to jobs quicker. As we approached the junction I checked left and saw something approaching and said, 'clear after the boat'. My colleague, thinking I was taking the piss drove off...... and drove straight into a car pulling a boat on a trailer.

1991

I had responded to a fight in a bar which was really getting out of hand. At the time I had only been issued with a wooden truncheon that you kept either in an inside pocket in your skirt or trousers. I used to wrap the rope at the end of the truncheon around my belt. As I grappled with a man, I could feel someone trying to grab at my truncheon and unwrap it from my belt. I managed to move out of his way and took hold of my truncheon also requesting immediate assistance. Those minutes waiting for your colleagues to turn up drag on forever and its frightening and exhilarating all at the same time.

1995

My colleague had driven our patrol car across some grass and the wheels had sunk in the mud. He asked me to get of the car and decided that if we put some weight on the bonnet that would help. Me being very naïve, got out of the car and got on all fours on the bonnet facing the windscreen. By this time a couple of other police cars had arrived to help/laugh at us. I continued to ride the bonnet then heard laughing behind me. It was at this point I realised they were taking the piss out of me when I turned to see them all doubled over laughing.

1997

It was Christmas Eve and I had been called to a domestic dispute. When we arrived the man in the house had run from the back, so we were left dealing with the woman who was less than pleased to see us. I could tell there was something wrong when I requested her personal details which she was less than willing to give. It turned out she was wanted on a 'no bail' warrant and had to be arrested. She pleaded with me as it was Christmas Eve, but I arrested her. She was not happy, and I got called all of the 'bitches!! She was taken to the police station and would stay there until boxing day which is when the next court was in session. We decided at about 3am to return to the house to see if her boyfriend had gone back because he was also wanted on a no bail warrant. We crept around the back of the house and looked in through the window where we saw him sleeping on the sofa. We went in through the open back door and managed to get the handcuffs on him before he woke up. The look on his face was very funny. He was taken to the same station and put in the adjacent cell to his girlfriend. Then the argument started. She called him all the 'stupid bastards' for the police getting called to their house in the first place. He'd ruined Christmas and she hated him.

I thought it would be fun to record what she was shouting on an old tape recorder. I balanced the tape machine on her cell door and recorded her ranting at him. She eventually shut up. Then an hour later I quietly balanced the tape machine on his cell door and pressed 'play'. Her voice burst though the silence ranting away. He was yelling from the inside of his cell for her to 'Shut the fuck up'. She was yelling at him that it wasn't her, even though it sounded like her. It was very funny, and it made the night pass quicker.

2014

I was working in a DV (domestic violence) unit and had dealt with an incident on where the lady alleged, she had been hit on the head by a man she had been in a relationship with for a while. She had an injury to her head so I no reason to disbelieve her. I interviewed the man and he 'no commented' the whole interview. He was a typical chauvinist, trying to tell me how to do my job. He was also angry he'd been arrested. I did notice during the interview that he had blood spots on his designer shirt so I informed him I would be seizing his shirt for forensic analysis as he couldn't confirm if the blood was his or hers due to his 'no comment' interview. Before he was released on bail, I seized his shirt and took a DNA sample from him. He was given a custody issue t shirt but wasn't happy. 'Did I know how much his shirt cost?' he shouted at me. I gathered all my evidence and submitted this to the CPS (crown prosecution service) only for them to NFA (no further action) the job. He rang me demanding his designer shirt back that had been found to have specs of his own blood on. I collected his shirt which was in a forensic bag, and with no reason to remove it from the bag I handed it to him still in the bag when he arrived outside the police station. He continued to rant at me about wasting his time and did I not know how busy he was. He pulled his shirt from the forensic bag and right in the middle of it was a massive hole. I started in disbelief wondering why on each the forensic investigators had cut the section out with blood on it rather than just take a swab of the blood. He exploded with anger, and it was all I could do not to laugh. It wasn't my fault someone had cut a hole in it. I'd never known the forensic department ever do this before. He stormed off shouting he was making a complaint, and true to his word he did.

119

1998

We had executed a drugs warrant at an address we had hit on numerous occasions. The occupants were dealing cannabis on a large scale, but we always struggled to find their stash. We had got inside the premises and had the occupants all sat handcuffed in the front room when there was a knock at the back door. As we were in plain clothes one of my male colleagues open the back door slightly and asked the visitor what he wanted. He replied that he had come to buy weed (cannabis bush). He was invited in only to be grabbed and sat on a chair and told he was under arrest for attempt possession of a controlled drug. As we searched the house the knocks on the back door continued to come with customers arriving to buy cannabis. Each man was arrested and sat in the kitchen. Even they found it funny in the end. A knock would come on the back door, and they would all shush each other laughing quietly as another customer would ask for cannabis. We eventually had to draw the line at 8 prisoners as we ran out of handcuffs.

2012

I was driving the police carrier. As I was older than most of the others in the van and had D1 on my driving license I had to drive all the time. The younger officers had to apply to have a carrier course, and as this would mean that they would have to drive around for most of the day they refused to put themselves on the course. Consequently, I had to drive for 10 hours a day every day. One day I was driving along, and it was very quiet in the back of the van. I turned around and everyone was playing on their mobile phones. No one was even looking around, looking for crimes that may be happening. Looking in vehicles spotting the boys out dealing drugs or people possibly driving with no insurance. I was so angry. This was not how I had been taught to police, or to do my job properly. A job came out on the radio of a drunk woman in the road causing a disturbance. I shouted up for it only to be asked by a colleague in the back of the van 'What was that'. He wasn't even listening to his radio. I drove along and spotted the drunk woman in the road. I positioned the carrier, so I pulled up and she was by my door. I noticed that one of the policemen stood up in the van to get out first, but I beat him to it, took hold of the woman who was shouting abuse to passing drivers and arrested her for being drunk and disorderly. I popped her in the secure cage, and we set off to the police station. The policemen in the carrier fell silent as I drove. My Sgt turned to me and said, 'Can you give this prisoner to John'. I questioned why I should do this and was told 'You're the only carrier driver'. To say I was angry was an understatement. I replied and said, 'well that's not my problem is it'. We continued to the police station in complete silence. I processed my own prisoner which took well over an hour. Not one of my colleagues helped me. It was then I decided I was leaving uniform and going to CID. I'd had enough.

1988

I was put in a panda car with a very old constable to be shown around. I hadn't been in the police long and was still in my probationary period. The constable drove around our division pointing things out as he weaved in and out of cars. I realised he was drunk. I could smell the alcohol on him, so I asked him to stop the car and I got out and walked back to the police station. I spoke to my Sgt and told me never to put me in a car with him because he was a drunk. He worked in the police for years after that as a community officer.

1999

We were in plain clothes and had executed a drugs warrant at a house and had detained all of the occupants inside. We were just about to start the search when there was a knock at the back door. I answered it and it was a drug addict asking to buy drugs. We invited him in and arrested him for attempt possession of a controlled drug. This continued throughout the search with numerous drug addicts knocking on the door asking for drugs. It got ridiculous, so I went outside and sat on the wall, intercepting the addicts as they walked down the path. I said to them, 'I wouldn't bother mate, it's full of bizzies in there'. On hearing this they turned on their heels and ran. At least this stopped them knocking on the door.

1999

I was working with a bunch of policemen on the vans, and we were asked to take part in a multiple warrant day. We arrived early at headquarters and got given our cooked breakfast along with multiple small sachets of brown and red sauce. The saying goes 'There's nothing worse than a bored bobbie'. After we had finished eating one of my colleagues started rolling one of the sachets and said, 'I wonder how much pressure you'd have to put on this before it popped'. Not that much it would appear as the brown sauce squirted sideways all over one of my colleagues white shirt.

1992

There was a detective Inspector that worked in my station that would stay after work and drink whiskey with colleagues. He would sleep in his office and then get changed in the morning. I went to a morning briefing with him in his office and halfway through the briefing he stood up and walked around his desk. He was wearing a shirt, tie, suit jacket and pyjama bottoms, and nobody said anything.

1996

I was posted to a child protection unit and dealt with a job where a small baby had been found in a house. The child was sat silently in a soiled cot, its hands wrapped around an empty feeding bottle. Neglected babies don't cry because there's no point. Nobody comes. I took the baby from the cot and prised the dirty feeding bottle from its hands. The baby had had hold of the bottle for so long that its hands were moulded as if still holding onto it. It broke my heart. I left my post in child protection after this job. I couldn't do it anymore. It never ceases to amaze me the horrors human beings do to each other.

1998

I was working with a male colleague at a premier league football ground and at the time we were in the police room processing a prisoner when the female chief superintendent came into the room for a chat. My colleague then said to me 'I think I've split my pants'. He bent over to show me, and he had indeed split his police trousers, along with his underpants, so showed me and the chief superintendent his hairy bum crack.

2007

I was executing a drugs warrant at a not very pleasant house. I walked through the kitchen and just as I reached the living room someone called me a 'fucking cunt'. I turned around but there was no one behind me. On closer inspection I noticed a parrot in a cage in the kitchen so walked towards it and stood looking at it as it then repeated what it said again to my face.

1994

I was dealing with a sudden death where the elderly lady had fallen and died on her kitchen floor. At the time you had to call out the FME (force medical officer) to pronounce life extinct. Nowadays this is done by the Ambulance service, so it could take hours waiting for the FME to show. On this occasion we were eventually joined by a rather eccentric Doctor who walked into the kitchen, checked for signs of life on the old lady and confirmed that she was indeed dead. The kitchen was a typical old lady kitchen with proper tea in a caddy, along with bone China cups and saucers. In the corner of the kitchen was a vegetable rack containing various vegetables and potatoes. As the Doctor walked past the veg rack they stopped and then selected several potatoes which they popped into their bag saying, 'She won't be needing these now, and it saves me stopping at the shops on the way home'. Just unbelievable.

1993

There was a stolen car razzing around our division looking for a chase. I had stopped in the area the car had been seen and my colleague and I got out to see if we could hear it as it was the dead of night and very quiet. We had been stood there for a few minutes when suddenly the stolen car appeared out of nowhere speeding past us with its windows wound down, the occupants flicking the 'V's' at us as it sped past. My colleague had hold of his police issue 'motorola' handheld radio which was very heavy. As the car past us, my colleague threw his radio at the stolen car out of frustration. The radio flew through the air and straight though the open window of the stolen car, landing inside the stolen car which then drove off with his radio. The evening and several evenings following this had the thieves shouting random obscenities on the radio until the battery ran out.

1999

I had attended a sudden death where a man had sadly died in his kitchen. At the house we found his body lying on his side. The ambulance was at scene as well and pronounced life extinct. Part of the Police's role at sudden deaths is to check the deceased body for any obvious signs of foul play or injuries. This usually involves lifting clothing up checking for injuries. We moved the man's body, and I immediately noticed a massive bulge in his trousers right by his zipper. I questioned the ambulance staff as to what they thought it was and were as confused as us. The bulge was the size of a grapefruit. Suddenly there was a popping sound followed by wetness spreading across the man's groin, then the smell followed. Now I'm not good with smells and this was rancid like rotten meat. What had happened was that one of the man's testicles had swollen to the size of a grapefruit after he had died and had burst when we moved him, spilling its contents all over the floor. The liquid oozed out and began forming a mini lake around his body. I had never seen anything like this in all the sudden deaths I'd ever attended. The smell just got worse, and I felt my mouth start to water and knew I was going to be sick. I ran from through the house and outside to the garden path where I retched and was sick in the front garden. I hadn't noticed the man's family who had arrived on hearing the news that their relative had died and were walking up the path. I wiped my mouth and offered my condolences explaining my sudden sick outburst on an upset stomach from something I must have eaten earlier.

2000

I had been asked to attend a report of an old lady who hadn't been seen for months. I arrived at the address which was a top floor flat. I got to the flat and did the obligatory sniff through the letter box and realised something was terribly wrong. Death smells sticky and sweet and the hundreds of flies exiting the letterbox sort of gave the game away. I forced an entry to the flat and the smell was something else. I'm not great with smells at the best of times and because of this I always carry a small bottle of Vicks Sinus rub which I hurriedly smeared underneath my nose. There were thousands of flies buzzing around the flat. I checked every room eventually ending up in the bedroom where I found the old lady, dead on her bed. It was now the end of March, and she hadn't been seen since Christmas the previous year. Due to it being cold in her flat she had used an electric blanket on her bed which had been switched on low when she died, so she had technically been 'cooking' for 3 months. She was only small to start with but now looked very skeletal, her eyes sunk back into her skull. Flies had laid maggots on her rotting flesh and her body looked like it was moving due to sheer mass of maggots on her. It was one of the worst sudden deaths I've ever been sent to. I requested an Ambulance to pronounce life extinct, which always amuses me, especially when you can clearly see the person is dead. I also requested the undertakers to remove her body to the city mortuary. I checked around the flat for any valuables or address books with next of kin details in for family to be contacted. I momentarily left the flat to return to my police car when a resident from the floor below appeared with a can of air freshener in hand and began frantically spraying the air saying, 'This smell has been here for weeks now'. I looked at her incredulously and wanted to say, 'Why the fuck didn't you ring us earlier then, you must have known she died'. But I didn't, I politely smiled and explained to her that the resident above her had sadly passed away. She continues spraying Lily of the Valley while I carry on dealing with this incident. The lady is eventually moved to the city mortuary and life carries on. I don't know if they ever did find her next of kin. I still think about her now. What a terrible way to die. No one cares, they just get on with their life because if you can't see it then it's not really happening, is it?

1985

We used to have BBQs on the flat roof of the police station when we were on nights. You could get to the roof through one of the windows in the CID office and we would all sit up there at 3am on a balmy summers evening eating our burgers and hot dogs.

1989

I went to a report of child neglect. We found the baby aged about 8 months in a cot upstairs lying on soiled blankets. I found the babies feeding bottle underneath the cot, lying on top of a load of used hypodermic syringes. Mum and dad were out of it on drugs and got arrested for child neglect and the baby got removed by social services. You never get to find out what happened to the child, and it plays on your mind.

1983

We used to play cricket matches against other officers from different police station on nights. We'd all turn up at the local park and have a few overs before going off duty at 7am.

1982

I was in my probation, and we were sent to a report of a fight at a Chinese chippy. There were 4 of us in an old plain Austin Allegro and with me at 6 foot 2 inches I was the smallest cop in the car. We were all struggling to sit as the car was driven at high speed along the road. Suddenly the driver stopped the car and one of the older policemen got out and started pulling at the front passenger seat ripping it from its attachment. He then threw the seat at the side of the road jumped back in and we carried on our way. At least now there was room for our legs.

1982

The FME (force medical examiner) would often be called out to examine a prisoner during a tour of nights. One FME would sleep in the police station doctor's room to save him driving from home every hour or so. You would go into the examination room, and he was curled up on the examination table fast asleep. You'd wake him up and then 5 minutes later you would take your prisoner to see him.

1992

PSD or the Professional Standards Department are not very well liked within the ranks of the police, especially the police constables. PSD investigate complaints made by the public against officers. The was an Inspector working for PSD who was not particularly well liked and whilst in his post he would continually attend our police station to 'serve' officers with numerous complaints, most of them malicious and he was always really smarmy when he did so. Months later he was posted to work with our group and so set up in his office at the end of our corridor. I heard that one day he was in his office, sat in his chair and opened his drawer to retrieve his police hat...... and someone had done a shit in it and then closed the drawer.

1990

I was working in the 'car squad' which basically meant you arrested people for stealing cars or stealing from cars. Theft of radio cassette players was particularly popular. On one such arrest my colleague mentioned in his statement that he observed the male stealing from the car for 60 seconds. Fast forward a few months and were all in Crown Court during the trial of the man observed for 60 seconds who stole from a parked car. The defending barrister made a bit of a meal of the 60 seconds, wondering how on earth the officer knew it was exactly 60 seconds if he wasn't wearing a watch? The officer explained that he just had this natural ability to count to 60 and be spot on. The barrister asked the officer to demonstrate this to the Court and the Jury who were sat watching the trial. My colleague stood in the witness box and when instructed by the barrister he stood silently and began counting in his head. At bang on 60 seconds, he said 'Now'. The barrister who had been timing the proceedings on his watch was amazed, as the officer had indeed stopped at exactly 60 seconds. 'How did you do that?' asked the amazed barrister. 'There's a clock on the wall behind you' replied my colleague.

1991

Again, in the car squad we were called to court last minute. My colleague who had been doing some plain clothes obvs was dressed like a tramp, very scruffy. He mentioned this but was told to get his arse to court straight away and just apologise to the magistrates when he arrived. He promptly arrived at Court and apologised for his appearance at which point one of the magistrates asked him why he was dressed like he was, he replied 'I can't remember'.

Nicknames for police officers

TAPS - Thick as pig shit

TAF – Thick as fuck

Thrush – Irritating cunt

Dolly Parton – because he only worked 9-5

Laptop – because he was a very small PC

1998

I was working lates and was off at 12pm so at 10.30 pm we were trying to keep our head down and not get involved in anything when we were flagged down by a member of the public who looked very distressed. He explained that he couldn't get hold of his friend and asked if we could help. We were directed to his friends flat a short distance away and I stood outside the door and opened the letter box to be greeted by a terrible smell. He must be dead, so we forced the door and went inside. As per usual no lights were working in the flat so we both fumbled around in the dark trying to find out way. I could see a small chink of light at the end of the hallway leading to what must be the living room. We edged closer, the smell overwhelming us and reached the living room door. I opened it and was confronted by a man standing in his dirty underpants who screamed at us 'Get out'. I almost shit myself. My colleague screamed and ran back up the hallway. It was the friend who we thought was dead. Turns out he just couldn't be bothered to go out and wanted to sit in his underpants on his own!!

1999

We had been issued with CS spray for the first time and this was a novelty. We had a lesson on how to use it. When it was first issued, you would just empty a can on someone, but now it must be a measured dose. During the training sessions you are given replica cans of CS spray which are filled with water and at the end of the training we kept a few to take out on patrol with us. We would use the cans of water when we were dealing with someone who was arsey. They would get a dose of CS and immediately put their hands to their face screaming ARRRRRRRRRRR then seconds later realise that the spray had no effect on them. They would walk away thinking they were invincible, often goading officers to spray them as it didn't affect them. They got a short sharp shock when they did get sprayed with real CS.

2002

I was seconded to work for MI5. I was removed from the police force I was working for under the guise of 'mental health' issues. I was asked to go due to my knowledge of custody procedures and firearms expertise. Some of the things I saw were shocking. I worked a lot with Counter Terrorism and was told some of the tactics used by terrorists in Afghanistan. When children are born to an extremist family the boys are ok, some of the baby girls are not so lucky. I've seen footage of suicide bombers, men dressed as women pushing a baby girl in a pram. The child is laden down with explosives as the man walks the child in the pram into a crowded marketplace and detonates the child. It's truly horrific.

2004

Dealing with 'dirty protests' in the cell. Basically, the prisoner would do a shit and then smear the shit all over themselves, the wall, the floor and the benches. You would then be sent in as a unit to take him out of the cell so that the specialist cleaners could come in and do a deep clean. You would have to get kitted up in your riot overalls with helmet and shield. The cell door is opened, and you do a rapid entry in to contain the prisoner up against the wall, pressing into them with your shields. You then must handcuff the prisoner and drag him out and forcibly shower him or her. It's not a pleasant job believe me, and the smell is indescribable.

1989

I was working on the vans with several other officers in the city centre. Occasionally you would hear of an office building that had been broken into. We knew who was doing these break ins, it was just a matter of time before we caught him. Then one night we saw him. The man we knew was responsible for the burglaries from the local offices. We grabbed him and put him in our van and blind folded him. We told him we knew it was him doing all the office burglaries and that we were going to put a stop to it. The city I was working in had a Port, and boats would regularly come in and out of the Port. The tide used to come in quite high and to assist with this there was a 'rolling road'. This was a section of road that moved up and down as if you were on the sea.

We parked our Police van up and got the blind folded burglar out of the van near to the 'rolling road'. We all remained silent as he was walked around the Police van a few times to disorientate him. The sounds and smell of the Ports all around us as ships sounded their horns and seagulls squawked. Then we stood him on the 'rolling road' and held onto him as he swayed up and down. We then told him that we were sick of him burgling and had put him on a ship that was due to leave. No one would know where he had gone. What happened then was the burglar panicked begging us not to put him on the boat and told us exactly where he had stashed all the stolen office and computer equipment, he had stolen the previous evening. Result!!!

2000

There was an old drunk who regularly got arrested for being drunk or just generally causing a nuisance. I found out through talking to him that he had been in the army many years before. When he had been discharged, he had been subject to a bad assault which resulted in him having extensive facial surgery where numerous metal plates were put in his face and head. The local children used to harass him by sticking fridge magnets on his face when he was drunk and had fallen asleep, and he would often be brought into the custody suite still sporting the magnets. He was arrested one day for causing a disturbance in a library. He had apparently gone in and shouted 'Can I have some Fish and Chips'. He was told in no uncertain terms by the staff that this was a library, and he couldn't come in here shouting, so he then whispered to the staff, 'Can I have some fish and chips'.

The sad thing is he probably had PTSD but wasn't diagnosed. I heard he died alone, and me and the other custody Sgt's wanted to go to his funeral because he had no one, but we didn't know when it was. I remember him with fondness.

2001

There was a drunk who was brought into custody. He had been thrown into a fountain near the pier head. Sometimes kids can be evil. I sat and chatted to him and gave him some hot food and got him a shower and some clean clothes. Sometimes you just have to show the prisoners a bit of compassion.

1994

When regular drug addicts or drunks would be brought into the custody suite, they would always ask to see the Doctor. The police stations all had a doctor's room complete with examination table. Rather than ring the Doctor in the middle of the night we would dress one of the Police constables up in the Doctors white coat complete with stethoscope, and send the drunk/ drug addict in to see them (no medicine was ever administered during this piss take)

1999

I was sent to a domestic dispute on a Sunday afternoon. The lady in the house was upset and had been assaulted by the man stood in the kitchen. He then walked out towards me holding a cup of steaming hot tea. He stood right next to me and began shouting that we should 'Get out' and that it was 'Nothing to do with us. I still don't know to this day why I did this, but I flipped his cup of scalding hot tea onto him. He went nuts jumping up and down, wafting his shirt which was covered in tea. He then decided he wanted to fight myself and my colleague. This resulted in him getting arrested and handcuffed seconds later. At least his wife had a quiet Sunday whilst he languished in the cells.

2001

I was working as a Sgt in the custody suites when a male was brought in for assaulting his wife who he had hit in the face. He was booked in and placed in a cell waiting to be interviewed. I was made aware that his wife had come into the front desk at the station and wanted to speak to me, so I made my way down to talk to her. On seeing me, she presented me with a frozen chicken covered in blood which I presumed was hers as she had a broken nose. She asked if I wanted it for 'evidence'. I politely declined.

1995

I was called to a report of a woman standing on the ledge of a building threatening to jump. When I arrived, I parked my police vehicle outside the building as did one of my colleagues who arrived and parked behind me. The woman was stood on a flat roof which surrounded the building about 30 foot up. From the flat roof she could also climb back into the flat in which she lived. As we began to speak to her, trying to talk her down she suddenly disappeared back into the flat climbing through the window only to return moments later with a bin bag full of empty milk bottles. She began throwing these at us with some ferocity as they smashed into thousands of pieces on the roadway. We all cowered behind a wall as she continues to hurl the milk bottles at us, the glass splintering all over us. There was no way we could get near her. She momentarily disappeared back into her flat again only to reappear seconds later with a can of paint. She took the lid off the paint and then poured it from height, all over my police car. I remember it was a deep red colour, and I watched as it oozed from the roof of the police car down the front windscreen and dripped onto the road. She then hopped back into her flat and we waited to see what she would reappear with next. She didn't disappoint. We could hear something heavy being moved and watched as she pushed through her window a chest of drawers. There was nothing we could do but watch as she pushed the drawers further and further to the edge of the flat roof, and then giving it one final shove, she let go of it, the chest of drawers landing with a thud on top of my colleague's police car, which smashed the front window and dented the bodywork beyond repair. I turned to him and said, 'My paint job doesn't seem too bad now'. She was eventually arrested by a team that did a 'rapid entry' into her flat' for Affray and Criminal damage. We had to get my colleagues police car towed to a repair shop and I managed to limp my car back to the station even though I managed to smear gloss paint all over the front window when I turned on the windscreen wipers. I had that red paint on my Dr Martin shoes for years after.

2002

One night I got called to the docks in the city I work in which has now all been renovated and has a lot of bars and restaurants and a very vibrant night life. A man walking home with his friends had jumped in the dock for a laugh. As I looked into the water, it was a good 4 metres down until you hit the water. I searched with my torch along with the fire fighters who had also attended and then I found him. He had landed feet first in metres of muddy silt and was basically stuck under the water by his feet, with his arms outstretched upwards. He had drowned. The firefighters fished him out while I consoled his friends who had seen him jump. Total waste of a life.

1997

We had a girl working on our section who was a bit naive to say the least. One day she was going to Crown Court for the first time and was understandably worried about the etiquette attached to appearing at the Crown and what to call the Judge. At Magistrates Court you would usually refer to the bench as 'Your worship' and in Crown Court 'Your honour'. I told her with a straight face that she should address the Judge as 'Your Grace' which should be accompanied by a curtsey which we practised before setting off for her first-time giving evidence. I wasn't present in Crown Court when she burst through the doors, did a curtsey and called the Judge 'Your Grace' but I wish I had been.

2014

I have attended many child post-mortems where children had died as a result of neglect or cot death. It always gets me when the tiny body is wheeled into the mortuary covered in a white sheet with the child's favourite cuddly toy lying next to their body.

2006

I was part of a team that used to execute a lot of search warrants mainly for drugs. On one occasion we were in the middle of searching a house and were in the upstairs bedrooms. One of my colleagues got a pair of crusty old knickers and hung them on the handcuffs of another colleague. The colleague with the handcuffs had no idea they had been hung on his utility belt and we then completely forgot about it until after the search when we got back in the van. He sits down with the old knickers hanging off his cuffs and we set off back to the station. We then decided to stop at a local Sayers bakery for lunch. Handcuff boy decides he wants to go into Sayers to get his lunch. I stopped him saying 'Just tell me what you want, and I'll get it'. No, he is adamant he's going to get his own lunch so off we all go. We're only in the shop a few minutes when an old lady tapped my colleague on the shoulder and says 'excuse me love, you've got some knickers on your handcuffs'.

2006

During another house search I was completing paperwork which documents who is in the house, where is searched and what is recovered. As I'm sat with the quite hostile family in a small, terraced house one of my colleagues who was searching an upstairs bedroom shouts down to me 'Do you need this seizing?' The house holder starts shouting 'What's he fucking found'. I make my way to the bottom of the stairs to see what it is while the house holder stays seated in the front room but in my eye line. I look up to see my colleague stood at the top of the stairs waving a massive dildo around his head. How I managed to keep my face straight I don't know but I calmly replied, 'No we won't be needing that'. I made my way back into the front room saying it was just some paperwork that wasn't needed.

1993

I was brand new in the job and was out in uniform when I was sexually assaulted by a male member of the public who grabbed my arse over my trousers. He got arrested and we all ended up in the police station cell area. The custody Sgt informed me that as I'd been sexually assaulted, I would have to be examined by the Police surgeon. Completely naive to procedure I agreed and duly made my way to the doctor's room that was in the custody area. As I walked in, the Dr was stood there with his white coat on, stethoscope around his neck. He was also wearing the thickest bottle bottom glasses. I was a bit taken aback by his appearance, but he told me to relax and stated he would have to examine my bottom as it had been grabbed by the prisoner. Even I was a bit dubious about this, and then I heard noise outside the Dr's door and the sound of laughter. I opened the door to find the Sgt and several other policemen laughing hysterically. They had dressed up one of their colleagues as a Dr for a laugh.... Bastards!!!

1997

I had applied to go to work at the firearms department as an AFO (area firearms officer). It was apparent when I arrived on the first day that the male instructors who were basically a bunch of sexist pigs did not want women in firearms. As part of the course, we had to shoot on the range, which is a long corridor inside the firearms training department. You had to fire your handgun towards a static paper target and your scores on the target were then assessed. There is a safety catch on the handgun that you must remove with your thumb before firing. My hands were only small, so I struggled to do this. The instructor shouted at me for not being able to do this, laughing at me with his colleagues. As a final insult he also looked at my stance as I held the gun and told me I needed to 'Stand more manly'. They failed me on the course after a couple of days. I found out some years later that I could have been offered a smaller gun which would have enabled me to reach the safety catch. This was never even offered to me.

1995

I was working in uniform on a section dealing with 999 Emergency response incidents. One afternoon I was sat on 'parade' waiting for our Sgt to come and give us or duties for the shift when I overheard a conversation between two male colleagues who were discussing a new WPC that was soon to join our section.' What's she like?' he asked. The reply 'She's got big tits'.

1998

I got called to a large music venue. Headlining that evening was 'Morrisey'. Off I headed inside the event to speak to Morrisey who apparently had been hit with an object that had been thrown on stage. The only problem with this is that I had no idea who Morrisey was. I was ushered into the dressing room which had several people in and introduced myself to the man 'holding court' thinking this must be him. I held my hand out and shock his hand enthusiastically introducing myself and saying what a pleasure it was to finally meet him. The man explained that he was one of the Roadie's for Mr Morrisey and pointed me to a quiet man sat in the corner. I wanted the ground to swallow me up.

1995

I had arrested a man for assaulting a sex worker. Just as I'd lodged him at the police station, I was called to deal with a woman who had made a rape allegation. Being the only woman on the section it was down to me to deal with her, so off I went to the rape suite for the lady's examination and to take her statement. I was then contacted a few hours later by the custody Sgt asking me to return to the station, to complete my paperwork for the male I had earlier arrested for assault. I explained I couldn't be in two places at once and the custody Sgt suggested that my male colleagues complete my paperwork for me. They agreed and the paperwork was subsequently completed, and the man charged with assault. Months later I received a court warning to attend magistrate's court as the man who had attacked the sex worker was pleading 'not guilty' and the job was going to trial. I attended the court on the day. The sex worker couldn't be bothered turning up so it was decided that I would read out the statements in her absence. I did this cringing, as they bore no resemblance to what had happened.

1995

I was working in the city in quite an old station that had wooden pigeonholes containing the police radios near the front desk where the public would attend. One night an old drunk had come into the station for a sleep and to get out of the cold. We decide for a laugh to put all of the radios on a 'back to back' channel and to whisper into them. The poor drunk woke up and thought he was hearing voices. I went out to see if he was ok and he told me about the voices. He was that shaken up I had to get some colleagues to drop him at a different police station after I'd made him a cuppa to calm him down.

2000

I was in my probation and had been sent to a job where a female shoplifter had been detained. When dealing with shoplifters, you arrest them, take them to the station where you interview them asking why they stole what they stole and what they intended to do with the items they stole. This shoplifter had been detained in a sex shop and when I arrived it transpired, she had stolen seven vibrators. I duly arrested her and a short time later we found ourselves sat opposite each other in the police interview room. It was very awkward when I asked her 'So what were you intending to do with them'? Both of us tried not to laugh.

2001

I was working on the vans with a load of policemen. I stood up as I'd got cramp and fell banging my utility belt on the seat in front of me. This set off my CS spray which sprayed everyone in the van.

2002

I was working on a unit that predominantly dealt with searches of venues before a stage show would commence. On one such occasion we were called to search a venue that the Queen would be attending. The show was Chinese acrobats performing amazing stunts. During the search I sent my all-male team backstage to search when I was suddenly aware that everything had gone quiet. Suspecting they were up to no good I made my way backstage to find that one of my colleagues who was 6 foot 4 inches tall, had stripped naked and was wearing one of the Chinese acrobats leotards which was obviously made for someone who was less than 5 foot tall, complete with his tackle hanging out!!

1997

I worked with a policeman who had a fetish for wearing women's underwear. During a house search I was working with him searching the main bedroom and rummaging through the householder's dildo drawer when something caught my eye. My male colleague had leant forward, and a pink bra strap had fallen below the arm of his police shirt. He had put one of the house holders' bras on. I had a word with him, and he took it off before we left.

1995

Whilst working in a police station my male colleagues must have been bored one night and opened all the tampons stored for the female prisoners and put them in water. They swelled up and were then dried on the radiators and then placed around the station in various places with little mouse faces drawn on them.

2001

We had a smelly Special Constable who had terrible personal hygiene working regularly on our section. The policemen working with me, put him up to asking me out. I felt terrible saying no to him so I agreed much to my colleague's amusement. Luckily for me he got sacked before our first date.

2018

I was working as an Inspector and was SIM (serious incident manager) cover. I dealt with so many sudden deaths in one shift I was known as the SIM Reaper!!! During my shift I was that up the wall I managed to deliver a death message to the wrong person.

2019

I got called to attend an incident where a man was 'feeling down'. There was some suggestion this man had doused himself in petrol, so I decided to take a fire extinguisher with me in case the worst happened. I arrived at the scene to be confronted with a distraught man who wanted to take his own life. As I was talking to him trying to calm him down still holding my fire extinguisher, it accidently went off covering him in foam.

2015

I was posted as a uniform Sgt to quite a rural location and was sent to a report of a pig in the road causing a danger to motorists. I arrived and saw the pig in the road. We stopped traffic going both ways and my master plan was to put a rope around the pig and lead it off the road. This didn't quite go to plan. I managed to get the rope around the pig that promptly ran off, dragging me off my feet and along the road in front of the public who had stopped in their cars to watch the unfolding pig debacle.

2004

There are posters up in the police custody suites relating to 'language line' with various languages and countries depicted on the poster. Somebody wrote 'Narnia' and a fake phone number on one of the posters. It always used to make me giggle.

2014

I attended a weird domestic incident where someone had thrown a hamster in the road. I got there, recovered the hamster which was returned to its cage and gave the pair of them a dressing down.

2012

I was working nights and was sent to a report of a hanging. I arrived with other colleagues to see a man hanging by his neck from a large tree. It was in a park, and it was dawn, with a strange mist covering the floor of the park. The swinging body looked eery against this backdrop. On seeing the body, I screamed 'He's dead'. One of my colleagues walked underneath the body and saw movement shouting 'This fuckers still alive'. I asked if anyone had a knife and luckily someone had a brand-new Stanley Knife which he passed to me. I climbed the tree with my colleague and hurriedly cut through the rope holding him. We hadn't checked below at the large 'V' shape in the tree and as I cut through the rope, he fell.... into the V on the tree banging his head and getting completely wedged in the tree. We had to call on the fire brigade to help us free him. I remember telling the Ambulance crew 'He may have a head injury'. I heard he lived.

1998

I was on patrol when I stopped a drug addict, I suspected had just been involved in a drugs deal. I remember he was wearing a shirt with both arms tucked in his pockets. I told him I was going to search him and told him to take his hands out of his pockets. He just ignored me so I asked him again. Again, he ignored me, so I took hold of his right arm to realise it was just material and he only had one arm.

1993

Various pranks are played on probationer Constables. Fake hangings would be set up in the crypt at the local cemetery on nights with the radio room staff in on the prank asking the probationer to go there alone on foot to attend. Colleagues have also hidden under sheets at the mortuary, and when probation Constables attend to book a dead body in, they would say from under the sheet 'It's cold in here'.

1994

A probationer was sent to a report of a suspicious item in a bin bag at the back of a theatre. When he got there, he found a fake head from the props department in a bin bag. We all thought it was hilarious, him not so much, after he screamed when he opened the bag up.

1996

I attended a neighbour dispute and arrived at the house to see a group of children playing on the pathway with a ball. As I walked up the path the ball rolled towards me, so I kicked it back to them. They screamed. Unbeknown to me the ball contained their pet hamster.

1993

I was working nights on foot patrol in the city centre with a male colleague. We decided to meet back up at 2am and it was agreed that he would get us a kebab each from the shop on his foot beat. 2am arrived and I stood at our meeting point waiting for him. Ten minutes later he came running around the corner towards me covered in kebab sauce which was all over his shirt. He was very flustered, and I initially thought he'd got involved in a fight which resulted in my dinner ending up all over the pavement. When he eventually calmed down, he explained that having bought the kebabs he took a short cut down an alleyway which was frequented by men from a local gay bar. He had inadvertently stumbled upon two men having sex in the entry which was pitch black. He said he 'shit himself' and ran dropping the contents of the kebabs all over himself.

2004

I was working nights in uniform in the city when I shouted at a man pissing in the street to stop. He saw me and ran so I chased him, but he was getting away from me. A passing black cab saw me chasing him and stopped saying 'jump in'. I told him to 'follow that guy' which he did. The guy hadn't seen me get in the taxi. I could see the guy running was getting tired, so I asked the driver to stop, thanked him and got out on foot to continue my chase. I caught up with the guy seconds later and grabbed him. I could tell by his face he was impressed with my fitness. I arrested him and never did tell him I'd jumped a taxi.

1996

We would often have to attend the local Chinese buffet to reports of fights. We would get there and the owners, who were very grateful for us attending, would ply us with various dishes of takeaway food. It was very hard fighting with someone and trying not to spill your food.

2014

I had to do constant observations (Con obvs) on a female prisoner who spent the whole of my shift flashing her fanny at me.

2013

I had to strip search a rather aggressive female prisoner in a cell at the custody suite. I was assisted by a Sgt who stood outside the cell door. I was literally rolling around getting the clothing off this woman who had said she was going to self-harm. Each time I removed an item I would throw it out of the cell. The last bit of clothing was in my hand as I threw the woman's dirty knickers out of the cell which hit the Sgt in the face. He wasn't very happy.

1994

I left a prisoner in the cage at the back of the van and completely forgot about him. It was winter. I remembered just in time, or he could have frozen to death.

1995

There was a spate of robberies in the city centre, so undercover officers were sent out to try and lure the robbers into attacking them. It worked and the robbers were detained. The uniform officer who attended to make the arrest asked for a police station for 3 males all of whom were black. There were in fact only 2 robbers and the officer had also arrested the black undercover cop for robbery!! He was quickly de-arrested.

1992

When we would attend jobs were the person being dealt with was a bit odd, we would result these jobs with the radio room as SIM (strange in manner). This was typed on the incident logs as the result.

1998

I was a uniform Sgt working on a response section dealing with emergency jobs. Every shift I would sit on parade at the front of my staff and every shift the same male officer would move his chair to the right-hand side of me which would disrupt the parade. It wasn't until months later that I realised he was doing this because he could then see inside the gap of my shirt and look at my bra.

On one night shift I was sat in my office when there was a knock at my window, and I looked up to see the same policeman standing at my window naked. He had been in the gym on his lunch break and as he'd gone for a shower someone had stolen his clothes which is why he was stood outside my office window asking for help. We got his clothes back eventually and he got dressed. Later that night I went outside in the yard as I heard a commotion only to see the same male officer hanging from some bars on a window. What his colleagues had done when he had got dressed was grab him and shove a broom handle through the shoulders of his body armour and then insert the broom handle through the bars on the raised cell windows of the police station leaving him dangling in mid-air. I let him stew for a bit before we got him down.

1995

A uniform Inspector who wasn't very well liked lost his briefcase and we found it. We always suspected he was a Mason (male only society of which a lot a Police officers were members) and the contents of his briefcase proved he was. We decided to photocopy some of the paperwork in his briefcase and send it through the internal mail to other colleagues.

buying some adult Pampers

The Inspector was frantic and had to go home early. He really shit his pants over losing his briefcase which resulted in someone buying some adult Pampers which were put on the chair in his office. We also got hold of his Police tunic and sewed all the buttons on the wrong way. It made us laugh anyway!!

1994

A male colleague used to ride a motorbike into work every shift. He would leave his motorbike helmet on top of his locker. Someone taped a condom to the back of it which he didn't see when he put it on to go home, then wondered what the 'flapping' noise was as he drove home.

1995

I was working on a uniform section and one of my male colleagues was a bit of a 'hob' (loved traffic related jobs). He took great pride in prosecuting people for having out of date tax discs. Another colleague on my section got hold of some headed HMRC paperwork and wrote a letter to the Chief Constable mentioning this officer and praising his outstanding work prosecuting so many members of the public for having no vehicle tax. This letter didn't go anywhere near the Chief Constable, it was sent directly to the officer issuing the tax disc tickets as he sat on parade with us all, inviting him and his wife to a prestigious civic reception for himself and his wife to attend, where his efforts would be recognised more formally by way of a commendation. We all thought this was hilarious and he was completely oblivious telling us over the coming days how he had bought a new tuxedo and his wife had bought a new evening gown. Our Inspector had to step in when he said he had organised babysitters for the evening while they attended the reception. He wasn't very happy when he found out it was a wind up.

2002

I was working in uniform and every briefing we had at the start of a shift would involve our Sgt briefing us on the previous day's events. This particular Sgt we had, had a bad speech impediment and couldn't pronounce his 'S'. We made up fake observations for him to read out on the briefing. We were all in on it and waited with bated breath for him to read this announcement out at the end of the shift. It read 'observations for a silver Sierra Sapphire registration number S123 SSR seen in suspicious circumstances on Smith Street. I nearly wet myself trying to stifle a laugh. The cop sat next to me had tears rolling down his face as the Sgt walked from the briefing room completely oblivious to what had just happened.

1996

I was asked to attend a repeat nuisance caller who would ring 999 with various complaints. I went to his house and removed the 9 button from his phone, telling the radio operator 'he won't be calling again'

2001

I was in uniform stood by the crime scene tape at the site of a recent murder. The victim had been found lying inside the scene and had been removed but the area still needed to be searched by a specialist team of officers who were yet to attend. I was bored as I had been there for hours, so I decided to plough my way through the prepacked lunch that is supplied to officers stood on scenes. This consists of a sandwich, a bag of crisps, a chocolate bar, a bottle of water and an apple which is rock hard. I was so bored I decided to eat my apple. As I was munching through the apple a wasp began to buzz overhead. I tried to swat it away, but it was very interested in my apple. Suddenly as it flew at me and I swiped my hand holding the apple, I let go of the apple which sailed through the air landing in the crime scene inside the tape. I panicked. I couldn't go inside the tape. The victim had been murdered and I couldn't risk my footprints contaminating the ground. Also, the apple containing my DNA was now in the murder scene. During the following hours I concocted a story where I had been eating the apple, dropped it and it casually rolled into the scene. The search officers duly arrived, and I told them my story about the apple. They weren't even bothered and casually strolled over, picked it up and threw it in the bin.

1994

I attended a suicide where a woman had jumped from the top of a block of flats. I got there and found the woman lying on the ground dead clutching a small teddy bear. Her back story was that social services had taken her children from her days before and she couldn't cope.

1993

I attended a report of burglary where an old lady had woken in the night to find a male offender stood over her. She laid in bed terrified as he laughed at her and pulled the phone from the wall. She was distraught when I was talking to her and said she had been absolutely terrified during the incident. Sometimes this job makes you so angry.

2008

I'd started work as a Detective Constable and one evening had got changed in work and gone out on the piss. I stayed out all night and had to turn up for work the following day wearing hot pants. I was sent home to change.

2004

I was working in uniform at a large indoor venue where Beyonce was playing and was asked along with another female colleague to act as security for Beyonce moving her from one part of the building to another. I was beside myself as we were both massive fans. That evening I asked if it would be possible to meet her and her team agreed. We were ushered into her dressing room and gave her a massive hug which she wasn't expecting, gushing over her and telling her what huge fans we were. We then got a photo taken with her. Her squashed in-between two over eager policewomen. We really did get in her personal space. She's quite tiny in real life.

1995

One summer I attended a report of a sudden death. It was in a flat, and the man's body had been there for quite some time. We got inside the flat and there were flies all over the inside of the windows. The man had died on a sofa bed in front of a large window where the sun was streaming in on him. As the probationer it was my job to search him. This is primarily done with probationers as a piss take to see if they can stomach it, also the body would need to be searched for any valuables or identification. I moved next to the man to move him, my face only inches from his when I saw his eyes move. I screamed when I looked closer and realised that his eyes were in fact full of maggots which were wriggling around making his eye lashes move. His body had also swollen beyond recognition in the intense heat. The paramedics arrived along with the funeral directors whose job it is to move the body to the funeral home. As they went to move him one of them shouted 'Get back he's going to blow'. I managed to run a few feet before I heard a 'popping' sound. He did indeed blow up.

1994

We had gone riot training one afternoon. This was situated in an old aeroplane hangar on an industrial estate. Numerous police vans had attended with dozens of officers, and we all spent the afternoon running around getting pelted with blocks. It came time to go home so we all changed back into our uniforms and got back into our respective police carriers. We eventually arrived back at our station to discover we were missing a colleague. He had mistakenly got into the wrong police carrier and had been driven 20 miles out to completely different station due to him falling asleep at the back of the van. No one had noticed him.

1999

One of my uniform colleagues had CS gassed his prisoner, and for a wind up we told him the man had died. Even our supervision was in on the joke. My colleague was told he would have to strip from his police uniform which would be bagged and tagged, and he would have to wear a forensic hazmat suit and wait in a locked cell while enquiries were on going. To our surprise he fell for it and spent the next few hours sat in cell in a forensic suit worrying, before we let him out and told him it was a joke. He didn't find it very funny.

2008

I attended an incident at an industrial unit where a worker had fallen into machinery and was trapped. We got there and realised along with the fire brigade and paramedics that it was impossible to release the man from the machinery and that he didn't have long to live. He was given strong pain relief by the attending Dr, and I held his hand while he died talking to him the whole time.

1990

One February I was asked to attend a report of a mother and daughter who had not been seen for some time. I arrived at the house which was a small terrace and to my surprise the front door was open. I walked in shouting 'hello it's the police' but the house was silent. I went into the front room on my right and saw it was decorated for Christmas with a tree, cards on the mantlepiece and streamers hanging from the ceiling. No one was in this room. I then made my way into the back room of the house. As I opened the door, I saw a dining table set out with Christmas dinner on it. At the head of the table was an elderly lady face down in a plate of dinner. I checked and she was dead. Then I saw lying behind her on the floor the body of a younger female that had been decapitated. It was at that point I heard a low growl and turned to my left to see an emaciated Alsatian dog sat in the kitchen growling at me. I slowly backed out of the room and closed the door, requesting CID and the RSPCA at scene as soon as possible. It transpired that both mother and daughter were alcoholics and had died sometime over Christmas. The dog, which had had no access to water had chewed through the neck of the younger female causing the lady's head to become detached. The dog had to be euthanised at the scene. I stepped from the house back onto the pavement trying to get my head around what I had just walked into when my radio crackled into life 'Can you make to a theft of a pedal cycle'. So off I went to my next job. I often speak to the CID officer who attended that scene and say to her 'Did that really happen'. You were offered no sort of counselling in those days, you just got on with it.

2004

I attended an incident in the city centre. A stolen car was being chased by an officer who was out with a probationer in her first week. The stolen car continued at high speed through a university area of the city. At this time three friends had left a local pub and were doing a 'three-legged race' as they walked home. The middle girl's legs being tied to her friends who were either side of her. The stolen car sped towards the three girls and hit them head on. The girls on either side of the middle girl tried to get out of the way but they had nowhere to go as their legs were all tied together. The bodies of the girls flew into the air as the stolen car crashed into them. One of the girls landed on the windscreen of the police vehicle as it came to a halt at the scene. All three girls sadly died. The female probationer left the job after that, and the driver of the police car was never the same after this happened. It was a terrible loss of life.

2003

I was working in uniform when I responded to a job where a man had tried to take his own life by slashing his wrists. I've attended many jobs like this over the years which are usually a cry for help. Superficial cuts that just require a night in hospital and a visit from the mental health team. It was clear when I arrived at this house that this was not the case. This man who lived with his mother had locked himself in the downstairs toilet and was refusing to open the door. Blood was seeping from under the door in a big crimson pool and I knew I had to get in there fast. I forced the door to find him sitting on the toilet. He had slashed his arms open lengthways from wrist to elbow and the wounds were deep. He had lost pints of blood which had gathered at his feet causing me to slip and slide as I got to him. It was obvious looking at him that he was dying, and I needed to do something fast. Me and my colleague took hold of one arm and wrapped a small towel around the top forming a tourniquet, and then did the same with the other arm, elevating both arms above his head in an attempt to stem the flow of blood. We'd asked for an ambulance who arrived quickly. We were all slipping and sliding on his blood as he manoeuvered him from the small downstairs toilet to the stretcher. The crew took him to the ambulance as I got some details from his mum, name address etc. It turned out this man worked for the church and has been caught weeks earlier downloading indecent images of children on his computer.... And I just saved his life. I still don't know how I feel about this!!

2015

I was sent to our local children's hospital to deal with a baby that had been admitted with a possible broken shoulder. When I got there, mum was less than impressed with the police attendance as she was adamant, she'd done nothing wrong. When I later interviewed her, it transpired she had got drunk/taken cocaine and had fallen on her child causing the child's shoulder injury.

When I initially saw the baby who was aged about 18 months, she was sat on a trolly looking very sad with a clearly broken shoulder. She was sent for x rays etc and then I had a bright idea. I asked the hospital staff to get a sample of urine from the baby which is no mean feat, considering she was still in nappies. After a painstaking couple of hours, we managed to collect a urine sample. The child was returned to the safety of relatives while the investigation was on going. I then set about interviewing mum and other family members and sent the urine sample away for analysis. To my joy this came back a few weeks later and had tested positive for cocaine. I deduced the mother had given the child cocaine on purpose to stop it crying. It was not unknown for people to rub cocaine on the gums of their babies. Or her bottles and formula had been contaminated when mum had prepared them on the kitchen worktop because this was where she informed me, she 'had a line (of cocaine)' I submitted my file to the Crown Prosecution Service in the hope they would charge mum with neglect and her child would be taken from her by social services and placed with a family that didn't put it in harm's way. CPS came back with quite a prompt decision. No Further Action. The child was returned to mum. Sometimes I give up!!

2015

I was working in CID and we had a Sgt attached to our department who told me a tale that he said if he hadn't seen this actually happen he wouldn't have believed it. He had been in the general CID office when one of the Detective Constables who was male, had gone to sit his promotion board to become a Sgt. He was very well liked amongst the bosses in the office who were sure he would pass with flying colours. When you sit your promotion board you are asked questions and are scored 1-4 depending on the strength of your answers. Asking the questions are usually two officers of rank, and a civilian member of staff. By the end of the day, he got his phone call and to his and the bosses surprise he had 'dipped' and had not passed. The bosses couldn't believe it. Phone calls were made and then a couple of hours later surprise surprise, his scores had been increased and he had passed his Sgts board to be made a substantive Sgt. I know the officer he is speaking about and in my opinion he's a dick. This type of over promoting people is a disgrace but it goes on. Phone calls are made, and people know people who are sitting on the promotion boards. It is 'jobs for the boys.

2009

I was working in a drugs squad when about an hour before going off duty I was handed a warrant by a Sgt who said 'This door needs putting in now, there's loads of gear there (drugs). I was less than impressed as I was looking forward to going home but instead, we gathered up our door opening equipment and headed off to the location in our van. When you get a warrant, usually from the courts, you must swear an oath that the information you're giving the magistrates is true. They then sign the warrant based on the intelligence you've given them about the address and what you are likely to find there.

We arrived at the address and knocked on first, but no one was home, so we set about forcing an entry. The house had a composite rock door which is held in place with several large bolts into the wall surrounding the front door. If the doors are fitted correctly there's no give when you hit them. After a few good hits then usually go through. This door however bounced when you hit it which means that it wasn't correctly fitted and took numerous hits to get any movement. Every time we hit it with the door opener it caused more and more damage to the plaster surrounding the door causing it to crumble away until we managed to crawl on hands and knees into the house through a flap we had created at the bottom of the door. A bit like a 'cat flap'. We got inside and began to search around and there was nothing. The house was extremely tidy (apart from the front door and surrounding plasterwork). We completed our search and left, leaving a copy of the search warrant in clear view for the occupier when he or she returned home.

The next day the phone calls started from the occupier. It transpired that the address on the warrant had been wrong, and it was the house next door that should have been subject to a search. The Sgt had spoken to me that morning and informed me that the intelligence was wrong. He seemed quite blasé about this and brushed it off. He also refused to take any phone calls from the house holder as we had been the ones that executed the search warrant. To make matters worse the house holder had to be told to obtain 3 quotes for the damage to his front door and the plaster in his hallway before the police would consider paying out.

Then the complaint arrived as he had quite rightly made a formal complaint. To my surprise the Sgt who had handed me the warrant took no responsibility, skirting over the fact that he had sworn out the warrant and it was his 'shitty' informant who had obviously given him false information in the first place. I took great pleasure in giving the full facts to the Professional Standards Department. One because I felt sorry for this house holder. Imagine coming home from work and finding a cat flap where your front door used to be and then enduring several weeks of phone calls to sort out a mess you didn't create in the first place. Also, the Sgt whose intelligence it had been had tried to shift the blame entirely from himself, probably because he didn't want to ruin his chances at this next promotion board. Him and I didn't see eye to eye at all after this incident and as far as I know the house holder got fully reimbursed for the damage to his house.

2002

I was working a night shift when I was asked to attend a report of a man who was continually ringing 999 and asking for the Armed Response officers to go round as he was going to shoot them. Armed Response or ARV's as we call them would not normally attend such trivial matters. This is down to your average uniform copper to attend and assess whether there is an actual threat before the ARV's set foot out of the warm police stations. This was the 4th time this man had made a call from his house issuing idle threats and the Sgt in the control room had had just about enough. I was told to make sure this man did not ring the police again. When I got to his house, we spoke in the living room about the nuisance he was causing constantly ringing the police, and then when he wasn't looking, I pulled all the phone wires out of the wall. He never did ring again!!

1990

I had attended a report of a noisy party and from what I could gather this wasn't the first time this evening that the police had been called. I was still in my probation and was still in awe of the more experienced officers. At the party there were a couple of officers from a different group that I hadn't seen working before, so being new and very young I tended to stand back and observe how things were getting dealt with. I remember the flat was above a shop with the only access being up a steep set of stairs which lead to the landing. I remember lots of shouting going on as the officers attempted to be heard over the banging house music. I then saw one of the older officers walking towards me down the landing pushing a large 'stack system', the ones that had the record deck on top followed by the equaliser, double tape deck and CD deck. He wheeled the decks to the top of the stairs and then lifted his leg back and kicked the whole lot down the stairs. It all smashed to pieces. I stood there, mouth open wondering what was going to happen next. Nothing happened. The party stopped and we all left. This was policing in the 90's.

1997

I attended a report of a sudden death in a care home on Christmas Eve. There had been a party for the residents and one of the males had choked to death on a sandwich. It was my job to deliver the 'death message' to his wife. I was told before I left the care home to be prepared, as the response I would get from his wife would not be what I was expecting. I attended the wife's house and was let inside, keeping a straight face ready to deliver the sad news that her husband had passed away. I sat her down and said, 'I'm sorry to tell you but your husband has died'. She asked me how he had died, and I explained he had choked on a sandwich. She looked at me for a few seconds and then burst out laughing. The lady then rang her daughter and shouted excitedly down the phone 'The fucking bastards dead'. The lady later explained to me that she and her daughter had been the victim of domestic violence for years at his hands. I remember as I left her house it had started to snow. She thanked me as I was leaving and said, 'This is going to be the best Christmas ever'!!

1999

I was working on the vans with a bunch of lads when we were sent to execute a drugs search warrant. It was the early hours of the morning, so we had to do a silent entry. We parked around the corner, and all got out of the van. The officer designated 'door opener' slung the large orange door opener over his shoulder and we all began the quiet jog around the corner to the target house. Just as we reached outside the property the officer carrying the door opener tripped over the kerb and fell over sending the heavy metal door opener crashing to the floor. We all started to laugh at him sprawled on the floor. The lights inside the target house came on and we managed to gain entry seconds later. The occupants told us they heard the crash and saw us all in fits of laughter, so they flushed what drugs they had down the toilet!!

1998

We were executing a drugs warrant and were doing a 'window entry'. To get through a patio window you must use a 'hoolie bar' which is a metal bar about 3 foot in length which has a large metal spike on one end and a flat metal edge on the other end. We approached the rear of the house and my colleague smashed through the patio window, raking the glass in a diagonal. Once all of the glass was out of the window we began to pile into the house. There was a couch with a duvet on it underneath the patio window and every time one of us landed on the couch we heard a voice saying 'Ouu you bastard'. It wasn't until we all got in that we realised that someone had been asleep on the couch and every officer had jumped on him as they came through the window.

2000

We used to do 'Training Days' on Saddleworth Moor. Plastic body parts would be hidden on the Moor, and we would spend the day using the 'Winthrop Theory' (The need for reference points to identify possible hide locations) to locate the hidden body parts. After a full day on the Moors, we drove back to our station with a plastic arm and hand sticking out of the van door. As we passed vehicles on the motorway the officer in the front would make a face like he was screaming in pain because his arm was stuck in the door, much to the horror of passing motorists.

1998

I was on my van driving course with other officers, so there was a convoy of 3 marked police vans driving around the city centre. I asked the instructor if we could stop by a scrap yard while we were driving around as I needed a part for my car. 'No problem' he said and instructed us to put the blue lights and klaxons on as the convoy of 3 vans sped through the city centre, traffic parting like the waves thinking we were going to a huge disturbance. No, we were just going to the scrap yard.

1990

I was sent to a concern for welfare as an old lady had not been seen for some time at home. I got to the house and had to force and entry to get inside. I began to search around the house shouting 'Hello it's the Police' as I slowly made my way from one room to another. I checked all the rooms downstairs but there was no one there. I made my way up the stairs shouting and began checking the bedrooms, still nothing. I then went into the bathroom and noticed the shower curtain pulled halfway across the bath and the bath full of water. I put my hand on the side of the bath and as I went to look around the shower curtain the old woman who had fallen in the bath suddenly grabbed my hand. I nearly shit myself, as I had been expecting to find the lady dead in the bath. She had fallen and had laid in the bath for 24 hours before I found her.

2008

Every year I would make my shift bacon and sausage butties on Christmas Day. To be prepared I bought the bacon and sausage a month before and froze them at home before bringing them into work on Christmas Eve ready for the following day. Unbeknown to me the cleaner had decided to clean out the fridge on Christmas Eve and bin all of the out-of-date food and had disposed of my sausage and bacon thinking they were out of date. So, on Christmas morning off I went to the local garage to buy more bacon with my flashing Christmas hat on. Later that day I was interviewing a prisoner who kept looking at me oddly. I asked him what the problem was, and he was said he was finding it weird being interviewed by a copper with a flashing hat on. I forgot I had it on when I went into the interview.

2010

I was working on a uniform group, in an office with a load of civilian staff. One of the civilians (or civvies as we're now not allowed to call them) smoked and would go outside to the designated smoking area at least 5 times a day for a cigarette. By the time she had got the lift to the ground floor, walked to the end of the car park to the smoking area, had a chat with her friends and had her cigarette and then come back up in the lift it was at least 20 minutes. She did this 5 times a day. I worked out one day that over the year all the times she went outside for a cigarette equated to 5 weeks extra leave for me (the non-smoker).

2012

I was walking around the station just stretching my legs. Every time I would walk past a certain office there was a terrible smell emanating from their office. One day curiosity got the better of me and I stuck my head into the office and asked what the smell was? 'It's my pet ferrets' came the reply. A police officer would bring her ferrets to work every day and walk them around on leads, and nobody ever challenged her over it.

1996

I was working with a fellow probationer. We had been allowed to stay back at the station to complete urgent paperwork rather than attend a 'Training Day' with our colleagues. We decided to make a coffee before starting our paperwork so made our way up to the small canteen. As I was making the coffee, I spilt some milk on the floor and as I bent down to wipe the milk up my belt kit caught the fire extinguisher which fell from the wall and exploded on the floor. The white powder covered us from head to toe as well as the canteen floor and the snooker room which was attached to the canteen. We spent the next 3 hours cleaning up the mess rather than doing any paperwork. The Sgt eventually returned and saw the state of the pair of us, still covered in white powder. She didn't believe us that it had been an accident and never let us stay behind again to complete reports.

2003

In the wake of a colleague, Stephen Oake being murdered in a block of flats, we were called into search the flat and surrounding flats for the possible deadly chemical Ricin which it was believed was being produced in the flats. It was a warm day and we all got kitted up in our CBRN Chemical suits. Ait was organised chaos when we arrived, and we were then told to make our way inside the stairwell to flats and to wait there. We stood on the stairwell for an hour and a half before our Sgt made representations to the command team that we would need a break as the temperature inside the CBRN suits can become unbearable. We were told to stay where we were and got told to search the flats. Another concern was how we would be decontaminated if we found ricin in the flats. We were told the Fire service were on their way and would be setting up a decontamination area outside the flats for us. Hours later we had searched the flats, found no ricin we were aware of, and the fire service had not attended. We were told that an Ambulance crew were now in attendance and had set up the decontamination area. I made my way downstairs, covered in sweat underneath my CBRN suit to see that the decontamination area consisted of a washing up bowl that you had to walk through and a toilet brush to scrub your boots off with.

2004

There was a bomb scare. So as is usual in the Police, you rush to the scene and then sit there for hours doing nothing. A bomb had been found underneath a car on a residential street. Usually, you would evacuate the residents of the street through the back of their house if possible and a cordon would be placed around the car of about 100 metres. Not so on this occasion. When we arrived, there were two uniform officers stood on either side of the car with residents from the surrounding houses walking right past the car with the suspect devise underneath it. It was organised chaos. There were no cordons up and people were just coming and going from their houses. This boils down to incompetent bosses who having been promoted have not got a clue what to do when situations like this arise. The device was later defused, and nobody was injured.

2004

I attended a sad job on Christmas Day. I had been called to a report of a sudden death. The family involved had all gone out for Christmas lunch to a nearby gastro pub. During the meal the mum had said she had left something at home that she needed and so walked home on her own. She didn't return to the pub, so the family all made their way home to find their mum in a bath full of water. She had put a hairdryer in the bath with her and switched it on causing her to be electrocuted. The family were distraught when I arrived realising that their mum had gone home to commit suicide. It was very sad, and it is something that has stuck with me since then.

1999

I was working at Aintree Racecourse for the Grand National and was attached to a group that were tasked with searching people's belongings when they arrived. We were all in uniform. I had told one of my colleagues that my sister was coming that day with a few friends to watch the racing, so he said, 'Let me know when she's here and I'll run up behind her and grab her to surprise her'. About an hour passed when I saw a group of ladies coming through the gates. It was ladies' day, and they were all dressed in their finery. I turned to my colleague and said 'that's her over there, the one in the red dress'. He left our group and crept up behind the group of unsuspecting ladies and then suddenly grabbed hold of the lady in the red dress and lifting her in the air scaring her half to death as she screamed 'what are you doing?'. What he didn't realise is that the lady I had pointed out wasn't in fact my sister it was just some random woman who was with her friends. My sister hadn't even arrived yet, I was just a bit bored. He apologetically put the lady back down on the ground as she brushed herself down. I nearly wet myself laughing, he didn't find it as funny!!

2017

I was working in CID and one of my colleagues had gone off sick again!! I had been tasked with sorting out a couple of her investigations and bringing them to a conclusion. For one of the investigations, all that was required was a 'capacity statement' from a social worker. A capacity statement is basically to determine if the person can make decisions on their own. In this particular case as the lady had dementia, she did not have capacity. The job involved a lady with dementia who had been assaulted by a care worker who had been witnessed by another care worker slapping her. All of the evidence was on the file, and it just needed this statement from the social worker and then it could be submitted to the Crown Prosecution Service for a charging decision. I managed after several attempts to get the capacity statement and the job was ready to send off as my colleague returned to work and asked me to reallocate her job back to her, which I did. I explained to her that I'd got the rest of the evidence and that it was ready to go. I thought nothing more of this until months later I remembered about it and thought I'd be nosey and check out her jobs on the force computer to see where this investigation was up to. I was gobsmacked to see that this officer had held onto the job until after 6 months, which is the cut off point for Summary investigations. She had then submitted it to her Sgt and had asked him to 'write it off' as the investigation had now basically run out of time. The lady who got smacked and her family got no justice. Some officers in my opinion should not be in the police as they are a disgrace. She is one of them.

2016

I received a phone call from a concerned daughter regarding her elderly father. She explained that he was using the services of a 'home help' which was a middle-aged lady who would come to his house once a week to do chores and assist him to 'shower'. This lady wasn't from a reputable company, it was a friend of a friend who would pop into the man's house to keep him company. The daughter was concerned as basically her father was spending quite a bit of cash on this lady and it was cutting into her inheritance. I ended up ringing the 'home help' lady and having a chat with her. She confirmed she would go round and do a bit of housework or shopping for the man in question and assist him to shower. I also went to see the man who confirmed the same story. Although he was in his 80's he still had all his faculties and had 'capacity' to make his own decisions. It was obvious reading between the lines that the lady in question was providing some sort of weekly sexual service to the elderly man and he was more than happy to pay for it. As you can imagine this was an incredibly awkward conversation to have with his daughter when I rang her back!!

2012

I was working in the city centre and part of my foot beat was a large shopping complex. One day I had witnessed a fight between two men and chased the offender as he ran through the shopping area past the shops. I was right behind him as he ran into the trendy clothing store, Hollister. It was a bright sunny day, and as I ran into Hollister it went from bright light to near darkness, as Hollister is known to have very little lighting inside its shops. Everything went completely black, and I couldn't see anything for several seconds. Luckily the same thing had happened to the man I was chasing so as I grabbed hold of him, we crashed into a clothing stand sending it flying to the floor. He tried to get away from me but I held on as we bumped into another table full of clothes, knocking the display to the floor. I eventually got him handcuffed and then looked around at the clothing carnage on the floor. The manager wasn't impressed but as I explained 'Put some bloody lights on then'.

1992

I was working as a civilian in a police station and was posted to the front desk, so mine was the face you would see when you first came into the police station. One day I was sat in the back office on a wheely chair when two policemen that I knew came into the station. They quickly grabbed me pinning my hands to the chair and then used masking tape to attach my arms to the arms of the chair. Just as they'd finished this somebody came into the front counter and pressed the buzzer. The policemen wheeled me to the door, opened it and then pushed me through on the chair into the front office. I wheeled slowly towards the member of the public, coming to a stop in front of him. Smiling I said, 'How can I help you?'

1994

A man and woman had been arrested in the city centre for outraging public decency. Basically, she had been caught giving him a 'blow job' in front of passing members of the public on a Saturday night. Many members of the public had gathered round to watch, and the couple seemed completely oblivious to this fact. Two policemen interviewed the female after she had been arrested and said to her 'did you not notice the crowd that had gathered around you?' to which she replied, 'Well I was a bit busy at the time'. Both officers burst into fits of laughter as the female remained deadly serious and said to them, 'pull yourselves together'.

1995

I had attended Crown Court to give evidence during a trial. After the trial the Judge contacted the Superintendent at my station and demanded to see my pocket notebook. I was a bit pissed off to say the least when I returned to the station and found that my locker had been searched to try and find the notebook in question. They never found it. To get my own back on this boss, who many other of my colleagues also didn't like we decided to play a joke on him. Whenever somebody went on holiday, they would send the boss a postcard from the notebook saying 'hope you're keeping well. Life is tough for a notebook on the run'. This continued for over a year with postcards sent from all over the world. By the end he was raging demanding to know who was sending all the postcards. One was even staged with a polaroid photograph of a notebook on a towel next to a Pina Colada with a straw in it. What the boss didn't know was that the last time I had seen the notebook he was trying to find, it was on a bonfire with me toasting marshmallows over it.

1995

Our Sgt was a legend and is sadly no longer with us. One day he went to the Superintendent's office to speak to her, and the pair ended up having words with each other. He sat there stubbornly with his arms folded as she said, 'well I've got work to be getting on with'. He remained sat, arms folded in the chair opposite her while she continued to work until 5pm and then left, closing her office door behind her as our Sgt remained sat in the chair by her desk. At this time, we were working a shift that had a short-change over time. You would finish work at 11pm and then be back into work at 7am the following morning. He waited until 5.30pm until she had left the building before leaving her office, and then the following morning at 7am he went back into her office and sat in the same chair with his arms folded waiting for her to get in. She arrived just before 9am and walked into her office seeing him sat arms folded, where she had left him the afternoon before. We all heard her scream at him 'Get out!!'

1995

The same Sgt, who didn't drive, would take his whole section down to the beach in the Police Van to get ice creams. One day we got the van stuck in the sand.

1996

We had gone riot training which was in an old aeroplane hangar we would run around while having small blocks of wood and car tyres thrown at us. As we arrived with a policeman who was new to our section we were told 'Go over there and grab yourselves a boiler suit'. These were basically flame proof overalls. The policeman who was new on our section said, 'Well that's lovely'. I asked him what he meant, and he said, 'We've only been here 5 minutes and they've already offered us a 'bowl of soup'. We all fell about laughing as he had completely misheard the instructor.

1988

I had just joined the police, and my Sgt decided to join me on my foot beat in the town centre. No sooner had we started walking than he directed me into a local pub. I followed saying nothing. When he asked me what I was having to drink, I thought this was a trick question. 'I'll just have a coke please' I said. 'Rubbish' replied the Sgt 'Get him a beer and I'll have one as well'. By the time we had finished walking around the city visiting various pubs I was absolutely bladdered as I'd had about 5 pints, and we both stumbled back to the police station at the end of my shift. He drove home. I walked back to my flat.

1988

I was collected on my foot beat by some older police officers and driven to the local hospital where I was then handed a prisoner. 'You've just caught him burgling the nurses' quarters. I agreed/ went along with this, and took him into the police station to book him in. The prisoner wasn't bothered. He had indeed been caught burgling the nurses' accommodation and didn't care who arrested him. I was so proud booking in my first burglar. You knew you'd been accepted by the group when things like this happened to you.

1997

Several colleagues had been served with papers from the internal investigation unit. Apparently, they had all driven down to Glastonbury music festival and had been getting paid on their rest days to work as private security. Internal investigations were not happy about this and wanted to get to the bottom of it. All of officers were interviewed and admitted they had been there to watch the music festival but denied getting paid. On the 2nd interview a few of them cracked and admitted they had been paid to work as security, as they had been threatened with the sack if they didn't admit they had been paid. One colleague was again interviewed for a 2nd time, and he was informed that his colleagues had admitted they had been paid, 'Well don't I fell the fool' was his reply. His colleagues kept their jobs and got fined, he didn't get fined. They had all worked doing security.

1995

We had gone to Catterick army barracks for a search training course. At the end of the course one of my colleagues managed to find a toilet that was waiting to be plumbed in. He put this in the back of the police van right in front of the sliding doors. It came complete with toilet brush holder and toilet roll holder. As the army lads were lined up on the parade square doing drill, we drove the police carrier slowly in front of them with the sliding side door open. My colleague was sat on the toilet, pants down reading the newspaper. The army were trying to hold it together and not laugh. We brought the toilet back to force with us and then set it up in our boss's office because we didn't like him. He arrived for work Monday morning wondering why there was a toilet, toilet brush and loo roll holder next to his desk.

1994

I'd lost my pocket notebook and when I was interviewed over it, I told the investigations department that I' definitely handed it to the admin lady in our station. I was re interviewed some weeks later over the same matter and asked the investigators if they had spoken to the admin lady. They informed me she had passed away some months earlier. She was a lovely lady and I think she would have liked that she got me out of the shit on that occasion.

1996

If we had performed well during the week and hit our arrest targets as a treat on Sunday, we would all go for a pint on duty or go to the bowling alley. This was done as a thankyou and an incentive for you to work hard during the week. This was all going swimmingly until a colleague grassed us up and loads of us got moved to different stations. Nobody like a grass!!

1992

If we were working late and finished at 4am our boss would often bring in a crate of beers. We would then stay until 7am drinking and talking about then day's events then all drive home.

1996

When we would go to the station bar (public houses were over each police station until they began to close them in 1998) we would play a game called 'Spoons'. One officer would put a dessert spoon in his mouth and the officer facing him would do the same. You would then take it in turns to shut your eyes as you were hit on the head with the spoon. If there was someone new on the group, they would usually watch and think 'I can do that'. When it came to their go to be hit, they would shut their eyes as a colleague would hit them hard on the head with a soup ladle.

1996

I, and about 20 other colleagues were on 'standby' to do security for a murder trial that was being tried at Crown Court in a different city. We were there for weeks eating from the canteen at the force's headquarters. At the end of our time there we had told the staff to send the bill to our boss. No one liked him. He was less than impressed to get a bill for £100's of pounds weeks later.

1995

We were on 'stand by' in a station that we were not posted to. It was late at night on a Saturday and the Lennox Lewis fight was being shown on Sky. One of my colleagues managed to crack the code on Sky Tv and ordered the fight. We all got in trouble weeks later when the bill for £800 came in.

1996

We nicked the Christmas decorations from a local police station over the festive period and put them in our police carrier which was now adorned with tinsel and twinkling lights. You should have seen the prisoners faces when they were arrested and put in the van.

1996

One year we had a brilliant idea. We got a huge list of people who were wanted on no bail warrants or for serious arrestable offences. These people were all sent letters to their home address on headed notepaper from a fictitious company telling them that they had won expensive electrical items, video recorders or TV's. We used policewomen from our group who dressed in matching red uniforms with clip boards. They were placed outside of the hall where the prizes would be given out, collating the names of the offenders as they arrived. They had been told to bring with them a form of photographic identification so we could verify it was them. The offenders arrived in their droves, handing over their passports, ready to claim their prizes. They were ushered through to a separate part of the building where their photo identification was checked and then finally into a separate room into the arms of the waiting police officers who promptly handcuffed them, arrested them and took them to the nearest police station. When the offenders had their photographs taken at the police station somebody had drawn a pair of Donkey ears on the photograph board because everyone who got arrested was a right 'Donkey'. We arrested 100's of offenders and all got commendations for our efforts.

1995

Me and two colleagues were in plain clothes and were stood by a local train station when we witnessed a priest being robbed by three men. The Priest was quite elderly and had been at a local hospital giving the 'last rights' to sick and dying patients. We chased the three men. Two of them jumped in the back of a black cab promptly followed by me. The taxi driver not realising I was a cop shouted for the Transport police to help with the fight going on in his cab. I shouted that I was a cop as I grabbed both men by the hair and banged their heads together. My colleague chased the third man and caught him, and we proudly took all three to the police station.

Two of the men admitted the robbery but when I interviewed the third man he said, 'no comment'. This was at the time when the 'special warnings' had come into play in the police. If suspects said no comment during a police interview but had been seen or found in possession of items you wished them to account for, you had to give them a special warning. Not that this makes a lot of difference when you get to court but we had to do it. Realising this offender was saying 'no comment' I told him I would have to give him a 'special warning'. Looking down onto the desk where the interview sheet prompt notes are sellotaped to the desk I realised that someone had removed the bit with the special warning on it. I tried to give myself some time telling the suspect that the warning I had to give him was very special and repeated this several times while frantically looking through drawers trying to find the actual warning. The suspects solicitor must have realised what I was doing and asked for a 5 minute break, thus giving me time to run to another interview room and rip the special warning from the desk.

1997

I was being interviewed by the Professional Standards Department and one of the detectives interviewing me was new to the role she was in. At the start of the interview the female detective read me the new caution which had recently changed from the old caution. She then said, 'You don't need me to explain that to you, do you?'. I looked at her and said, 'Do you know what, yeah go on explain it to me'. She panicked as she obviously had no idea how to explain the convoluted new caution. She floundered through an explanation which just sounded ridiculous. At the end of her explanation, I sat back in my chair and said 'Well I'll be honest, that's not what I thought it meant. And I'm so glad you've explained it to me'. She looked completely embarrassed, and we then carried on with my interview.

I bumped into her at a party some years later and she called me a fucking arsehole but did laugh and said I made her look stupid in the interview, which I did. She is now retired and has been seen on those 'Hunted' programmes as an investigating detective. I'll leave that with you!!

2000

I was again being interviewed with three colleagues by the Professional Standards Department. The first officer went into the interview room and complained before the interview started that the room was oppressively hot. The interview was suspended, and windows were opened before his interview continued. The second officer went in and came out shortly after saying he had complained that the room was oppressively cold. Interview stopped and heating put back on before he was again invited in. Then it was my turn to go in. I sat there and was asked 'before we start is the room temperature alright for me? I replied, 'Do you know what it's just right'. We later called this the 3 bear's interview.

2002

I was working on a team and one of the officers who had been attached to our team had been arrested for possession of indecent images of children. We were obviously disgusted by this and wanted nothing more to do with him. When he was part of our team his job had been to collate the arrest files some of which had now gone missing, so there was now to be an investigation into these missing files.

As part of this investigation, I was interviewed and told the interviewing officer that all the paperwork had been handed to the officer who had now been convicted of possession of indecent images of children. The interviewing officer told me that this wasn't the case and that he had spoken to the ex-officer in question who had denied being responsible for these files. I asked if he had spoken to this man in prison and he confirmed he had done. I then said 'He's lying, we gave him the files. I was again told this wasn't the case. I asked, 'You know when he was first arrested, did he deny possession of the indecent images he was found with'. It was confirmed that he had indeed denied possession these images. I then pointed out that the ex-officer had then admitted his guilt at a later Crown Court appearance…which meant he was a liar. We never did find those missing files.

1995

I was asked to work in plain clothes to stake out a possible brothel on our area. I walked into the brothel and spoke to the lady on the front desk. I was then handed a menu which included massages etc.

I noticed at the bottom of the menu it said, 'blow job' and extras. I said to the lady that I would have to go to the cash point as I had not brought enough cash in with me. I would then make my way outside the premises; tell my boss it was a brothel and minutes later it would be raided. It was all going to plan until I turned and saw a man inside the brothel I recognised as a police colleague who had obviously gone to use the services of the brothel. Realising that if it got raided, he would get arrested I smiled at him. He smiled back and obviously thought I was a punter. I was staring at him and moving my head towards the door. Thankfully he caught on to what I was doing and realised there would be an imminent raid on the premises and quickly made an exit through the front door. The problem was he was running so fast he tripped and fell banging his head on the pavement.

1994

We used to have an Inspector we called 'Dog biscuit'. This was because he was always pinching sweets off your desk when he walked past, just helping himself. To have a bit of a laugh we started bringing dog biscuits into work and would leave them on our desk. The idiot ate them as well.

He also had an addiction to fruit machines and would gamble his earnings away. Because of this he was seen by a colleague of mine waiting tables in a local Chinese restaurant. Then another colleague ordered a children's entertainer for a party she was having for her kids. He turned up dressed as a clown. He was also then known as 'Coco the clown'.

1990

We had a uniform Inspector that used to come in on a night shift and go upstairs in the station to go to sleep. We didn't see him all night.

1994

There was a uniform WPC who left policing after a few years to work in the adult entertainment industry. Sometime after this, one of our colleagues was hospitalised after being assaulted on duty and a few of the lads went into hospital to see him. They took him some adult magazines to help while away the hours. As he was laid in bed, he opened one of them up and said 'bloody hell I used to tutor her when she was a policewoman'. We knew that her brother was also in the police and worked as a custody Sgt. He had a reputation for being a bit of an arsehole. One day while he was being particularly frosty with me as I was booking my prisoner in with him, I said 'How's your sister doing, I hear she left the cops'. He was nice as pie with me after that.

1995

There was a house on our patch. It was a large Victorian three-story house and the man living on the top floor was dealing drugs on a big scale. The trouble was that every time we executed a warrant at the house the drugs would have disappeared by the time we got in there, as he could see and hear us coming. We came up with an ingenious plan. We would move into the flat below him. Three policemen and three policewomen. The six of us were all quite young. Moving day arrived and we pulled up in a clapped-out old van, music blaring out, carrying some old chairs we'd borrowed from the police canteen. Suitcases that contained our police issue search overalls and we had picked up an old fridge from the tip that had our riot helmets inside it. We carried all of this into the flat below his, music still blaring. We then carried up the crates of larger to the flat and continued to party, throwing beers cans out of the window singing loudly. To our surprise he came down to check us out. We invited him in and gave him a beer. Seemingly happy with what he saw he returned to his flat thanking us for the beer.

That evening we all got changed into our police gear and using the door opener we'd stashed in a suitcase, went up to his flat, smashed his door open and recovered all of his drugs. Result.

2006

We did a warrant at a cannabis factory and found out later that day that the room we had been in had a high concentration of asbestos so all our own clothes we had been wearing at the time would have to be bagged and destroyed. We were invited to put in a 'chitty' with the admin department for our clothes. My bill came to £620.

1994

During a house search when we had finished and then got bored, we used to swap the rooms around. We would move the front room to the upstairs bedroom and the bedroom to the downstairs front room. It always used to make us laugh thinking of the house holder returning home to find this and wondering what the hell had happened. We also used to prise the skirting boards off and hide frozen fish or crab sticks behind them and then neatly put them back.

1996

During a Junior Conservative Party Conference, we were called into search the premises prior to the conference going ahead. On the outdoor billboard it spelled out 'Junior Conservative Party Conference'. We thought it would be funny to remove some of these letters to spell CUNT underneath this. Obviously, we put everything back in its rightful place when we left. I was watching the news that night and reporter was stood in front of this billboard as the letters C..U..N..T fell off. It was obvious to anyone watching what it spelled out.

1995

Working at The Grand National we were bored. One of my colleagues lay down on the conveyor belt and went through the X Ray machine you put your bags on, like you have at the airport 3 times while we cheered him on.

1988

It was customary to wind up the probationers at the city mortuary. We would go into the mortuary and tell the probationer to lie on a slab with a sheet over them because a colleague was coming in shortly after, and to then jump up and scare them. The probationer obliged and laid on the slab covered in the sheet. He was then locked in the room waiting for the arrival of his unsuspecting colleague. As he laid there the probationer said out loud 'God it's cold in here', to which the body lying next to him replied 'You're not kidding'. We had hidden another colleague in the same room under a sheet next to him. He shit himself and jumped up banging on the door to be let out.

1990

Someone got hold of a shop window dummy. Fake jobs would be sent out by the radio room to probationers on foot patrol to attend the flyover in the city as there was a male stood on the bridge. As the probationer arrived the dummy would be thrown off with a rope around it. This was called character building.

1993

I worked with a colleague who couldn't pronounce his 'R's properly. One day he was assigned the call sign R33 (Romeo 33) and pleaded with the driver of M22 (Mike 22) to swap with him as he knew the radio room staff would just take the piss out of him when he shouted up as R33. His colleague obliged, but later that shift M22 became involved in a vehicle chase. Every road he turned into as he gave commentary began with an R. The radio room staff dissolved into fits of laughter listening to him.

1994

Another colleague had a nervous twitch which made him quickly move his head to the side and rub his chin on his shoulder. For a laugh one shift we composed a letter from this officer requesting an attachment with the firearms department. As part of the letter we put 'I understand there may be some concerns regarding my twitch, and that I may have an episode and accidently shoot down the force helicopter, but I am confident that with my medication I can overcome this'. He was called into speak with the Sgt who didn't know it was a wind up. He didn't get his firearms attachment.

2006

The Euro football games were upon us and as part of a plain clothes team we were tasked with infiltrating the crowds that were gathering in the city centre as there had been widespread disorder at previous games. We had a policeman working with us who was a right knob. On the day of the match, we all arrived in our jeans and t shirts ready to be deployed with the crowds. He arrived wearing a full England kit complete with shorts and socks and then proceeded to put on face paint in the form of little England flags. He hasn't changed. He's still a dick.

2006

Same officer as above!! Had written a statement that was needed by the CID urgently. He left his computer open, and we decided to change a couple of bits. At the top of your statement is a 'declaration' which basically says that what you write, must be the truth to the best of your knowledge and belief. This was changed to 'I realise that if I don't tell the truth I may be liable to a stint in the pokey'. He hurried upstairs to the CID office and handed his statement over only to be phoned a few minutes later and told to change it immediately.

1993

I went to Crown Court. We were spoken to by the prosecution barrister who said that the defendant was pleading guilty and would be sentenced after lunch. Great we thought. We headed out for lunch complete with 3 pints to celebrate our guilty plea and then went back to court after lunch to see what sentence the culprit was getting. 'Change of plan' said the barrister. The defendant had now changed his mind and was pleading not guilty so there would now be a trial. I gave the most animated evidence I had ever given that afternoon curtesy of my 3 pints.

1992

Adding song lyrics to your evidence may seem like a good idea but it's not so funny when the defendant pleads not guilty, and you end up giving evidence in court. Meatloaf featured heavily this year.

1993

My colleague had taken a suspect's fingerprints. It was the old ink prints you had to do one at a time. For some reason there was a random single fingerprint on the back of the form that had to be pressed on and not rolled. When we got to court the solicitor spoke to us and mentioned the fingerprint forms pointing out that the fingerprint on the back of the suspects forms was in fact the officers. My colleague then admitted he had forgotten to do it and the suspect had left the station, so he popped his own on there.

1992

We used to photograph suspects on proper cameras with film in them. For a laugh sometimes we would make them turn around and photograph the back of their head. They would often ask why we did this to which we replied, 'In case you're running away then we can identify you'.

1990

Interviewing a suspect once we put a metal food colander on his head and sellotaped some wires to it which we then attached to his finger. We told him this was a lie detector, and he believed us. He coughed everything during that interview.

1994

I got sent to a nuisance caller who had rung 999 over 20 times in a day. We arrived and my colleague went straight to the phone, ripped it out of the wall along with the wires and then threw the phone in the washing machine and put it on a spin cycle. We then left the house. He didn't ring again.

1995

I worked with an officer who constantly made funny innuendos. We went to a report of burglary once and he said to the lady occupier, 'Can I just squeeze up your back passage'. He then asked, 'Did he come round the front or batter your back doors in?' The householders didn't know if he was taking the piss or not.

1989

I had applied to become the first SOCO (scenes of crime officer) in our force. These departments are now almost solely staffed by civilian staff but back then they were staffed by Police officers. The night before my job interview, I swatted up on everything to do with scenes of crime, wanting to be ready for every eventuality during the interview. The morning arrived and I was sat in front of my interviewers. The first question I was asked 'Can you pick up the Scenes of Crime kit?'. I stared at the interviewer. The SOCO kit was in a large metal box, and it could be quite heavy. I looked at the interviewers, confused, and realised that the question was just blatantly sexist. I thought I'd play them at their own game so

I answered, 'I wouldn't have to pick it up, I'd just bat my eyelids and get one of the men to pick it up'. It was obvious they didn't know how to take this answer as I was then asked, 'Would you be sick at a post-mortem?'. I understood at every home office post-mortem, a SOCO would attend to photograph the corpse during the examination. I answered that it depends how much I had to drink the night before. No other questions of note were really asked of me, and I got the job.

When I arrived in my new station in my role as a SOCO it was obvious that one of the other men in the office was not happy that a woman was now working in the department. The policemen in the SOCO department were very old school, wearing jackets with leather patches on the sleeves. I feel that when this happens in any department, I was posted to there is self-pressure to be the best. To prove yourself.

A few weeks after this I had to attend my first post-mortem as a SOCO, to photograph the corpse. The SOCO would normally attend with the senior investigating officer, The mortuary technician who assists the pathologist and the pathologist. On this occasion, when I arrived at the mortuary, everyone had turned up, not to see the post-mortem, it was to watch me.

I remember that the murder victim had been strangled using a scarf and that it was a domestic violence murder. I volunteered to 'scribe' in other words make all the notes for the pathologist as he performed the examination. All eyes were on me as the 'only girl' in the room. I got the impression they were only there to see if I was going to faint. The pathologist was known as 'fast Eddie' because he would do examinations very fast, and it was hard to keep up with him. In the 80's pathologist examination tables were porcelain, and the block on which the head of the corpse was placed was made of wood. The wood would slide around on the table. Nowadays examination tables and blocks are made of metal. I was sat on a stool at the foot of the examination table as Fast Eddie shouted his findings over to me and I frantically made notes. There was a bucket by his feet which contained various body parts and a large quantity of blood. I could see that the wooden block on which the head was resting was starting to slip on the porcelain surface so I began to slowly move my chair away as I could see what was going to happen. As I predicted, minutes later the wooden block slipped and landed in the overflowing bucket causing a small tidal wave of blood and guts. I had managed to avoid this by moving backwards, but some of my colleagues weren't so lucky and were splashed by the contents. I smiled inwardly. This is how things continued for some time until I proved myself and was accepted as 'one of the lads.

1990

As a SOCO officer we had moved stations to work in the force Headquarters. The SOCO van was a long wheel-based carrier and was quite cumbersome to drive. The men in our office hated driving it due to the fact they could not park it. One evening as I pulled up at headquarters gate house, the officer in the gate house motioned for me to wind the window down. He then informed me that the men in the office had asked him to give them a ring when I arrived at the station as they wanted to 'see if I could park the van'. I decided that I could do this in one of two ways. I could either take my time parking, or just go for it. I put the van in gear and set off driving fast towards the parking space. I drove forward, rammed it in reverse and shot backwards turning the wheel frantically as I reverse parked perfectly in the space. I then got out and hooked the van up to the electric point. When I walked into the office no one said a word!!

1991

I went to a fight in a local chippy. When I arrived on my own there was a huge fella kicking off. He paid no attention to me whatsoever when I told him to 'calm down', laughing at me saying 'What are you going to do. All I could think was 'hot fat!!' which I didn't fancy getting covered in if we started fighting. He continued to shout and swear so I told him he was locked up and to stand there, pointing to a back wall well away from the deep fat fryer. I could see my colleague who was 6'5" had arrived and was peeling himself out of his panda car. The drunk man shouted over 'Oh yeah how are you going to arrest me'. My colleague then walked into the chippy and said to me 'which one?'. I pointed to the angry man and said, 'him' as he was dragged from the chippy screaming.

1988

I was policing a very white area and one day while driving around we spotted a black lad walking around. This was very unusual in this area as it was my beat and knew everyone who lived here. He was so nervous when we spoke to him, and I'd seen him fiddling with his pockets, so I knew it had to be drugs. He looked like he was going to run and there's no way I would have caught him, so I said 'look I know what you're thinking. Should I run? The thing is, how embarrassing is it for you to be caught by a woman if you do run'. 'What's more embarrassing, getting arrested by 2 girls or being caught by one?'. He gave himself up and I searched him finding quite a large amount of heroin in his pockets. Later in the station he said to me 'so are you some sort of Olympic runner or something? I replied 'No, and I definitely wouldn't have caught you'. He was gutted.

1989

I had been told to stay in the station answering the front desk and the phones by my Sgt. As I was driving to this designated station to carry out this task, I saw a lad running across the road in front of me. I knew the Sgt and the rest of my team where executing a drugs warrant at a nearby property, and putting two and two together I suspected he was from the flats where my colleagues were. I pulled the panda car up and got out, tossing my police hat in the car because I never could run with it on. I started chasing him along the road. He didn't realise I was behind him until he heard my radio go off. We continued through the rabbit warren of back entries and small streets until he finally slowed down and I caught up to him. We both stopped, grabbing hold of a wall and breathing heavily as he looked at me. He then took out his inhaler taking a long drag on it and then said to me 'do you want a puff miss?' and went to hand me his inhaler. I declined and put him in handcuffs instead.

1989

I had a proper male chauvinist as a Sgt. He didn't like having a female on his block. One day there was a stolen car being chased around our subdivision. I managed to catch up to the car as both lads bailed from it and began running away. I chased after them, running past people who were sat in a bus stop watching the drama unfold. I managed to grab one lad and slammed him up against the bus stop handcuffing him. I then saw my Sgt who had pulled up some distance down the road and was running in my direction. Seeing the second car thief not too far away I thought 'I can catch him as well', so I dragged the first prisoner with me as I began to run after the second lad catching him seconds later. My Sgt caught up to me as I had hold of both men and helped me with them. He had a bit more respect for me after that.

1988

I got sent to a large-scale disturbance in a rough club. I had a probationer with me at the time and as we ran into the club it was carnage. Chairs being thrown, people rolling around on the floor fighting each other. A girl ran up to me screaming, fists flying at me as I grabbed her by the hair, wrapping it around my hand and dragging her to the floor. The probationer, who was quite a big fella stood there wide eyed and shouted to me, 'what shall I do?'. I could see a drunk man running towards him, so I shouted 'hit him' pointing to the man. He did as he was told and knocked him right out.

1987

I had passed my promotion board to Inspector which was no mean feat for a woman. My promotion party was in the station bar, and so we all gathered after work for drinks and food. My boss was a Chinese Chief Inspector we called 'Hong Kong Phooey'. He was a particular pain in the arse as he used to leave 'post it' notes all over your paperwork and in your pigeonhole. He approached me in the bar and said to me 'I'm confused. Did you ever get the notes I used to leave you on your paperwork because you never replied to them'. The people standing around me had fallen silent as they listened. I replied 'yes, I did get them, and do you know what I did with them. I collected them all together, put a hole in the corner with the hole punch and put some string through them. Then I used them to wipe my arse'. The whole bar fell about laughing.

1985

I had a terrible male Sgt who did his best to get me sacked because I was a woman. He didn't think that women should be in the police force. He gave me a dog's life and put me on report which meant I had to report weekly to the station superintendent. What he didn't know is that the superintendent couldn't stand him either, so I just used to sit and have a cuppa in his office while we chatted until he said, 'I reckon that would be enough time for me to have given you a telling off don't you?'. Then I would leave until the next week. He never did get me sacked.

1985

The same Sgt would send me out on endless foot patrol and would 'peg' me on my beat, meeting me to basically check up on me'. I would walk for miles in my skirt and stockings, with my thick Henley overcoat rubbing on my tights. I'd often have to stop by the local hospital just to go to the ladies and pull my tights up as I looked like Nora Batty with them all wrinkled down my leg. One night at 4am he shouted up on the radio that he was coming out to meet me. Sure enough 30 minutes later he's walking towards me, his custodian helmet shining in the moonlight, tapping his night stick on the floor. He then starts lecturing me on stopping cars and tells me he's going to show me the correct way to stop a car. He walks out into the roadway and does his finest number one stop signal, raising his right arm in the air towards the oncoming car which stops in front of him. I stood on the pavement watching this unfold as the Sgt goes to speak to the driver. There must have been 8 people in the car, all crammed in the back lying on top of each other. He tried to communicate with the driver who spoke no English. Getting angry the Sgt shouts 'where are you from'. A little head popped out from the back and shouted 'Vietnam'. At this point I was now sat on a nearby wall laughing, as the Sgt tried to get some sense out of the driver and passengers. He eventually gave up and let them go then angrily shouted up for someone to collect him and take him back to the police station. That was the last time he pegged me on my beat.

1984

There was me and two other female WPC probationers on our group, and we got really bullied by our Sgt. You never forget things like this and how people treat you when you first join the police. 30 years later when we had all retired, I had met up with my ex-cop friends for coffee and she told me that she had seen this Sgt at a Koi Carp fish show. She had been stood with her husband, and he pointed out an elderly man with a big beard who kept looking over at her. Eventually this old man came over to her and it was indeed our old section Sgt who had bullied us all through our probation. He was all friendly saying 'Hi, Hello' to which my friend said to him, 'When I was in the police, and you were my Sgt I had to be polite to you even though you bullied me. Well, I'm not in the police now so fuck off'. Apparently, his face was a picture as he turned and walked away.

1998

I was one of the first females to join SO15, the bomb squad. We would attend incident where bombs had exploded or were unexploded, and this job took me all over the UK and the world. One day back in the UK and in my force, I attended a report of a car bomb. We arrived first and I as the OIC (officer in charge) set up a 100-metre cordon around the burnt-out vehicle. It transpired that the vehicle had contained a large quantity of fireworks which had exploded, and due to the fireworks being confined to such a small area meant that this had given the appearance of a car bomb. Shortly after we had arrived, the force riot/assistance van with a Sgt and several Constables had arrived on scene. He was less than impressed that we had taken over and that a woman was in charge. After we left the scene me and my two colleagues headed to a local police station for a cuppa when the phone rang. I answered it to a man shouting at me, 'who the fuck do you think you are?' It was the Sgt from the van. I lost it with him and shouted, 'what expertise do you have?' I explained I was a lot more qualified than him to be dealing with the vehicle explosion and then I said, 'I haven't got a dick, but if I did have one, I'd still be able to piss higher up the wall than you'. I then put the phone down.

1998

I had to go to young offender's institute to speak to them about the error of their ways and to try and put them on the straight and narrow. Accompanying me was a colleague who was a regular at these kinds of talks. I had no idea what he was going to do as it was my first time doing this. We stood in front of them as my colleague produces a flip chart with three circles drawn on it. Two larger circles with a small circle in the middle of them. The offenders including me looked at this confused as my colleague said, 'This small circle is your arse hole now. The size of this big circle is what your arse will look like if you go to prison'. I think this may have shocked some of them into not committing any more crime.

2002

There were rumours on my team that people were going to be let go which meant that unless you found yourself a new posting, you'd be back out on the street with a big hat on. I spoke to our Inspector, and he confirmed this, telling me 'Well you'll have to go first, because we can't be showing favouritism keeping a female on the staff'. So, I applied out to Special Branch. When my Inspector found this out, he saw his arse which ended with me saying to him 'You can't have it both ways'. I left shortly after this as I got the job in Special Branch'.

2014

I got sent to look at an explosion. A young male had been making homemade fireworks in his flat and it had exploded causing massive damage to the flat but also blowing both of his hands off up to his elbows. He was in a right mess, but I suspect he wouldn't be doing that again.

2007

I was part of the team that investigated the unexploded bombs on the London underground. I remember seeing the suspects who were black and noticing that their hair had gone orange from the toxicity of the chemicals they were working with. I was told I'd have to attend the Old Bailey to give evidence. I replied, 'Not a problem but I'm off on maternity and I'm breastfeeding at the moment, so I'll bring my baby with me'. Luckily my evidence was 'served'(agreed) so I didn't have to attend.

2004

I refused to watch the video of hostage Ken Bigley being executed. I was possibly going to be on the team investigating his murder, but until I knew I was on it I refused to watch. Some things you just can't unsee.

1990

I attended a fatal stabbing as a SOCO (scenes of crime officer). I got to the location of where the man had been found. I had heard minutes earlier a policewoman on the radio desperately trying to give mouth to mouth to the victim who had been stabbed. The victim had then been taken to hospital, and as I arrived at the scene, I heard on the radio that the victim who had been stabbed in the neck had died. At the scene I noticed that although there was some blood there wasn't enough for this to be the murder scene. I followed the drips of blood on the pavement in the back alley until I found stairs leading to a small flat. There on the bed was a massive pool of blood. I'll always remember touching that blood because it was still warm.

2011

I attended a fatal shooting where the victim had been shot in the chest at point black range and then 'knee capped'. This is where he had also been shot behind his knees. He had lost a huge amount of blood and had died at the scene. As the SOCO I dealt with the body. Any murder victim always has their hands and head placed in a forensic bag to preserve any evidence. I did always used to slightly panic placing the head in a plastic bag in case the bag started steaming up and the victim was still alive. In this case he was definitely dead.

1991

When I first joined SOCO I was the only female. The lads were very excepting of me eventually, and one evening when I was the only person working nights, I found their home phone numbers written on some paper inside my paperwork drawers. This meant a lot because it meant I was accepted by them, and they were there to give me advise if I needed it. I had to attend a post-mortem on this set of nights. The pathologist wasn't a very pleasant man to work with. The victim had committed suicide by putting a shot gun to his chest. During the examination of the body, I was trying to photograph the injuries with the pathologist huffing and puffing at me, so I said to him' look, you stick to cutting the bodies and I'll do the photographs'. Shortly after this at another post-mortem the same pathologist was examining a dead body and had placed a ruler into the cavity of the person lying on the mortuary slab. On closer inspection of this ruler, I could see my collar number written on the back of it. I pointed this out to the pathologist and cautioned him telling him he was under arrest for theft. He replied, 'Well you can have it back then'. I pointed out that why would I want a ruler back that had been inside a dead person? Also the ruler had obviously been inside my SOCO box which contained all of my kit. He was very apologetic and polite to me after this, and we got on just fine.

1990

I was the SOCO at another post-mortem with a different pathologist. He's mellowed a lot in old age but to start with he was a bit uppity. The victim subject to his examination was a bombing victim whose legs had been blown off. He started to examine the remains of the victim's legs that had been recovered, when I reminded him that we would have to X Ray the legs first. When he questioned this, I pointed out that they would be full of shrapnel, which they were when we X Rayed them.

When he'd chilled out a bit, we used to have fun with him. I would often forensically bag his shoes up with tags on them when he would leave them in the changing room after he had changed into his scrubs and wellies.

I did have to go back to being a SOCO years later when there was a national SOCO strike. I was phoned by the Deputy Chief Constable who said to me that I was one of only two qualified police officers who worked as a SOCO and they needed me to go back to doing this role whilst the strike was on going. I hadn't done it for years, but it was like riding a bike once I got back into it. My first shift I was called in early to deal with a murder victim and had to attend the post-mortem. The pathologist to my surprise was the same man. We were both now a lot greyer and wiser. He recognised me when I arrived, and we chatted. During the examination I stood on a chair over the top of the victim using my new digital camera. Gone were the days of proper film in cameras. He questioned why I was standing on a chair because apparently 'we don't do that now'.

As we chatted, I told the pathologist that I was going to have my sinuses drilling in an upcoming operation and he helpfully showed me on the body he was examining exactly what would be happening to me. I find that with pathologists, just talk to them. They are incredibly clever people and the work they do is just fascinating. They are always willing to show you how a body works if you have a question.

As part of being a SOCO I also attended a 'bone identification course'. I learnt to distinguish bones structure from European and African ethnicities. As part of the course, we had to attend a 'dig', where bones would be found and dug up by us and then identified. I was heavily pregnant at this point but there was no way I wasn't going to complete this course. At the end of the day, one of my male colleagues said to me 'I've not seen you go for a wee all day, and I can't believe you've done this being nearly 8 months pregnant'. I did tell him that I had disappeared off on several occasions throughout the day to have a wee behind a tree.

I would say that although this may seem alien to policewomen nowadays or feminists, but to be classed as 'one of the lads' was one of the biggest compliments.

1995

Attending Post-mortems used to make me incredibly hungry. I put this down to adrenaline.

1996

There was a Chief Inspector working in CID who was involved in the criminal underworld. This had been suspected for a long time and so the police station in which I was working was bugged. Nobody apart from the anti-corruption police investigation team knew this. The bug was placed in the Inspectors office where it was known this corrupt Chief Inspector would go and make phone calls. Listening equipment was placed in the office along with a covert camera. The everyday occurrences of the police carried on with everybody who went into this office, unaware that their every move was being watched.

On one set of nights the office in question was occupied by the covering night Inspector. It must have been a particularly slow set of nights for him because he decided to borrow a small TV with an in-built video recorder and watch some porn on one of his VHS tapes. His wanking escapade was captured on the recording. He left the police shortly after.

1968

I had joined the police cadets as a female WP (woman Police) Constable. As a cadet we didn't get involved in any sort of policing. In July 1970 I joined the regular police as a WP Constable. I went to Bruche, the central police training college for all forces but was sent back to force after a hosepipe fight in the women's block on the first floor. We didn't realise that the water had gone through the ceiling. I was allowed back a few weeks later and completed my training until I 'passed out' some months later.

1970

Woman Police worked out of a totally different police station to the men. We were based at the Pier Head, near to the docks. My main duties were school crossing patrols and looking after lost children. Sometimes I was sent to work at the Main Bridewell (large city centre police station) as the 'wardress' looking after the needs of the female prisoners. My uniform consisted of a skirt, tights, shirt and police tunic, along with an old style fuzzy felt police hat. We were also issued with a handbag. I just kept stationery in mine and my pocket notebook. One of my female colleagues used to keep a wheel brace in her handbag in case she got in trouble. She would then hit the offender with her handbag. We were not issued with a baton or handcuffs because we were female but also as we were not expected to be actively involved in arresting suspects. I also only received 9/10ths of the pay my male counterparts received. I basically patrolled the city centre with my female tutor Constable who I have an incredible amount of respect for. She was very switched on and taught me a lot. We were expected to deal with the copious amounts of shoplifters in the city and basically became the first 'shoplifting squad'.

1971

Policewomen had to work in pairs. It was expected of us and was also for safety reasons. The men didn't want women on the force, and I lost count of the numbers of dead rats I received through the internal post. I just used to seal them back up in an internal envelope and send them through to the women's superintendent to deal with. The women in the police at this time were seen as a 'necessary evil' and we were literally given all the shit jobs to deal with.

1970

I was being tutored by my female tutor Constable, and we were walking around the city centre when she noticed a CID car parked up at the back of a pub. I asked what was going on as the licensee was stood with two CID officers and they were loading alcohol into the boot of the CID car. She told me that the CID took booze off the landlords for their own Christmas party. Basically, everyone was on 'the take'.

1972

Outside the Crown Court was a large monument to Queen Victoria. Underneath this monument there is a fabulous public toilet which is ornately decorated, and in 1972 it was open to the public. I used to go down there when on my foot beat and speak to the lady that worked as the toilet attendant. She was an amazing informant and knew everything that was going on.

1978

When I worked on the 'Task Force' we had a 'traffic light system'. Basically, the next person you saw wearing red was getting arrested, usually a drunk for being drunk and disorderly. Then we moved onto yellow and green. This was commonplace in the police.

1979

There was a policeman I worked with who had an unusual way of dealing with car thieves. He would get hold of their hands and place them in the crease of the car door and then slam the car door shut on their hands, thus usually breaking their fingers. It stopped them stealing cars for a while.

1968

I was in the cadets and had got into trouble. As a result, I'd been told to report to the commander's office. I was marched in at double time and came to a halt on a mat inside his door. I raised my arm to salute him, but I had come to such an abrupt halt that I slipped on the mat going flying on my arse.

1981

The riots had started, and policewomen were not allowed to be actively involved in policing the riots. I had been promoted to the rank of Sgt in 1981 and went to the clothing store to get my stripes. The usual procedure would be to hand over your tunic and then collect it in a week's time with the 3 Sgts stripes having been sewn on the arms. I told them in stores why I was there and was handed a set of felt stripes. I questioned why the tailer would not be sewing them on for me and it was explained to me that as I was a woman, I could sew my own on. I said, 'would you ask a male Sgt to sew his own stripes on?' He took them back from me and said they would sew them on for me. I then asked for my 'night stick'. This is basically a cumbersome stick about 2 foot in length with a carved handle and a metal tip on the end of it. It dates back hundreds of years and any officer Sgt or above has a night stick. I was told that women don't get night sticks, and he refused to hand one over. It took me months of report writing to eventually get my night stick, but it was the principal of it.

I was told by my Inspector that I couldn't go out on patrol during the riots unless I had a custodian helmet, and as I was a woman, I didn't have a helmet. A custodian helmet is a male police officers' helmet, the tall ones with the metal tip on them. I found an old custodian helmet in the station and took it out in the car with me when I would go out on patrol, placing it on the seat next to me. He was raging when he found out.

You'd go out in the police cars during the riots, and I remember there were big potholes all over the road. Rioters would throw bricks at the police cars as we passed, some of the bricks smashing the car windows. I had glass in my hair one night from a smashed police car window, and just drove into the police station, shook the glass from my hair and then got another police car and went out again.

1982

Armed with my new night stick I would 'peg' the local public houses that were having illegal stay behinds. Pubs in those days would be shut by 11pm and last orders was 10.30pm. I would walk in put my night stick on the bar and then swipe it left and right sending the glasses of beer and wine flying and smashing to the floor, while telling the publican to 'get everyone out now or I'll shut you down'.

1973

I applied to go to the 'Mounted division' in the police. Mounted is where horses are used for public order situations commonly at football matches, and ceremonial duties as well as basically being a beat bobby on a horse. I was told 'No women, no toilets'. There were not toilet facilities for women in either the mounted department or the police dog handler department until the late 1970's. They then had to make one of the small rooms into a toilet solely for the use of the policewomen. The policemen hated women being in their department and would regularly put cling film over our toilets so that we pissed all over ourselves.

1971

There were a few women detective constables in our force but there would only be one WDC per area. There were never two WDC's put in the same station. Even on drug squads years later there was always the token woman. There was never 5 women and one man, it was always just one woman on the squads.

1981

The riots had started, and I was asked to drive our station superintendent to the briefing room. When we arrived, he told me to come inside with him and I walked into the briefing room where a uniform Inspector shouted at me in front of hundreds of male colleagues 'WHAT'S A FUCKING WOMAN DOING HERE?

The riots weren't all bad though. I made enough money doing over time to buy my first house. We used to work 12 hours on and 12 hours off for months with no rest days. We also had to man the casualty bureau on the phones, ringing the wives of injured officers and telling them which hospital their husbands were in and how bad their injuries were.

We were eventually allowed to drive police vehicles during the riots, just to answer the day-to-day calls, not to actually get involved in any confrontation with the riots. No driving courses were needed, we were just asked, 'can you drive?' and then given a set of keys.

1973

Prior to the riots in Liverpool happening, there was a smaller disturbance that happened in the early 70's. We had no riot kit as such and were just given dustbin lids and pickaxe handles. As we were deployed to deal with the disturbances we were told 'No prisoners, just send them to hospital'.

1981

We heard that the Liverpool riots started when a CID officer who attended a house in the Toxteth area of Liverpool, beat to death a family dog on the doorstep of the house. The riots started after that.

1981

As a male officer, I was working during the riots driving the police carriers. The vans would be taken to a police station situated near the town centre to have the tyres removed and the wheels fitted with solid rubber tyres. I was driving along a road during the riots. The smoke was thick in the air and bins were on fire in the roadway. I had the metal grill down on the front window of the carrier which makes it incredibly difficult to see. I didn't see the man sitting with his legs stretched out in the roadway and I'm sure to this day that I accidently drove over his legs as I passed him.

1978

I was involved in a car chase. We got alongside him and my colleague just side swiped the stolen car and ran it off the road.

1975

I went to the local docks with a male colleague as there was report of a man causing a disturbance. When we got there, he was stood close to the drop off into the water waving his arms around calling us all the stupid fuckers. This continued for a few minutes until my colleague wondered over to him and said 'can you swim? The angry man looked at him confused as my colleague pushed him in the chest and into the water. That shut him up.

1982

The wife of a policeman I worked with came into the station one morning to report him missing. We later found out that he hadn't gone missing, he'd taken some RDL's (rest days in lieu) and had gone to Spain with his girlfriend.

1981

When I was promoted to the rank of Sgt I was sent to work in my new post. The first morning I arrived there I overheard the Inspector on the phone saying, 'They've sent me a woman'.

I was also sent to this station in my new role as there had been an issue with 'station stamping' where young policewomen would be forced to have their arse or breasts stamped with the station stamp. They thought that by sending me as a woman Sgt it would put a stop to this behaviour. It didn't happen when I was on duty, but I am aware this 'ritual' occurred in many police stations for years.

1982

We were driving around one night and came across a male and female having a domestic in the street. He was trying to strangle the woman and so he got arrested. When we got him into the police station he kept saying' can I speak please?'. Eventually the custody Sgt said, 'what is it?'. The man lifted his jumper and showed us a broken bottle that was sticking out of his stomach that the woman had stabbed him with. Turns out he was the victim not the offender.

1974

It was the 70's and women police officers weren't issued with handcuffs or batons. I was out on patrol in a panda car and had arrested a male for being drunk and disorderly. I got back into the police station yard and went inside asking one of the policemen to come and help me got my prisoner into the custody suite. He came outside with me and looked in the rear seat of the panda car and said, 'looks like he's done one and run off'. 'Oh no he hasn't' I replied opening the car boot where I'd stuffed him inside. You had to be resourceful.

1985

We used to regularly visit the local pubs when we were walking the beat and just have drink after drink, often ending up drunk at the end of our shifts.

1983

There was a policeman who worked in our station, and he would wear slippers on a night shift and sit in an old wheelchair that someone had found. If a member of the public would come into the front desk at the station, he would wheel himself out in the wheelchair and ask 'how can I help you? You should have seen the looks on their faces.

1980

I would often attend Crown Court where colleagues had typed my evidential statement for me. I would be asked to confirm my name that had been read out to me by the barrister. This name would usually contain several fictitious middle names that the lads would type for me as a joke.

1978

We would regularly pick up known burglars and thieves when we saw them walking around the streets and then drive them miles out of town and dump them off telling them to make their own way home.

1980

We had a Sgt who was a right dickhead so we would glue the balls of paper from the telex machine inside his hat. One of my female colleagues also broke into his office one night and took the Sgt stripes from his police tunic and then sewed them upside down for a laugh.

1972

I was one of the first women in the 'Task Force' who drove round in pale blue and white jeeps. Nowadays this is a unit who deal with public order issues. It was well known with the local criminal fraternity back in the 70's that 'You don't fuck with them'.

1993

I was working as a mounted officer (police horses). I used to 'borrow' the police horses on my rest days or duty days to go to friend's special occasions like weddings and christenings wearing full regalia as a little treat for them. We also attend police funerals, where officers who die either in service or when they have retired can have a full police funeral complete with horses, hearse, coffin with national police flag draped over it and a guard of honour usually done by former colleagues of the deceased officer. On one such occasion I was leading the parade of horses in front of the officer's funeral car. We were trotting along slowly when we were joined by a Scottish piper who proceeded to strike up his bag pipes to accompany us on the final stretch to the crematorium where 100's of former colleagues and family where waiting. What I didn't realise was that the horse I was riding didn't like bag pipes and so when the piper struck up the horse reared back and then bolted with me on it. It galloped towards the waiting congregation who looked horrified as we sped past them nearly knocking them flying. I eventually managed to bring the horse to a halt in the garden of remembrance.

1991

I was 40 and was joining the mounted police and had to take the fitness test. The test comprised of as many sit ups and push ups as you could do in a minute, a standing long jump, a grip strength test and the 'bleep test' where you run in between two static points, probably the width of two tennis courts and just keep running as long as you can, usually until you vomit. Candidates were also subject to a 'body fat test' which is where callipers are used to measure the body fat on the back of your arms, under your bra strap on your back and your stomach. As women have a higher percentage of body fat than men this meant that we would have to do more press up, sits up and run further during the bleep test to offset the fact that we naturally have more body fat. I was determined to pass and so enlisted the help of my male colleagues in the police station who would take me out running and practise other aspects of the fitness test with me. I eventually passed first time. This fitness test is now obselete thankfully.

1981

We used to be called upon to assist with drug searches. I was being tutored by my female colleague at the time who was very switched on. She used to tell me to watch where had already been searched and to not search that area again. This was because male officers would plant drugs during the search and then hope that the WPC would find them. This always looked better in court if the woman found the drugs. Who's not going to believe her?

1973

Pre PACE (The Police and Criminal Evidence Act that was introduced in 1984) we used to have specific cells that were bugged. We would arrest the offenders and then place them in the same cell and then listen in on them. Their statements would then be written for them which they would sign. The offenders made full admissions when they knew we had been listening to their conversations.

1994

There was a very well-known Judge in the Crown Courts who had a massive following. Regulars would come to court and sit and watch as he passed sentence. If offenders knew he was their trial judge, they would often change their pleas last minute to avoid a trial and almost inevitable higher sentence. One day he was passing sentence on a female drug addict who was up before him on yet another shop lifting charge. This was the umpteenth court appearance for this lady who had obviously never been up before this judge before. He passed sentence on her giving her 6 months in custody. She shouted over to him 'I'll do that standing on me fucking head'. He replied, 'In that case I'll make it 12 months, which will give you time to get back on your feet again'.

On another occasion an elderly sex offender was up before the same judge for sentencing. His barrister was putting the man's case forward, and pointed out to the judge that his client was elderly and could your honour consider a sentence in months rather than years. Looking over at the frail man stood in the dock the judge replied '60 months, do as much as you can'.

2010

I worked in the same police station as a male colleague who in the 1970's and 80's had been a member of the dance troop 'hot gossip' and regularly appeared on Top of the Pops. He used to say to the probationers 'I was wearing spandex before you were born'.

1985

I was the only female in the drugs squad and over the course of several months I arrested 6 people for possession with intent to supply. I would be in plain clothes and would get so close to the dealers doing their transactions and made all the arrests. Nobody suspected me because I was a female. I attended all the trials and gave damming evidence against the drugs gang who at the conclusion of the trial all received substantial custodial sentences. The men who oversaw the operation all received commendations for their work. I didn't.

1988

A well-known burglar in our area was back at it. He burgled an elderly lady one night, confronting her while she slept and ripped the wedding ring from her finger. She died not long after this incident and although a partial fingerprint was lifted from her house the lazy CID officer dealing with the job did nothing with it this and the burglar wasn't arrested. I saw this man years later in a custody suite. I ran up to him and kicked him as hard as I could in the balls.

1984

There was a 'rolling road' in our city, built because the tide would come in so high it covered the road. A very strong male Sgt I worked with would blindfold suspects and hold them by their ankles whilst stood on the rolling road, telling them that he couldn't hold on much longer and was going to drop them in the dock. Thinking they were going to drown they were very forthcoming with information about where they had stashed their ill-gotten gains.

1982

Whilst on duty I've met Ken Dodd. He linked arms with me and walked me and my colleague back to his dressing room where we sat and had a glass of sherry from his 'globe' cocktail cabinet. He also gave us tickets for his show along with a tickling stick and a large bag of marshmallows. I had to walk through the city centre on the way back to my station with the tickling stick.

I've met comedian Dave Allen who stopped traffic for me while I was on my foot beat to allow me to cross the road.

I've met Glen Campbell (country singer) who was lovely and signed my pocket notebook.

I've met Tony Christie while on my foot beat and he gave me a ride round in his Rolls Royce and then gave me a lift back to my beat.

1976

I worked in uniform on the same group as a male colleague all the policewomen used to call 'The Moth', because all he did was flutter around the women. He had no idea we all called him this.

1975

I was on my foot beat in the early hours of the morning walking past a local park when I heard a woman screaming. It transpired that she had been raped. I then saw a male, pants around his ankles running from the park. I chased and caught him and arrested him on suspicion of rape. I later found out that the male CID officers the victim had dealt with had talked the woman out of making a complaint by scaring her so much about a future court case. Nothing happened to the man I arrested.

1979

I was working as the BP (bridewell patrol) at the front desk in the police station when a young woman walked in and threw a knife on the counter saying to me 'I've done for him'. It transpired that she had been sexually abused by her own father for years. When the young lady found out that her dad had now started sexually abusing her younger sister, she lost it and stabbed him as she couldn't have it happening to her sister as well as her.

1976

I was working at an old police station on the outskirts of the city. This is now no longer a police station. One of the policemen working on our shift was arrested one day for sexually abusing his own daughter. Thankfully this was investigated properly, and he was sent to prison.

1968

In the same police station, if you paid a 'tanner' or a 'shilling' you could have your dog put down in the gas chamber that was inside the station. One of the officers would do it for you. Due to the police station being next to a very busy road this was quite a regular occurrence.

1988

When you're sent to a report of 'persons on premises', meaning there's a possible burglar reported breaking in somewhere, you usually attend and after a search around you find there is no one there and result the incident with the radio room as 'premises appears correct' or PAC for short. There was a policeman on our shift who was incredibly lazy and would attend every job he was ever sent to with the result 'premises appear correct'. We knew that half the time he didn't even attend the jobs he was sent too. He would merely walk past the jobs he was sent to, wait around for a bit and then result them as PAC. As a result of this we called him PAC Man.

We found a starter pistol that somebody had handed in at the police station and decided to play a prank on the lazy officer. One of the younger policemen who could run very fast got dressed up all in black with a balaclava on took the starter pistol out with him to the bowling green that was next to the police station. We watched the lazy officer (PAC man) walking down the road on his beat and then I made a phone call to the police pretending to be a concerned member of the public. I said that I was a local neighbour and could see a man who had broken into the bowling green. I stayed on the phone to the police and said that I could see an officer right by the bowling green now. The radio operator by this time is on the radio to PAC man directing him into the back of the bowling green. We could see through the window in the police station PAC man creeping down the pathway at the side of the bowling club approaching our colleague who was clad in black stood in the middle of the bowling green. As PAC man reached the bowling green, our colleague raised the starter pistol, pointing it directly at him making threats to him. PAC man shit himself and ran away. What we didn't factor in was that the radio message to PAC man was also heard by several other officers who were hot footing it to the scene. Those officers arrived on scene and ran through to the bowling green and began to chase the intruder (the young policeman). I had to get a patrol car and drive it round to the back of the bowling green and hurriedly collect our young colleague before he got caught. The weird thing is that PAC man arrived back at the station minutes later and didn't say a word.

1978

I went to a domestic dispute in a small, terraced house. When I got there with my male colleague, I managed to separate the couple with no help from my colleague. The man then quickly grabbed an item from the counter and thrust it towards my stomach. This was all pre body armour in the police. I doubled over in pain and thought 'Oh god I've been stabbed'. I reached out and grabbed the first thing that came to hand which was a kettle. I took a swing at the man and clobbered him round the head with the kettle, hitting him several times until he fell on the floor. I straightened up and looked at my stomach. There was no blood. I then saw what I'd been stabbed with. It was a spoon. Throughout this whole fight my male colleague didn't help me at all.

1988

Policewomen used to be made to do a cycling proficiency course as a piss take. You were made to cycle between two police stations that were about 2 miles apart, holding a stop sign that would be used at school crossing patrols. When you reached the station on your pedal cycle you were then subject to being sprayed with a hose pipe to simulate inclement weather.

1976

There was a policeman working on our section who was known as Dr Death. This was because he would willingly volunteer to attend every sudden death that was called in. This went on for years, until another colleague attended the sudden death shortly after Dr Death got there and caught the officer going through the dead woman's purse taking her cash. Then it became clear as to why he always volunteered to go to every sudden death. He'd been taking money from the dead for years.

1975

There was a FMO (force medical officer) who would attend police stations to deal with prisoners and officers who had injuries. If the prisoner had assaulted the police officer who had arrested him, the Doctor would stitch up their wounds with no anaesthetic. The screams from the prisoners were horrific.

1984

I stopped a car that was driving erratically. When I went to speak to the driver, I reached in through the open driver's window and tried to remove the car keys as the driver took off with me hanging out of the car window. I was dragged about 100 yards down the road until I finally fell away from the car.

1988

The first female had applied to go to the dog section. A room had to be converted into a female toilet as there were only male toilets and showers. As part of the physical test when becoming a dog handler for the police you must be able to pick your German Shepherd dog up to be able to do things like lift the dog through a loft hatch during a house search. The training school gave this female officer the biggest and heaviest dog they could find in the hope that she would fail the course. She didn't fail. She managed to pick up the dog and became a very competent dog handler.

2002

I was sat on parade one day when we were joined by the Chief Constable who would often go to random police stations in his force to see how things were going. As usual, the old arse on the group started spouting off about 'how shit the job was' and 'how the wheel was going to come off'. He told the Chief Constable 'How could you possibly know what is going on when you don't come out on patrol with us? To our surprise the Chief Constable agreed to do a night shift with our patrol group the following week. The night arrived and the Chief Con turned up for parade. We all expected that the mouthpiece of the group would partner up with the Chief Con, but to my surprise he refused. This was because in my opinion he was just a 'gob on a stick' who would never follow through with what he was saying'.

One of the younger Constables offered to take the Chief out with him and got him kitted out with a utility belt and a stab vest. During the shift the Chief got stuck in and ended up in a foot chase and caught his own prisoner. The Constable and the Chief made their way to a custody suite with their prisoners. They arrived and had to sit in the holding room with the prisoners before being allowed entry to the custody suite to book their prisoners in. The young Constable was going to buzz through to the custody Sgt's to let them know that the Chief Con was with him, but he was stopped by the Chief who said 'Let's see what happens? What happened was that the pair of them were left in the holding area for over an hour. The Chief could see through the spy hole in the door that the custody Sgt's were having a cuppa and a chocolate muffin with their feet up on the desk, making the officers wait.

When the custody Sgt eventually buzzed the officers through with their prisoners, he apparently shit himself when he saw it was the Chief Constable he had made wait for over an hour. The Chief was apparently not overly impressed, but this was the reality of what officers are faced with daily.

2001

The same Chief Constable said that he wanted to learn to ride horses and contacted the Mounted Section to arrange this. He was told by the Inspector of the mounted section that if he wanted to do this, he should come down to the stables at 7am on a Saturday morning and start by 'mucking out' the horses. He would then be taught about horse management before he would be taken for a riding lesson by one of the instructors. To his credit the Chief continued with this for 6 months, turning up at 7am every Saturday to help before his lessons. I later heard that he learnt to ride and took part in the Lord Mayors Parade. He was a good Chief.

2014

I was working in a child protection unit and delt with a rather odd job. The daughter of this man had come forward to say she had been touched sexually by her father. He was interviewed and completely denied this allegation. On the strength of her evidence, he was charged and eventually appeared at Crown Court. During his evidence he admitted he had knelt on the bed, naked with his daughter lying on top of the bed and had rubbed talcum powder into her body to calm her down. I couldn't believe what I was hearing. This evidence had never come out during the investigation. The problem is that there must be a sexual motive for the offence of sexual assault to be proven. He was saying he was doing this to calm her down. I mean, what father kneels on the bed, naked and does this? The jury returned their verdict of Not Guilty (a unanimous decision). I couldn't believe it, and the barristers on both sides couldn't believe it. That Christmas I received a massive tub of talc for my secret Santa.

2015

I was working in child protection and dealt with another interesting investigation. It was between a father and a daughter. He had a daughter with a previous partner over 20 years before and had not seen her since she was 2 years old. She contacted him through a family friend and the pair met up. It was clear that a short time after they met, there was a physical attraction between the two and they began to have a sexual relationship. Apparently, this can be a common occurrence called genetic sexual attraction. One evening this culminated in an horrific rape, committed by the dad on his daughter. He was arrested and interviewed. He denied all the allegations put to him about the sexual offences he had allegedly committed with his daughter. Throughout the questioning he remained calm denying everything that we asked him about the sexual activity that was alleged to have taken place between them. We then put to him that during the rape, he had used a lubricant to assist him in committing his offence. He went ballistic, shouting and swearing at us that he 'would never use lubricant', 'how dare we say this'. It was very odd. I think it was because we were questioning his masculinity suggesting he would need to use lubricant. He was found guilty by the jury and got 13 years in custody. I got a bottle of lubricant that year for my secret Santa present.

2003

I had to attend a job at a retired social worker's house. The lady was having psychotic episode and believed there were pixies in her loft that were stealing her milk. The problem we had is that she knew the law in relation to mental health with her background in social work. I can only arrest a person under section 136 of the mental health act if they're in a public place. I can then detain them to be sectioned for their own welfare, usually meaning they will be placed on a 28-day section and be medicated and monitored. I could have detained her in the house under section 135, but this would have meant getting a warrant from the courts and this would take time. This lady needed help now.

I managed to entice her out of her house by basically winding her up. She followed me down the path shouting at me and followed me outside onto the pavement where she then punched me in the face. We detained her and got her in the police car. My face hurt, but sometimes you have to take one for the team.

2014

I was working in the Domestic Violence Unit. When categorising victims, we use the colours Gold for serious repeat offender, Silver for moderate offenders and Bronze for new offenders of domestic violence. The lady who rang me was a repeat victim of domestic violence and as I spoke to her, she said 'Hi, I'm a Gold Award'.

1993

One of my colleagues who is sadly no longer with us was involved in a brilliant incident. He stopped a guy in the local park who was wanted on a no bail warrant. This meant that the man would be arrested and taken to a custody suite and then put before the next available court. My colleague gave the man a choice. Either come with me now or I'll give you a 10 second head start to run away from me and if I catch you, you're coming in anyway. The man took the option to run and legged it across the park away from the officer who started to count to 10. My colleague then took off running like the wind after the wanted man, catching him with ease seconds later. He handcuffed the man and took him into custody. This colleague was one of the nicest men I've ever had the pleasure of working with.

1995

I was on my police driving course. For the first 5 weeks I had a civilian instructor who was a lovely man, then for the final week I did my pursuit and response course with a police driving instructor who was a complete dickhead. He took every opportunity to ball me out, shouting at me and basically being a bully. It was obvious that he didn't like policewomen. One day we went to an old airport where a course had been set up for us to drive around. This entailed driving round cones very fast and coming to a controlled stop 'without making your tyres screech'. The test ended with parallel parking as quick as you could. The two boys in my car went first and put on an admirable show. It was then my go and I smashed it, beating the time of my male colleagues by 14 seconds. Then the instructor decided to have a go at the course. He razzed around as fast as he could, desperate to beat the only woman in his car. He even screeched his tyres on the controlled stop. We all commented on this but didn't say anything to him when he finished 8 seconds ahead of my time. None of us mentioned this to him when he got back to us as we didn't want to give him any reason to fail us. I was so glad when this week was over.

I found my police driving course very hard as I got incredibly car sick in the back of the unmarked police car and was often sick on the side of a country road before it was my turn to take the wheel.

1996

I was working on a response group and dealt with an interesting job. A couple who had been married for nearly 50 years were getting divorced because the husband was having an affair with a woman 30 years younger than himself. He and his wife were both in their 70's. He had moved out and was living with his new girlfriend, leaving his wife in their marital home. One day his wife was walking down the road when she saw her soon to be ex-husband on the pavement. They had an argument during which she hit him and ripped from his neck a necklace she had bought him years earlier. She did this in anger, clearly devastated their marriage had come to an end.

I was called to the new girlfriend's house to speak to the husband about the assault committed on him. The girlfriend was the one who had phoned the police and was obviously loving this, winding the husband up so much that he said he wanted to make an official complaint. I took his statement and told him I would follow this up. I then went to their marital home and spoke to the daughters of the couple who were all in their 40's and told them that I would have to arrest their mum for assault and robbery but that I would put the file into the Crown Prosecution Service and request that it be filed as No Further Action as I could see this incident needed some common sense applying to it. I assured them I would do my best.

About a week later, having arrested and interviewed the lady who fully admitted she had hit her soon to be ex-husband out of frustration (it was only a slap) and ripped the chain from his neck because it was something she had bought him for a present and she no longer wanted him to have anything on him that represented her love for him, I submitted this file via the Detective Chief Inspector for him to endorse and send onto the CPS for a charging decision. I had written my NFA recommendations all over it. As I was driving into the police station a few days later I noticed the DCI (detective chief inspector) stood on the back step. He beckoned me over to him and spoke to me about this job. He told me that he wasn't sending this job to the CPS, and that he had made the decision to prosecute the woman for Robbery and Affray. Affray is a violence offence committed by one or more persons which would put other people in the immediate area in fear of their own safety. Robbery is stealing property belonging to another whilst using violence.

I couldn't believe his decision and being 5 years into my service I did question his decision to prosecute, but he wasn't a man to be argued with and told me to do it as soon as possible, telling me to not go back out on patrol until I had completed the charge sheet for the accused lady and put it on his desk ASAP.

You may ask yourself why he made this decision. The simple fact was that it was the end of the month, and he needed his Crime Detections for the month. It's all to do with figures, and he needed to look good at his monthly meetings. This job was 2 detections for violent crime. Never mind that this job just needed a bit of common sense applying to it. I felt completely embarrassed having to ring the lady's daughters and tell them that their mum was going to be prosecuted for Affray and Robbery. They cried on the phone, and I profusely apologised. This was an Indictable Offence (serious, carrying a sentence longer than 6 months) so the lady had to appear at Crown Court to be sentenced. She pleaded guilty and was 'bound over' to keep the peace, which is a very lenient sentence for such charges. She obviously had a very good barrister, and the Judge saw this job for what it really was. The lady would then have had a conviction against her name for the rest of her life.

I had no respect for this DCI after that. He was a prick who continued to rise through the ranks before he retired. He wouldn't even have remembered this job, but I still do, 26 years later!!

1988

I was a new WPC and arrived on my shift to be allocated my tutor constable. Before tutoring me, he has previously tutored a black policeman and a white policeman. His first words to me were 'Oh great. I've had a nigga, a nonce and now they've given me a nympho'.

1989

There was a Sgt on our shift who worked in the custody suite booking in the arrested prisoners. He was known to be a pervert. I was stood with a new female WPC one day in the custody suite when he turned to her and said 'Do you want to walk my snail? She looked confused as he placed a long piece of string on the countertop and said to her 'give it a tug'. She took hold of the string and pulled it. The string was attached to the Sgt's penis that then popped out of his trousers. He did this with all the female recruits, and everyone thought it was funny, apart from the women. We couldn't say anything because you just learnt to keep your mouth shut and take it.

1988

I had finished at Bruche, the central police training establishment and had been sent back to force to begin shifts with my tutor constable. There was a policeman who had also finished his training with me and returned to my station. You get a report written about you by the training Sgt's in Bruche that is sent back to force with you. This policeman's said 'This man spends an inordinate amount of time hanging around the male locker room and showers'. The Sgt's in the station thought this was very funny and told everyone that the policeman was gay. He wasn't gay, he was married with children, but because of the rumours and abuse he received from fellow colleagues he left the police shortly after.

1996

I was being tutored by a male tutor Constable who was an idiot. He had arrested a man for being drunk and disorderly and had put him in the back of the van in the secure cage. Whilst driving to the police station with the prisoner he started to brake hard, causing the prisoner to fall from his seat while handcuffed and bang his head on the cage wall. He continued with this heavy braking all the way to the police station. As we arrived, he said to me, 'he's your prisoner'. I told him to 'fuck off' as I knew what he had been doing. Deliberately braking to make the prisoner get injured. This is a common trick the police do, and I was having no part in it. I said to him 'you can explain to the custody Sgt why your prisoner has injuries'. We didn't get on much after that, but he knew not to take the piss with me.

2010

There was a report of a lad on a stolen pedal cycle, and I was quite close by in my patrol car. As I reached the junction, I could see him riding to my left along the pavement. I don't know what possessed me to do this, but I turned left, mounted the pavement and drove straight at him. He hit the front of the police car and landed in a heap on the pavement and was arrested. I managed to get the police car wedged between the wall and a raised brick flower bed. Still don't know how I got away with that one.

2011

I was working on a foot beat in the city centre, and part of my foot beat was a huge shopping and cinema complex. One afternoon the radio room put a call out that a man and woman had been detained in the cinema having sex. As you can imagine there was a lot of patrols wanting to go to this, mainly because it's very funny. I insisted I go as it was on my beat, but my Sgt also turned up because he knew this was going to be funny. On my arrival, the couple were stood in the foyer. The lady was in her late 50's as was the man. He was smartly dressed, and she was wearing a long fur coat. Taking the usher to one side I asked him what had happened. He explained that a dad and his young son had gone into the afternoon showing of the 'Incredible Mr Fox' and thought they were the only 2 in the cinema. The film started and minutes later the dad heard noises coming from over his shoulder and realised on turning around that there was a couple having sex several rows back from where he was sitting with his child. He left the cinema and made the usher aware of what was going on.

Cinemas nowadays have infrared cameras to spot patrons who make illegal recordings of films to sell. On checking this infrared camera, it had indeed captured the middle-aged couple having sex. I spoke to the detained couple and pointed out what had been seen. The woman was most indignant, denying that anything untoward had taken place between her and her man friend. To set the record straight I told them I would be going to the security office to see the captured footage for myself. The couple were shown sitting next to each other while the woman then proceeded to give the man a 'blow job'. Shortly after, when the man was suitably aroused, he got the woman to sit on his lap while he bounced her up and down. The finish to the film was the man on all fours behind his female companion engaging in a bit of 'doggy style'.

Having viewed this I went back to speak to the couple again, informing them that I had just watched her give him a blow job, then the pair of them have sex. The woman was still shouting 'How dare you say that'. She then said, 'I wasn't giving him a blow job, I had dropped my M and M's in his lap and was picking them up'. I said to her 'were you picking them up one at a time? I had heard enough and arrested the pair of them for outraging public decency. At the custody suite the pair continued to protest their innocence. Even after the interview, during which I played the footage that had been captured they were still having none of it.

I decided to tell them that I would be going to their respective home addresses to verify who they were before they were charged with the offence of outraging public decency. This is a common practise with prisoners. I would like to point out that the couple lived a considerable distance apart from each other. The pair suddenly changed their tune and admitted they were having an affair and accepted a 'caution'. This remains one of the funniest jobs I've ever been sent to.

2010

I was working on shift with an incredibly funny policeman, and we loved working together. It was late in the evening and there was a stolen car razzing around the city centre. As we had both recently completed our 'Stop Stick' (stinger) course we shouted up to the radio room that we would head down to the main road leading out of the city to deploy the stop stick and puncture the stolen vehicle's tyres.

We arrived at the main road and got the stop sick out of the boot. These are elongated pieces of metal on a bungee that has spikes on it to puncture the car tyres. The road was quiet, and I could hear the approaching police sirens chasing the car. I threw the stop stick into the road with as much strength as I could and then quickly ran back to safety behind a wall. As I was running, I could see the stolen car and police car approaching. They quickly raced past our location as we waited for the explosion of car tyres. It was then that I realised I'd got the stop stick caught on my shoe and as I ran to safety behind the wall, I had dragged it back across the road with me. Me and my colleague couldn't stop laughing.

2010

I always used to dress up in the occupier's clothes for a laugh when we did a search warrant. My funniest outfit was a dress, complete with hat and handbag. We always put everything back afterwards, but it lightened the mood.

2009

I was sat in the front passenger seat of a police carrier. I was the only woman in the van, with a male driver and several male colleagues in the back of the van. As we were driving along one of the men said, 'Can you pass me ......' and held his hand out behind him to receive the item he had asked a colleague for. I then heard him say 'That's your dick, isn't it? One of my colleagues had put his penis in the outstretched hand offered to him. When you see a police carrier on your travels please don't panic because they are more than likely just messing around.

2009

I was sat in the Constable's writing room with my head buried in a prisoner file when a request came over the tannoid for me to go and speak to one of the Sgt's. I didn't immediately move and remained sat down typing as one of the policemen in the room with me said, 'I've shagged her' meaning me. I remained sat listening, as he went on about his escapades with me for a good few minutes. He obviously had no idea who I was and was a complete liar because I'd never met him let alone shagged him. After a few minutes I stood up and introduced myself to him. His face was a picture as I pointed out to him and his fellow male officers that he had never shagged me and that he was a big dickhead.

2007

Shortly after the London bombings in 2007 I arrived at my police station early one morning to find a probationer policeman sat at the entrance to the police station with a clip board. He stopped me as I went to drive in, taking my name and my vehicle details. I thought this was a bit odd but let him get on with it. I was taking over from him as the station officer that morning as he had been working the night shift. Minutes later he walked into the front office to brief me holding an old drainpipe with a car wing mirror sellotaped onto it. He proceeded to tell me that he had been checking underneath all the cars in the carpark overnight, making a note of their registration numbers and vehicle details, and that I would have to do the same during my day shift. I looked at him like he was stupid and said 'They're taking the piss out of you. I am not going round the carpark with an old piece of drainpipe with a cracked wingmirror sellotaped onto it' He refused to believe this was true and thought he was part of some big terrorist plot. I eventually told him to 'fuck off' and go home to bed.

2011

I was working in the 'licensing department' where you would dress smartly and visit pubs and clubs in the city centre identifying hot spots for violence, making sure the clubs had the right alcohol licenses and occasionally applying to the council to shut a venue down because of excessive noise/violence on the premises. One Saturday night early on I visited a Lap dancing bar with my Sgt, or a 'lappy bar' as it was more commonly known. He was busy chatting to the licensee, and I got talking to the lap dancers who were stood around the pole practising their moves. They are amazing ladies, very fit and athletic. I asked them I if I could 'have a go' on the pole and they agreed, teaching me how to run at the bar, twirl round and then go upside down. After ten minutes I was like a pro and they thought it was hysterical that a 'bizzie' was pole dancing. My Sgt was less than impressed when he saw me hanging upside down.

2022

The CID departments are decimated in our force. CID Officers have applied for and have been posted to other departments within our force but are unable to be let go from their existing department as there is no one to replace them. Retired detectives have been called back to work as civilian investigators due to the lack of CID officers and it will only get worse.

Every week we have an e mail called 'orders', which details the comings and goings of different officers and new legislation that we must read. Every week there are more and more officers resigning and retiring, and there's very few new recruits replacing them.

There are specific teams set up within CID to deal with GUN crime. These officers work 8am-4pm Monday to Friday because obviously no gun crime happens after 4pm or at the weekend. Officers continually 'shaft' each other by arranging for gun nominals to be arrested at 3.45pm and then going off duty leaving the prisoners to be dealt with by Main Office CID departments who are already understaffed and over worked.

When uniform officers arrest a suspect a 'score' sheet as to the severity of the crime is filled out. Officers will continually over score offences when filling out this paperwork, meaning it will be passed to the CID to deal with it. For example, a male arrested in possession of 4 very small wraps of cocaine. This would normally be for his or her own personal use and would be classed as possession of a controlled drug. Officers are over scoring these offences as possession with intent to supply. Officers are also arresting these suspects, then illegally going through the suspects phone stating there were messages on the phone consistent with the officer being involved in the supply of controlled drugs. The officers then over classify this arrest as possession with intent to supply, meaning it now must be dealt with by CID officers who are already carrying a huge workload. These uniform officers are 'gung-ho' and it's only a matter of time before civil litigation suits are brought against them for unlawfully accessing a person's phone. I've tried to tell them, but they won't listen.

Prior to being in the CID I worked my time in uniform and I loved my job. If you were in the middle of a meal break and an emergency job came out, you would put down your food and go. I now listen in to my police radio and hear numerous unanswered jobs daily, with uniform officers refusing to attend as they are eating or doing their paperwork. Their Sgt's aren't even pulling them up on this. The police really has gone to shit.

2022

Uniform attended a report of a male who had been attacked by his ex's partner. The man had been hit numerous times with a baseball bat and this assault was captured on CCTV. The officers attended and arrested the offender at his home address but didn't search his house or car for the bat used in the offence. This incident was then handed to CID the following morning with loads of outstanding enquiries to be completed because lazy uniform officers couldn't be bothered.

I arranged for the offender's house to be searched the following day. The keys for his car couldn't be found and we knew the bat used in the assault was in the car. On the 'Ring' doorbell the officer could be seen loading the offender's car on to the back of a tow truck and then putting the car keys in his own pocket. The officer then went home and was on 'rest day' for 2 days and I couldn't get hold of him to retrieve the car keys to get in the car and recover the bat.

The offender was interviewed and said 'no comment' as we had no evidence of the bat because we couldn't get in his car which was being held securely. As a result, we had to bail the offender, which then gives them time to intimidate the witness who will then drop the complaint, all because uniform officers who attended couldn't be bothered to do a proper job in the first place.

2022

Weeks ago, again our CID office had to deal with another job handed to us by uniform. A 77-year-old man was arrested for threats to kill his next-door neighbour. The incident had happened 'the day before' when the neighbour arrived home from work and the old man shouted out of his window that he was going to kill him. Neighbour rings the police who don't attend until the following day. There's no immediate threat as the threat was made the day before and not carried out. Another monumental uniform job!!

1999

There is a gay area in the city centre with numerous gay bars and clubs. The alley behind the clubs was known as 'sausage alley' because there was always so many gay men either shagging or sucking each other off when you walked down it.

2002

I had attended a domestic incident and had arrested the male offender for assault. At the police station when he was being booked in by the custody Sgt he made threats to his own life and so was placed on 'con obvs' (constant observations). With Con Obvs you must sit outside the open cell door with the prisoner inside, usually they are dressed in a safety blanket.

This day there were no male civilian custody assistants available to sit with my prisoner, so the task fell to me. I sat on a chair outside his open cell door. The prisoner stood in front of me calling me terrible names like 'fucking bitch'. He then started to masturbate holding his penis and shouted at me 'look at this'. He continued to masturbate until he ejaculated all over the cell floor. Obviously by this time I had called the custody Sgt to make him aware of what had happened. The prisoner was then arrested for a public order offence due to him masturbating in front of me.

223

He appeared at court some weeks later and pleaded guilty. As part of his punishment/rehabilitation the magistrate ordered that he should apologise to me face to face. I refused to do this and pointed out 'would you ask a female member of the public who had been sexually assaulted to meet their abuser? The magistrates agreed they had made a bad decision asking this of me.

2003

There was a couple on our division who were always having domestics. I lost count of the number of times we got sent to this address to break up fights. One day me and a male colleague attended this address again. We could hear shouting and screaming coming from inside the house and no matter how hard we banged on the door they wouldn't open it. My colleague eventually kicked the door down and we got inside. He went straight over to the male offender who was pushing his wife around and picked him up, turning him upside down. I remember the prisoner had really big pointy teeth like a vampire and my colleague shouted at him as he put him in the cage of the van upside down 'next time Dracula, open the fucking door'.

2003

Another domestic I attended was in quite a rough area. We got into the house and the couple were really going at it, shouting and screaming at each other with the man grabbing at his partner. Me and my colleague took hold of the man and were wrestling with him on the floor trying to get him handcuffed. The woman obviously then decided that she didn't want her partner arresting and jumped on my back trying to pull me off her boyfriend. She was screaming down my ear 'let him go, he's me world'. I then had to turn my attentions to her, and after a struggle managed to handcuff her. As we lead them both from the house the woman screamed 'I rang you for help'. My colleague screamed back at her 'This is help. If you don't want it, then don't ring us.'

2002

When I was working in uniform, our section would meet up in the local park at 3am on nights to play on the swings.

2004

At our local police station, we had a civilian BP (bridewell patrol) officer who would answer the phones and the front desk enquiries. We all used to pop in for a brew when our shift was on and sit and chat with her. We used to prank her all the time. If a customer came into the front desk for advice, she would go out to speak to them. Just as she reached the front counter, we would press the emergency shutter on the front desk which would cause a heavy metal shutter to shoot up from the front desk right in front of her making her scream.

There was also a life size cardboard cut-out of a policeman we worked with for a PR stunt that was in the front office of the police station. We used to get the cut out and hide it in the female toilets and turn the lights out then wait for the her to go to the toilet. She always used to scream when she walked in and switched the lights on.

2002

I was dealing with a domestic incident with a colleague one day. The domestic was on the pavement right in front of us and the couple were pushing each other around calling each other all the twats going. I got out with my colleague to grab the male who was the aggressor, but he wasn't coming quietly. We ended up rolling around on the pavement with him and when I eventually got up, I was covered in dog shit.

2014

I had to interview a sex offender for a horrendous rape on a female. The lady in question had alleged that she had been 'fisted' (fist forced up her vagina) during this ordeal by the male. During the interview the male denied doing any kind of 'fisting'. Then his solicitor, quite an old fella got involved asking how it was possible to 'fit a fist up there' and demonstrated this by making a punching motion in the air. It was so difficult to keep a straight face as he's sat there punching the air several times. I pointed out to the ignorant solicitor that I had had two children, and it is quite natural for a vagina to expand enough to fit a baby's head out. That shut him up.

2016

I was working in child protection and was out on enquiries with my colleague. Every job we went to always seemed to turn to shit. On this evening, she asked me to go with her to get a couple of statements for a 'baby shaking' job she was dealing with. I agreed thinking what could go wrong? When we got to the house it was minging. I went into the back room with a witness to get his statement. The room was bare apart from a rusty old wheelchair. He asked me if I wanted to sit down and pointed to the wheelchair, I refused, taking this statement at record speed. I then went into the front room where my colleague is sat in a haze of cigarette smoke, several family members all smoking stood around her, as well as a couple of small dogs pottering around. I motioned to her to get a bloody move on. What I didn't know was that halfway through taking her statement from a different family member, a young child had snatched the paper statement from her and had taken off with it, running around the house. She had eventually retrieved it and sat down again on the couch. I watched as the young child, who was kneeling in front of my colleague appeared to be playing with something on the floor, rolling it around. He then let go of what he was rolling around which I then realised was dog shit and wiped both of his hands down my partners trousers. She was trying not

226

to flinch, and I was trying not to laugh. I remember looking up at the small crappy glass chandelier they had hanging in the living room and wondering what the brown substance was dripping from it. Turns out it was nicotine.

We left the house stinking of cigarette smoke and with me telling her she now owed me big time for this.

2014

Another job in child protection. I went to speak with an elderly man to let him know that an allegation had been made against him of historic sexual abuse. He lived in flats and had come down to answer the door. I didn't want the world knowing his business so said I would speak to him in his flat. I followed him up the stairs a couple of steps behind him when he farted in my face.

2014

Me and a colleague had to go to prison to interview a prisoner about historic sex abuse allegations. Prior to going into the prison, we popped into a pub that was literally next to the prison. There was nothing else for miles around, and we only went in for soup and a sandwich and a soft drink. I popped to the toilet before we left noticing the yellow and black hazard tape on the floor indicating a small step. On coming back, I said to my colleague 'be careful you don't fall'. She came back a few minutes later informing me that she had indeed fallen down the small step and had gone over on her ankle which immediately started to swell up. We left the pub and went to the prison to do the interview, returning to the police station some hours later. By this time her foot had swelled up to the size of an elephant's foot which we both thought was very funny.

I had to borrow a crutch to get my colleague up in the lift to our office where we told everyone what had happened. We had a bitch of a Sgt who made a right meal out of the fact we had gone in a pub for lunch. Going to great pains to say she had 'sorted it' and for us not to do that again. What pissed me off about this was that a male officer from our office had gone on enquiries down south the week before and had done the same thing by going to a pub for lunch and nothing was said to him. This Sgt just wanted to flex her muscles. No one had any respect for her. My colleague who was signed off by her GP for two weeks with torn ligaments in her foot was also forced to come back to work as it had been 'her fault' she had fallen, and arrangements were made to pick her up and take her home after the shift.

2014

We had to interview a lady who was making allegations of historic sexual abuse from the 1970's. She was quite a large lady who wore inappropriately tight-fitting T shirts with cats on them and spent the whole interview telling us 'I were born with a club foot'. She just kept shouting that out. The job went nowhere.

2013

I split my pants in the office one day and one of the male officers kept chasing me round with a camera, trying to get a photograph of my knickers.

2014

Whilst working in the CID there was a detective on our section who would say he was 'going out on enquiries', then 30 minutes later post on Facebook that he was in Costa coffee. Big mug of flat white sat on the table while he was obviously just sat in the coffee shop, and nothing was ever said to him by supervision.

2017

I worked with a right head worker in CID. She put in a special shift request to work different hours because of childcare so would start her shift an hour earlier and finish an hour before everyone else. So, 7-5pm instead of 8-6pm or 12-10pm instead of 1-11pm. When we eventually got a Sgt with some backbone who questioned her about this the officer replied, 'well I don't like finishing at 6pm or 11pm because I don't like getting home that late'. Again, nothing was done about this. She left early one day and said she had an appointment and was going in her own car and then going straight home after. This wasn't an unusual thing to do. She turned up the following day with a completely different hairstyle. She had obviously finished work early to go and get her hair cut. Again, nothing was done about this. She now works as a trainer of new police officers... God help them!!! This is what happens in the police. If somebody is crap, they get moved on, to work in a different department. At least she's away from investigations because she was useless. Oh, and she recently got promoted to the rank of Sgt, to work with officers who are on restricted duties. You seriously couldn't make this up.

2013

Whilst working in child protection I assisted a colleague with a job she had. A lady had come forward saying she had been sexually assaulted by her grandfather who was in his 90's. What then came to light is that she had been blackmailing him for years, and when his cash finally ran out, she made a complaint to the police because she wanted to get CICA (criminal injuries compensation), which can run into the £1000,s for sexual assaults. She was even talking about all the holidays she was going to book with the cash she would receive. We didn't have a lot of evidence from the lady involved but had to invite her grandfather in for an interview anyway. It was basically going to be one word against another. He declined to have a solicitor present and started to talk to us. During the interview he started admitting to sexual offences against his granddaughter that hadn't even come to light. Things that even she hadn't remembered. He was convicted and eventually died in prison. She got her money from CICA as expected and no doubt went on all of her holidays.

2015

My colleague was doing a video recorded interview with a child. These are conducted in a room designed to put the victim at ease, usually with couches and a table. I was acting as 'tech' sitting behind the 2-way glass screen making notes. It wasn't until we were 20 minutes into the interview that I realised I hadn't pressed record on the machine. I hurriedly knocked on the door and ushered my colleague outside to tell her my 'fuck up'. She eventually laughed about this after calling me a dick head and had to go through the whole interview again.

2017

I had to produce a child sex offender from prison and then interview him about the horrific rape of another very small child. At the time there was a solicitors strike on and try as he might, the custody Sgt could not get hold of a solicitor to represent this man. He decided to just come into the interview without legal representation and speak to me. This was because I had taken the time to ask how he was and shown an interest in his life and he thought I was his friend. Truth be told I couldn't have given less of a shit about him, but if I start behaving like an idiot, he's not going to talk to me, so I put on the smiles and made him a cup of tea and we sat down to chat.

During the interview he described to me and my colleague in graphic detail how he raped the small child. Hearing this was honestly one of the worse things I have ever heard. I asked him what it was about a child that he found arousing and he looked at me and said, 'no one has ever asked me that before'. He then thought about it and said, 'it's their little bums when they're running around naked'. Although what you are being told by these paedophiles is terrible it is also very intriguing to get a glimpse into their world and to try and understand why they do what they do to children. I don't think I'll ever understand it. I get the feeling sometimes that the offenders want to get things off their chest. They have been carrying around this terrible secret for years and finally it's out, and in some respects it's a relief for them. My primary concern for getting a paedophile to admit what he's done is that the child won't have to be cross examined in Crown Court. New measures have been brought in to assist the children who are cross examined via a video link, with a set of pre agreed (by the judge) questions. Although things are a lot better for child victims nowadays with 'special measures' where barristers remove their wigs and gowns, it's still a massive ordeal for children to be cross examined. If investigations with paedophiles means spending a couple of hours being nice to them and making him a brew, then I'll do it. For anyone who is interested he did plead guilty at crown court and got 20 years in custody.

After this interview and returning the suspect back to prison I returned to the office with my colleague. We were both in shock with what we had just heard. Most paedophiles either give you a 'no comment' interview or completely deny the allegations you put to them. We had been sat there for a few minutes when our Inspector came into the room and told us to go to the local children's hospital and meet two parents who had to formally identify their dead child. My colleague pointed out that we had just been sat in an horrific interview with a paedophile and asked if somebody else could go. We were told to 'Just do as you're told'. I didn't have a lot of respect for that Inspector after this day, and yes, we did both go and sit with the parents of a dead child while they sat and cried. It's hard being a child protection officer. You see and hear things that most police officers let alone members of the public don't see and hear. You can only really talk to your colleagues in the office you work in about things that get you down. You can't be putting the terrible things you see on your wife, husband or partner when you get home.

It's only when I retired that it all came crashing down for me a few years later. I was cutting up a cooked chicken one day at home and had to cut through the string holding the legs of the chicken together. At this precise moment an image came into my head of an indecent video of a child I had had to view one day in work. The image was of a small female child whose wrists were tied to her ankles, and she was being raped by an old man. It was horrific at the time I was categorising them years before, but you just got on and did your job. Now I was retired I had time to think. 'I wonder what happened to that child. I went to pieces crying and sobbing and realised at that moment I needed help. I can't fault the police and counselling service for the retrospective help I received about the trauma I was dealing with, but maybe counselling should be given to officers on a regular basis when they are working in these departments. It's the same with everything nowadays, cutbacks mean counselling has stopped.

I'm immensely proud of what I achieved during my time in the child protection department, and I hope I did make a difference in the children's lives.

2016

An officer had sadly been killed in our force one year. There was a female officer working in a totally different division to him who didn't know the deceased officer. She moved to the division he had been working in over a year later and suddenly went off work with 'stress'. This was because she was so distraught over the death of this officer..... that she didn't know. The job allowed her to retire and claim her pension as well as an injury pension because she had PTSD because this officer had died. I know that sometimes it's good to get rid of dead wood, but she was totally taking the piss.

2017

I dealt with a paedophile who was contacting children through their games consoles and chatting to them. He would then send indecent images of himself and ask them to do the same, which all of them did. These children were aged between 7 and 12 years old and the man was 20. It came to light when we interviewed the children that they all said the same thing 'he had a mole above his willy'. I had remembered years earlier watching a documentary on Michael Jackson and remembered that he had photographs taken of a distinguishing mark near his penis. My colleague rang our legal department, and we could indeed take photographs of this suspects penis, by force if necessary. I contacted the SOCO (scenes of crime) department and arranged for a SOCO to come and take the pictures. It was so hard not to laugh, getting the suspect to pose with no underpants on, legs apart. He did indeed have a identifying mole right above his penis. His willy was so small it was like a walnut whip. He got convicted months later for causing a child to be involved in sexual acts. For Christmas I bought my colleague a new mouse mat, with a walnut whip on it.

2016

I was working in a firearms department and me and my colleague were tasked with stopping a sex offender when his car landed in our division. We waited patiently and saw his car emerge from the tunnel and pulled him over. I got him out of his car and sat him in the back of the police vehicle while my colleague went to have a look in his car. My colleague returned a few minutes later holding what I can only describe as a silver sparkly Michael Jackson glove. He asked the paedophile what the glove was and got the reply, ' It's my vibrating masturbating glove'. I noticed my colleague wasn't wearing gloves. 'Why is it wet? Asked my colleague, to which the man replied, 'I like to urinate before I orgasm'.

2018

A colleague of ours was conducting a child video interview. These are usually done in a room that is decked out like a comfy living room with an adjoining room where a second officer will sit behind two-way glass and make notes for the interviewing officer. My colleague was coming to the end of her interview and stood up to leave the room and speak to her colleague and see if she had any further questions. What my colleague didn't realise is that because she had been sat on her leg during the lengthy interview, it had gone dead, and she stumbled and fell into the wall by the door. Even the little boy being interviewed laughed.

2005

I was asked to attend a possible break in at the Carphone warehouse. I pulled up, got out to check, had a look in through the front window and it all appeared correct. There was no way I could get around the back of the shop, so I resulted the job as 'premises appear correct'. I found out when I came on duty the following day that the burglars had got into the car phone shop through the roof and had cleared the shop out.

1998

I was in my probationary period but was out on foot patrol on my own when I attended a report of a man with an air rifle in a disused building. When I got there, I found the man and spoke to him. He did indeed have an air rifle and was struggling to remove the safety catch on it, so I showed him what to do and removed the safety. I then offered to show the man it was working just fine and took aim through an open window at a tree, firing and blowing the head clean off a magpie sitting in a tree. I then handed the gun back to him and left, feeling pleased with myself that I'd helped a member of the public. I got back to the station and told my Sgt what I'd done and got a right bollocking from him. Apparently, there were loads of firearms offences this man had committed, and I had basically aided and abetted him.

2016

I had to deal with a report of rape, child on child and was working in the child protection unit at the time. The 12-year-old boy accused of this rape lived at home with his seven other siblings and they all looked similar. I knew that the rape allegation was going to be very hard to prove, but on top of this the social worker allocated to this family was mental. She constantly rang me in work saying that the 12-year-old suspect and his 13-year-old brother had swapped identities in school and were in the wrong year. She had a proper bee in her bonnet about this and wanted to meet with the family who spoke no English. I wasn't particularly bothered if they had swapped years, because at least they were in school. I arranged for an interpreter to attend with me, a colleague, and the social worker.

We all sat in mum and dad's front room and chatted about the children. The 12-year-old boy had been caught in school watching pornography in the school library which had been witnessed by other students in school, and this was brought up in the conversation by then social worker, to the boy's parents. They looked at her confused as the interpreter attempted to decipher what the social worker was saying. She then repeated 'your son was seen MASHUATING in school'. I could see my colleague's shoulders starting to shake as she stifled a laugh. Again, she repeated that he had been 'mashuating' until I butted in and said, 'Look he was playing with his willy in school'. The parents looked horrified, denying their son had done this. The conversation carried on as I looked around the front room and tried to work out what the hell was going on with the wallpaper. It appeared that the mother of the boy had gone to the same wallpaper shop on numerous occasions and rather than buy a roll of paper, she had taken a 2-foot sample each time she had gone and then returned home where she had pinned the samples to the wall with drawing pins.

The result for this job was that we never did establish if the boys had swapped years in school and the rape allegation didn't go anywhere. I submitted the girl's underwear for analysis, and it sadly turned out that she had 5 different types of semen in her underwear, none of which matched the phantom school wanker.

2016

My friend and colleague who worked in a different office in our building used to come into our office when I was out on enquiries and go through my diary adding things like 'anal bleaching' and 'back, sack and crack' to my daily enquiries. This was interesting when I was asked what appointments I had during the day on our morning briefing.

2006

I was working in a drugs squad and one day we executed a warrant at a hoarder's house. I remember searching the fridge and seeing it was full of bottles of piss. I picked one of the bottles up as I had noticed there was something weird floating on top of it. As I was looking at it, the male house holder shouted over at me, 'LEAVE MY BABIES ALONE'. Turns out the weirdo had been wanking into the bottles of piss, and the stuff floating on the top of the urine was in fact semen.

2017

I attended the Manchester Arena bombing. It was carnage when we got there. I walked into the foyer and saw a child blown in two on the floor. She was obviously dead. I noticed next to her by her hand was a mobile phone and the screen continually lit up with the word 'Daddy'.

The day after the bombing we all paraded on for work in the firearms unit. The mood was very sombre, and we were asked to meet with the force therapist. She had no idea we had all been to the bombing the night before and was horrified that we were on duty the following day. She recommended that we were all suspended from duty awaiting an evaluation of our mental health due to the horrors we saw. This never happened. It couldn't because it would have meant a whole section getting wiped out. We just got on with it.

2013

I went to deal with a sudden infant death with a colleague. I had just returned from maternity leave and when we got there and saw the dead infant, she looked just like my new-born daughter. The public don't realise this when we attend these jobs, but this one really affected me.

1985

I was in the large old police station in the city centre. As I'm dealing with my prisoner one of my colleagues said 'Do you want to see our Christmas Tree? I looked at him confused as he opened the large wooden door that was in the cell area. There was a scrawny looking drug addict handcuffed to the door with tinsel and lights on his head.

2001

I was driving around the city centre in a police van with my tutor constable when a drunk man banged loudly on the side of the police van. My colleague did a U turn in the van and drove up slowly behind this drunk and put his arm out of the police van. As we reached the drunk, he slapped him hard on the back of the head and shouted, 'Don't slap my van'. Then we drive away leaving the man rubbing his head.

2001

We were again driving around the city centre one night in a large yellow carrier when I noticed a drunk stood directly in front of our van. He held his arms up to stop the police van and my colleague ran straight over him. Nothing happened to the man. Once the van drove slowly over him, he picked himself up and walked off down the road.

2003

My nickname in work was either Big tits or Bangers.

2016

I phoned a woman to give her result for the investigation I was dealing with when she said to me 'You live by the saw, you die by the saw'. I didn't have the heart to tell her it was sword and not saw.

2017

I went with a colleague to the local hospital A and E department where a young teenager had been brought in as he'd overdosed on heroin and alcohol and had died. We were taken to the cubicle he was in, the oxygen mask still attached to his face, his body now lifeless. I had noticed when we arrived at the hospital that there were about 40 people stood outside and had a feeling they were something to do with the death of this young man. I was correct as they were his immediate family and loads of extended family. Suddenly the curtain moved, and we were greeted by a weeping mum and dad. I offered my condolences and put my hand on theirs. There was paperwork we also needed to complete so I set about doing that as suddenly more family began to trapse through the cubicle gawping at the lifeless teenager. It all came to a head when a young mother came into the cubicle carrying her 5-year-old child, who on seeing his dead 'uncle' began to scream hysterically. I asked her what she was doing bringing a small child into the cubicle. She replied, 'he needs to see him'. I pointed out her child does not need to see things like this and ushered her out. I ended up shouting at the family and refusing to let anyone else in apart from his parents. In my opinion they were just coming in to gawp at him and I wasn't having it.

2009

I was called to deal with a fight in town. There I was rolling around on the floor with this drunken male when suddenly I noticed a retired colleague I used to work with. He was carrying a tray of chips and gravy and was on his way home. He saw me, came over, put his chips down in the road and said, 'Ay up chuck' and then punched the man hard in the face knocking him out. He then picked his chips back up and carried on home. I handcuffed the man and took him to the station. Months later the drunk man had made a complaint of assault as his nose had been broken. I was interviewed by the police professional standards department who had viewed the grainy CCTV and asked me who the mystery man was who had assisted me. I told them I had no idea and said he was just a random member of the public who had come to assist me. I didn't hear anything more about this.

1994

We used to get taxi's that would pull up outside the police station and frantically honk their horns. I went outside with a colleague one evening when this happened to see what the problem was. As usual it was a problem punter refusing to pay for his taxi fare. Rather than tie the taxi driver up taking a statement from him about 'making off without payment', we got the punter out of the back of the cab and tipped him upside down making the money fall from his pockets. I asked the cabby how much the fare was, and got that money for him, along with a little tip. By this time the drunk had started kicking off, so he just got arrested for being drunk and disorderly. Job sorted.

1995

I was working a night patrol in the summer, so it was light by 4am. I was due off at 7am and at 6.30am while driving down the road I suddenly became aware of a woman running down the road after my police car. I stopped to speak to her, and she was hysterical saying her baby was dead. I ran into their house and up the stairs to find the baby lying dead on a dirty bed. I remember the bed was full of tools like you'd use in a garage. The child was so dirty, like it had been in a house fire, and it was obvious looking at the child that it had been neglected. The house was chaotic with several other undressed children running around with full nappies. I tried to do mouth to mouth on the child and requested an ambulance, but it was all to no avail as the child had obviously been dead for some time. In the back garden there were a couple of couches and the remnants of a bonfire from the night before. The garden was also littered with empty cans of lager. I thought that both parents were still drunk. A post-mortem was carried out on the baby and nothing suspicious was found. My theory is they left their child outside all night and only realised in the morning when it had died and brought it inside the house. You'll never prove it though, and nothing ever happened to the parents.

1992

I was continually getting told off for using prisoner blankets for the dogs in the police kennels. I'd much rather have given the blankets to the dogs.

2017

I was working in child protection and dealt with a terrible job. A woman was seeing this new boyfriend, and they had a very violent relationship where he would constantly abuse and hit her. Alcohol also played a very large part in the relationship. One evening after a drunken argument he left the house and returned a few hours later having drunk a bottle of vodka. He went up the stairs and into the child's bedroom where he then performed a sex act on the child. The child woke up, screamed, which alerted mum who came into the room. She realised something was terribly wrong and threw him out of the house. The child admitted to mum that mum's boyfriend had touched her.

He gets arrested and answers 'no comment' to every question. I sent the child's underwear off for analysis which contained his DNA. I re-arrest him and he admits everything but says he was drunk and thought he was performing a sex act on his partner. He eventually goes to court and pleads guilty with the mitigation that he didn't realise it was a child in bed with him and gets a suspended prison sentence. I could not believe this. The only way a suspended prison sentence can be activated and the offender goes to prison, is if the offender commits a further offence within the time limit of the suspended sentence.

I made it my mission to send him to prison. I knew he was staying in a hostel and kept in contact with the staff there to check up on this man. I found out some months later that he had been involved in a fight in the hostel where he had punched another male that was living there. I found the man he had been in a fight with and persuaded him to give me a statement of complaint. Then I arrested the 'sex offender' for assault which put him in breach of his suspended sentence. He went straight to prison. Sometimes you have to think outside the box.

Thinking that was the end of this case I was contacted over a year later by a family member who told me that the mother of this child was secretly meeting up with the now released from prison sex offender who had sexually assaulted her own daughter!! They were meeting in a hotel in the city for sex. Obviously, I was livid about this, predominantly because how could you want to have anything to do with him after what he did to your child. I spent time one afternoon just visiting hotels in a certain area asking if they had checked in. I found the hotel. They had indeed checked in on several occasions, often having drunken arguments with each other in reception. I took a statement from the hotel manager and then informed social services and whoever else I could think of. I hope the woman got her children removed from her as my opinion of her is she is totally unfit to be a mother.

2009

I was working in a drugs team, and we were clearing up at the end of the day after doing a drugs warrant earlier that day and seizing a quantity of cocaine. We were filling all the exhibit bags in and booking the drugs and cash we seized into the property system. As it was the end of the day, and we were having a cup of tea and a donut while filling out this paperwork. A few minutes later, one of my colleagues said, 'I feel a bit weird'. He then realised that the powder on his desk that he had mopped up with his finger had not been sugar coating from his donut, it was in fact cocaine that had spilled from one of the exhibits. We had to give him a lift home!!

2007

When I was working on a drugs team we would often execute warrants at premises that were being used to grow cannabis plants. Some of the houses had hundreds of fully mature plants in them and on a sunny day you could see the spores filling the air. Half the time you left those jobs high as a kite with all the cannabis you'd breathed in.

2008

I executed a drugs warrant with my colleagues on a house known to have several drug addicts living there. Once you've forced the front door open you must get inside quickly, and to the different rooms as soon as possible to stop the householders from flushing the gear away down the toilet or throwing it out of windows etc. This day we got in the house fast. I ran through to the back kitchen where I found one of the drug addicts, a man, frantically injecting himself in the arm with a dirty syringe full of heroin. I tried to stop him, but it was too late. His eyes rolled back in his head, and he slumped back into the chair, the dirty needle still hanging from his arm. I caught him before he fell on the floor and called for an ambulance via our radio room. Luckily, he didn't go into cardiac arrest, and I stayed with him until he was taken to hospital. Turns out he was wanted on warrant and panicked when the door went in realising it was the police, so took as much heroin as he could before being arrested. The house was so bad and was obviously being used as a drugs den. I ended up doing a 'crack house closure notice' for this address and evicted the tenants some weeks later.

2003

I was working nights near Christmas time with a male colleague and said to him 'I've never done a handbrake turn'. He decided to teach me how to do this as it was a quiet night. We drove to a huge empty carpark. The ground was frosty white as I sped up along the car park. Just as I was going quite fast, he says 'right, turn the wheel and pull the handbrake on'. I turned the wheel to the left as he quickly grabbed the handbrake and wrenched it upwards causing the car to go into a massive spin. We spun around three or four times on the carpark before coming to a stop. It was so much fun, so I did it another few times to get the hang of it. You couldn't do that now with all the GPS on the police cars. The radio room would be able to see you on their little screens pulling donuts in the carpark.

2002

I was a probationary constable, and I was at the custody suite dealing with my prisoner. When you have booked your prisoner into custody you make your way to the Constables writing room to complete your paperwork. As I went into the writing room there were four male colleagues messing around. One of them asked me if I wanted to play 'human cannonball' which when explained to me was a game where you would sit in a wheely chair then push yourself backwards off the photocopier using your feet and see how far back you could go. This particular policeman explained that he was the reigning champion and offered to demonstrate while I watched. He lined himself up on the chair and pushed himself backwards as hard as he could. He shot back from the photocopier as his chair toppled over and he smashed his head on the floor. We all burst out laughing, but he was absolutely fuming.

1995

I was working on a burglary squad. When an offender would get arrested for burglary on a dwelling or commercial property you would go into the cell with them and have a quiet word asking them if they would be willing to admit to other burglaries they had committed on your area with a similar MO (Modus operandi (method of committing the burglary). This is called a TIC (taken into consideration). The burglar would only ever be sentenced for the burglary he has committed and not the TIC's, but the judge would be made aware he has cooperated and would reduce the offender's sentence to reflect this.

One this day the burglar I chatted to agreed he would TICa load of jobs. This meant that it would clear up the outstanding burglaries on our patch and look good for the bosses and their detection rates in the next monthly meeting. You were also guaranteed a 'work through', meaning you would get at least 12 hours overtime which wasn't to be sniffed at.

We got in the interview, which he had agreed to do without a solicitor being present...result!! I had in front of me a list of outstanding burglary dwelling incidents that this young man in front of me was going to admit to. As the interview started, he admits to the burglary he was arrested for and then starts to reel off burglaries he's committed in the past, supposedly from memory. The burglar then says, 'you'll have to move your finger, it's covering up that address and I can't read it'. The interview was ended shortly after this before we all got in trouble, I still got my work through.

1998

Years ago, when offenders appeared in court and were fined for the offence they had committed, if they didn't pay the fine a 'money payment warrant' would be issued for them. This carried a power of arrest, and on arrest you either paid the fine which could be anywhere from £25 to hundreds or thousands of pounds. If you couldn't pay the fine then you were sent to prison to serve a short sentence, usually weeks, and then be released with the debt paid off.

I used to go to the office that held the money payment warrants regularly, especially on Christmas Eve. I would select the warrants for all of the handbag thieves, house burglars and general scum. Then, along with my colleagues we would go to the offender's houses. They are much like any normal member of the public on Christmas Eve, wanting to spend time with their family. We would front and back the house so that they couldn't escape and then knock on the window. The look of horror on their faces will always make me smile. This was payback for all the shitty things they had done to regular members of the public. You would see them frantically running around the house trying to escape and realising they had nowhere to go. They never had the money to pay for the outstanding fines so would be arrested and put before the next available court on Boxing Day before being remanded to custody to serve the remainder of their sentence in prison.

I remember after our team had arrested several offenders for non-payment of fines one Christmas eve when I was contacted by the shift Inspector who told me to 'stop it'. This decision still confuses me. I was only doing my job. Maybe if he had had his house burgled, or his mum had had her handbag snatched from her, he may have had a different view.

2015

We worked with a detective who would constantly fall asleep at his desk in the office. His desk faced away from our supervision, and he would sit bolt upright and fall asleep. He even fell asleep during a suspect interview one day. The prisoner was laughing with the interviewing officer and pointing at him. This officer eventually moved to work as a 'trainer' in the police training school. I attended a 3-week training course, and he was one of my trainers. One day the lead trainer was taking the lesson, and sleeping beauty was sat at the back of the classroom. I looked around and he was fast asleep in his chair. He is still a trainer!

THE GRADUATE
ENTRY SCHEME

When I joined the police in 1992 you needed 5 O levels, CSE's at grade 1 which were equivalent to an O level, or 5 GCSE's grade A-C. You initially had to pass a basic entrance exam which comprised of English and Maths questions. You had to pass a physical examination which comprised of a bleep test, fat test, grip strength test, sit ups, push ups and standing long jump. You then had your family checked out with a home visit and then you had your final interview, and if you passed all of that you were in.

Granted, some police officers back then weren't academically bright, but they had intuition that you couldn't teach. I've worked with cops who were born and raised on the same subdivisions they policed in. They knew who the bad lads were, and they could speak to them on their level. I mentioned earlier in this book about officers without degrees who were brought up poor. They had nothing. They understand what it is to go to bed hungry.

You now enter the police and must complete a level 6 post graduate diploma. If you have a degree in any subject, you can enter the police on a two-year work-based training programme where you'll focus on specialist areas of study, from Investigation, Intelligence, Community Roads or Response policing. You will then earn a level 6 post-Graduate diploma in Professional Policing Practise once you've completed your probation. There is no other student debt to take on because the police will foot the bill for your new policing degree.

Alternatively, there is a Detective Degree Holder Entry Programme which as you'd expect is learning biased towards an investigative perspective. This is a more intense programme as you also need to pass your National Investigator Exam and become PIP 2 qualified (Professional Investigation Programme). Every CID officer must pass this exam to become an accredited detective.

Some forces offer a 'Fast track Detective Pathway' where candidates spend a period in uniform before they start their investigators pathway. Other forces have a 'Direct Entry Detective Pathway' where candidates will start in an investigation role. I'd like to point out that having spent most of my career in uniform and then moving to CID, you get no more money for being a Detective Constable than a Uniform Constable, although the public seem to think that being a detective is a promotion. Believe me when I say that the CID are incredibly understaffed, and everybody is over worked. I also spent a large chunk of my career as a Response officer which is just draining. After 10 hours of driving around going from job to job and arresting self-generated crime prisoners it is exhausting. Alternatively work in CID as I did carrying over 20 serious investigations, having to stay on duty if someone is murdered, there's a sudden infant death or a 'joint visit' with social services that needs doing out of hours because a child is being abused, physically or sexually. All these shifts take a massive toll on your body.

On top of your everyday workload, probationary officers have to complete their degree and if you're wanting to become a detective you must pass the NIE exam as well. This puts an incredible amount of pressure on these young probationers. Understandably the dropout rate is quite high.

I'm still in touch with some of the officers I worked with who very kindly contributed their stories to this book. Some of these officers are still serving uniform officers or detectives. I have been dumbfounded at what I have recently heard about our new graduate police officers. When I and many of my other colleagues joined the police, it was a vocation for the next 30 years. Nowadays this isn't the case with many new recruits seeing the police as a stepping stone to other occupations. New officers are openly saying that they are pacifists and will not partake in violence of any kind. They are writing this on their application forms and are refusing to handcuff prisoners or use their batons on a violent suspect. I say, let's see how you feel about this when some lunatic comes running at you with a big knife!! Probationary officers are also using the police to pay for their level 6 post graduate diploma and then resigning.

What follows now as I complete this book, are stories of our new recruits. These graduate entry men and women who are now protecting our streets. You won't believe it.

GRADUATE STORIES

2022

The policing degree done by new recruits is completed 'online' with officers often in a 'what's app' group to discuss the different topics raised during the course. One male recruit was on a video call with other officers while at home and for some unknown reason, shared a video clip of himself with his 'penis in a brace' while also having an 'item' lodged up his bum. This was shared with 18 members of the group including police staff trainers. He has since resigned.

2022

A tutor Constable was driving around with his female probationer. Throughout the shift he realised she was becoming less and less lucid and was slurring her words. When he checked her 'water bottle' he discovered it was full of vodka. The tutor confronted her about this, at which she 'kicked off' and was arrested for being drunk on duty. She had to be restrained and placed in a safety blanket she was that pissed. When she eventually came too, she admitted she was a functioning alcoholic and had been for years. She resigned.

2022

During a fight at a house the probationer took off his belt kit and left it at the front door of the premises because he is a pacifist and does not want to get involved in any violence. He left his colleagues in the house fighting and went back to the station. He has now been found a job in an office away from the public because he refused to go back out on the streets. He will probably spend the next 29 years in an office-based job because it is his right to be a pacifist.

2022

A tutor constable was working with his male probationer when they attended a domestic disturbance at a house. As they went to enter the house the tutor says, 'you can deal with this, and I'll watch'. They get into the house and the male householder is kicking off, shoving his wife and shouting and swearing at the officers. The probationer stands there like a rabbit caught in headlights and does nothing even after being prompted by the officer to 'put hands on' the male. Still the probationer does nothing so the tutor steps in and arrests the male. A violent struggle ensues between the two with the tutor eventually getting the better of the man and handcuffing him. The probationer does not help at all. They get to the custody suite and the tutor puts the male before the custody Sgt and explains that he has arrested the offender for assault and a breach of the peace. At the conclusion of this the probationer turns round and cautions his tutor constable and arrests him for assault on the prisoner. At this point the Sgt stepped in and 'had a word' with the probationary officer. I presume he is still in the police as I've not heard otherwise.

2022

A probationer who is a class 5 (basic) driver was tasked by the radio room to go and obtain a witness statement from a victim of crime. He requested 'back up'. The radio operator, confused, explained that it was just a statement he was taking. The householder was expecting him, and he wouldn't need any backup. It later transpired that the probationer drove to his home address and collected his own father who he took with him to the house to get the witness statement.

2022

Probationary officers are now resigning because they didn't know that they had to work night shifts or at weekends.

2022

There was a 'large scale disturbance' in the city centre, so in other words a big fight. There was a van load of police officers who had with them a male probationary officer. When they arrived, they all piled out of the carrier and got stuck in, arresting several people for drunkenness and public order offences. When they all got back into the police carrier, they realised that the probationary officer wasn't with them. They shouted up on his police radio but got no reply. The new encrypted police radios mean that if you lose them, they can be disabled to stop them falling into the wrong hands. Alternatively, to find someone whose radio it is, the radio room staff can use the GPS system to see where the officer's location is. The officers did this and were told of the location of the radio which was miles away. A supervisor then made his way round to the location given by the GPS to find that it was in fact the officers home address. The Sgt knocked on the door which was opened by the probationary officer's father who stated that his son was indeed at home and was in bed. He refused to let the Sgt speak to him and said 'I told my son if he was ever scared when he was at work, he was to ring me straight away and come home'. It transpired that the probationary officer got scared when confronted with a fight and had got an Uber home!!

2023

An officer was working a night shift and rang his mum to tell her he was stood outside a house at 3am. Inside the house was a sudden death and the officer was waiting for the undertakers to arrive and collect the body. The officer's mother took it upon herself to drive to the house her son was stood outside just as his Sgt arrived to check everything was ok. The mother was incensed and complained to the Sgt that her son was stood outside a house on his own at 3am. The Sgt pointed out that her son was a policeman and this was his job!

THE END

Acknowledgments

To my wife, for championing me over the last 3 years. You are amazing. To my friends and colleagues who took the time to talk to me, your support means everything. To my counsellor Beverley for listening and putting me back together. And to the very talented Gareth. Without you this book wouldn't exist.

Printed in Dunstable, United Kingdom

71486837R00147